7

ROB WALKER

To Wooty and Moo

with very best wishes

from

Rob

ROB WALKER

By Michael Cooper-Evans

HAZLETON PUBLISHING

PUBLISHER
Richard Poulter
EXECUTIVE PUBLISHER
Elizabeth Le Breton
PRODUCTION MANAGER
George Greenfield
ART EDITOR
Steve Small
HOUSE EDITOR
Peter Lovering

© Hazleton Securities Ltd 1993

This first edition published in 1993
by Hazleton Publishing,
3 Richmond Hill, Richmond,
Surrey TW10 6RE.

Printed in Hong Kong by World Print Ltd.

ISBN: 1-874557-35-7

DISTRIBUTORS

United Kingdom
Bookpoint Ltd
39 Milton Park
Abingdon
Oxfordshire OX14 4TD

North America
Motorbooks International
PO Box 2
729 Prospect Avenue
Osceola
Wisconsin 54020, USA

Australia
Technical Book and Magazine Co. Pty
289-299 Swanston Street
Melbourne
Victoria 3000

Universal Motor Publications
c/o Automoto Motoring Bookshop
152-154 Clarence Street
Sydney 2000
New South Wales

New Zealand
David Bateman Ltd
'Golden Heights'
32-34 View Road
Glenfield
Auckland 10

South Africa
Motorbooks
341 Jan Smuts Avenue
Craighall Park
Johannesburg

Acknowledgements

Many of the photographs in this book have been borrowed from Rob Walker's private collection. Where this is the case every effort has been made to identify the photographer and to seek permission for reproduction. However, this has not always proved possible. I hope that anyone who has not been consulted but recognises his work will accept this belated acknowledgement and the thanks of Rob and myself. Meanwhile we wish to give particular thanks to both *Autosport* and *Road & Track* for their generous co-operation.

M C-E

The publishers are grateful to LAT Photographic and the Trustees of the Imperial War Museum, London, for providing additional photographic material from their archives.

By the same author:

PRIVATE ENTRANT

SIX DAYS IN AUGUST

RISK LIFE, RISK LIMB

Contents

Foreword
by Stirling Moss

I read this book while I was recovering from pneumonia and I must say it cheered me up a lot. As I read it, many happy memories of my association with Rob came flooding back to me. The seven Grand Prix victories which we shared demonstrate that both Rob and I were very serious about our motor racing, but you will see that we also had terrific fun.

Having driven for him for almost five years, I thought I knew Rob pretty well. He has a great sense of humour, he enjoys being teased and, above all, he is, as his passport lists him, a gentleman. However, there is so much in this entertaining book that was new to me, so many fresh insights, some of them quite amazing, that I wish I had known when we were travelling the world together.

Rob is a remarkable man who has lived a remarkable life and enjoyed it to the full. His wit, his sense of fair play, his chivalry and his courtesy endear him to all who know him, and command their respect and loyalty. Had I continued racing I would never have driven for anyone else so long as Rob had offered me a car.

Everyone who is seriously interested in what I regard as the golden, fun era of motor racing should get this book – if only for the pictures which, as you can see, are wonderful.

Stirling Moss
London
1993

Introduction
Rob Walker

Rob Walker was the first private entrant to defeat the factory teams in World Championship Grand Prix racing. Between 1958 and 1968, he did it nine times.

Rob grew up at Sutton Veny, a magnificent early Georgian mansion in Wiltshire boasting more than a hundred rooms, several hundred acres, and a full complement of staff drawn directly from the cast of *Upstairs, Downstairs*. Initially taught by his governess, Rob's subsequent school career was marred by his inability to pass exams. He was a good athlete but a poor scholar.

The genesis of Rob's interest in cars and racing was a visit to the 1924 Boulogne Grand Prix during a family holiday in the Pas-de-Calais, when he was seven. From that moment on he seldom thought of anything else. Only four years later he was racing up and down the drive at Sutton Veny in an Austin Chummy, aided and abetted by the family's second chauffeur. Later, as a Cambridge undergraduate, he became not only a notable *bon viveur* but also a qualified pilot and an amateur racing driver of some distinction, driving his own Delahaye into eighth place at Le Mans in 1939.

Life suspension of his pilot's licence for low flying (he 'jumped' the Cottenham National Hunt course in a Tiger Moth during the lunch interval) did not prevent Rob from serving as a Fleet Air Arm fighter pilot during the war. He survived the torpedoing of his ship during the invasion of Sicily, several hair-raising accidents and numerous lesser escapades before discarding his Naval uniform in 1945.

Rob married Betty Duncan in 1940. An important part of their marriage contract was that he should give up race driving. Thus, after the war, he became an entrant, providing cars for drivers such as Tony Rolt, Reg Parnell, Peter Collins, Tony Brooks, Jack Brabham, Maurice Trintignant, Jo Bonnier, Graham Hill, Jochen Rindt and Jo Siffert. But his most productive relationship – with Stirling Moss – was cut short by Stirling's accident at Goodwood in 1962.

Rob was fortunate to be involved in Grand Prix racing when it was still fun, still a sport rather than a serious, multi-million dollar business, when competition was fierce but chivalrous, rivalry between teams intense but friendly. In those days Rob Walker epitomised all that was best about British sportsmanship.

Equally, it is fortunate for all of us that Rob chose to invest huge sums of his own money in motor racing at a time when British teams played second fiddle to the Italians. His vision, his generosity, his ambition and his commitment all contributed to the emergence of the teams which dominate the sport today.

Rob Walker is one of a kind. His retirement from motor racing marked the end of an heroic era. How lucky we are that as he sits in his trophy-lined study surrounded by the ephemera of a motor racing career which spans more than fifty years, he has forgotten none of the flavour of those days long past.

For Rob and Betty, without whom this book would never have been finished, and for Victoria, Alexander and Sue, without whom it would never have been started.

Chapter 1
La Mer to La Sarthe

It all began in September 1924.

Rob Walker was seven when, while their long-suffering governess enjoyed her annual two-week respite from her unruly charges, he and his older brother John were allowed to accompany their mother on a visit to the Pas-de-Calais, where Mrs Walker graced the roulette tables of the casino at Wimereux.

The boys quickly explored and exhausted the limited pleasures of the windswept beaches and chilly waters of the English Channel, and there was therefore considerable relief all round when it was discovered that a series of motor races was to be held at nearby Boulogne-sur-Mer on the final Sunday of their holiday. On race day the preliminary voiturette handicap event was won by a Type 37A Bugatti driven by an Englishman called Marshall whose wife happened to be sitting next to young Rob Walker in the stands, tirelessly answering his eager small boy's questions and explaining to him exactly what was going on. Then came the main event, the Boulogne Grand Prix for the Georges Boillot Cup, and the Walker brothers shivered with excitement each time the titanic cars and their heroic drivers rushed past in a cacophony of exhaust noise and clouds of billowing dust from the ill-surfaced road. The Grand Prix was won by a Chenard-Walcker driven by Léonard, with Robert Sénéchal driving another Chenard-Walcker – a coincidence of name not lost upon young Rob – in second place.

After the races were over it only needed the driver of their aged Citroën taxi to make a complete lap of the circuit while returning them to their hotel, responding enthusiastically to the boys' shouts of 'Faster! Faster!' (while a terrified Mrs Walker cried 'Slower! Slower!') and pointing out where drivers had been killed or gone off the road, for Rob to be completely hooked. From that day on, racing cars were seldom far from his thoughts.

In the years which ensued, as we shall see, Rob's interest in cars and racing flourished. He watched motor racing whenever he possibly could, travelling the length and breadth of both England and France in order to do so, but it was not until October 1938 that another driver ignited his imagination as had Léonard and Sénéchal at Boulogne fourteen years earlier. He was in his second year at Cambridge when he and a number of undergraduate friends journeyed to Donington Park to see the awesome Mercedes and Auto Unions in action. The sight was something which Rob will never forget.

The Grand Prix circus assembled for the Donington Park race in the shadow of the 1938 Munich crisis. As the Mercedes and Auto Union teams arrived in England, trenches were being dug in Hyde Park, soldiers were erecting sandbag barricades in front of Buckingham Palace, and every newspaper headline spoke of war. On 28th September things looked so bad that the German Embassy in London ordered their teams home, the race was cancelled, and passages for cars, drivers and mechanics were booked on the ferry from Harwich to the Hook of Holland. But after Mr Chamberlain had been deceived by Hitler and Mussolini at their 'peace in our time' conference at Munich normality, at least for the time being, was restored.

Almost a month later than originally scheduled, on 22nd October, the day of the Donington Park race dawned cold and damp. Mercedes and Auto Union were both back in full strength; Caracciola – the favourite to win – Lang, von Brauchitsch and Britain's Dick Seaman for Mercedes, and Nuvolari, Hasse, Kautz and Muller for Auto Union. Early in the race an old Alta, rented from Thompson & Taylor by Robin Hansan, blew its engine and left a large puddle of oil on the downhill section before the hairpin; Rob clearly remembers seeking refuge behind a conveniently placed tree – there was little protection provided for spectators in those days – to watch Hasse hitting the oil and spinning three times before leaving the track and demolishing a marshals' hut. Next in the queue was Dick Seaman, who slithered onto the grass, stalling his engine. Kautz crashed. And then came Tazio Nuvolari; he crested the hill flat out as usual, hit the oil at 140 mph, corrected a slide to the right, held a slide to the left as far as the hairpin, calmly selected first gear, and drove on to win the race. Rob was so impressed by this performance that he still rates Nuvolari as one of the five greatest racing drivers he has ever seen in action.

Rob's first competition car was this 1928 supercharged Ulster TT Lea-Francis.

However, his role model at this time was Whitney Straight, a young Anglo-American of considerable means who had been at Trinity College a year or two before Rob went up to Cambridge. Perhaps as a result of his close friendship with classmate Dick Seaman, Straight raced a 3$\frac{1}{2}$-litre supercharged Maserati and regularly flew down from Cambridge to Brooklands in his De Havilland Moth to be met by Dewdenay, his chauffeur and chief mechanic, and driven to the pits in his Bentley. Straight's lifestyle was so extravagant that even his considerable resources began to dwindle alarmingly as time went on; he was, perhaps, rescued from financial disaster by the war, in which he served with great distinction before becoming a successful commercial figure – and a Director of many blue-chip public companies – in later years.

Rob's first serious competition car was a 1928 supercharged Ulster TT Lea-Francis which was said to be the car driven to victory in the Tourist Trophy by Kaye Don – but then, as Rob says, 'they all were, weren't they?' In any event it looked the part with a fold-flat windscreen and two little aero-screens, straps over the bonnet, a huge pressurised petrol tank with quick-lift filler caps, an external exhaust pipe and a Brooklands silencer. When Rob bought it, it had a blocked radiator and boiled with irritating frequency. He soon fixed that by running into the back of the Countess of Denbigh while she was parked outside her London house, sitting in her car and minding her own business. The impact destroyed the blocked radiator of the Lea-Francis and the replacement never boiled again. The poor Countess, however, claimed to have suffered severe shock and subsequently won £100 in damages from Rob's insurance company.

Meanwhile, Rob entered the Lea-Francis in the Lewes Speed Trials – a major meeting in those days, attracting such driving stars as Raymond Mays and Prince Bira – but failed to complete his first competitive run for some mechanical reason now lost in the mists of time.

Rob's 3¹/₂-litre Delahaye Type 135S Course.

Late in 1938 Rob, as usual playing truant from Cambridge, happened to be wandering down London's Park Lane when he spotted, glistening in a showroom window, the most beautiful sports car he had ever seen in his life. He recognised it at once as a 3¹/₂-litre Delahaye Type 135S Course with a very distinguished pedigree. Originally brought into the country by Tommy Clark for the 1936 TT, the car had later been acquired by Prince Bira who, when his ERA was not ready for the Brooklands 500 in 1937, entered the Delahaye instead.

He finished seventh, unable to compete on equal terms with the field of out-and-out racing cars, even though his race average was 114.5 mph and his fastest lap 126.1 mph. Delighted with the spectacular speed and reliability of the Delahaye, Bira went on to win many sports car races with it, including the 1937 Donington 12 Hours. Now the car was for sale, repossessed by Count Doric Heyden from its latest, unfortunate owner who seemed destined to spend some time at His Majesty's pleasure over an unconnected matter.

There was absolutely no doubt in Rob's mind but that he would buy the Delahaye, although there was one small problem. Money. The Delahaye wore a very reasonable price tag of £400, but Rob hadn't got anything like that much money to his name. In fact his total annual allowance – with which he had to support himself at Cambridge – amounted to no more than £360. It was at this point that he was introduced to something he had not encountered before; it was called hire purchase, and after nothing more immediately painful than a signature on a piece of paper, the car was his.

Three days later Rob drove the Delahaye to Cambridge, wildly exhilarated by its tremendous speed and acceleration, quite unlike anything he had ever experienced before. 'I think the most noticeable thing about driving a car as fast as that in those days – it would do over 100 mph in third gear and had a top speed of 130 mph – was that you just didn't realise how quickly you were going until suddenly you were right on top of a lorry or something which only a moment ago had seemed to be miles ahead, and you had to stand on the brakes to avoid hitting it. The brakes were the only real weakness on the Delahaye, and you soon learned that you had to brake or slow down pretty early or you were going to have an accident. Actually, I don't think I ever did have a road accident in that car – a few dicey moments, maybe, but no accidents.'

Rob driving the Delahaye in the Inter-Varsity speed trials at Syston in 1939.

Rob could hardly wait to enter the Delahaye in the first suitable race of the 1939 season at Brooklands, at that time the Mecca of British motor racing. However, with his finances stretched by his hire purchase commitment, he could not afford the five-guinea subscription to the British Automobile Racing Club, of which membership was required before an entry could be accepted. Count Heyden came to the rescue again; he was a member of long standing, so the Delahaye was entered in his name with Rob nominated as driver.

Only one remaining obstacle now stood between Rob and his first real motor race; at Brooklands there was a very sensible rule that every novice driver had to complete five laps under the scrutiny of two experienced Brooklands drivers to ensure that his conduct would not seriously threaten his own safety or that of others. Rob decided to approach Charles Bracken-bury and George Harvey Noble to act as his scrutineers. These two were reputed to be fairly dedicated drinkers and Rob found them in the bar, as he knew he would, before lunch on the day he had chosen for his test. 'I went up to them and asked if they would be kind enough to observe my five laps to see if I was a fit person to drive at Brooklands. I knew that they could see the whole circuit from the bar, which was at the top of the tower, so it wasn't really asking too much of them. Anyway, they said of course they would, and turned back to their gins and tonics, or whatever. So I went out and did my five laps, and on the last lap I lost it and spun, and I thought, "Oh Lord, that's probably torn it." When I went back to the bar they were still there, and rather nervously I asked if everything had been all right. They said, "Yes, of course, my dear chap – absolutely perfect," and then I realised that they had been stuck into their drinks all the time and hadn't seen a thing – they

*Reg Parnell passes
Rob's Delahaye
at the 1939
BARC Whitsun
meeting at
Brooklands.*

Left: *Rob and
the Delahaye at
Brooklands in
August 1939.*

hadn't even looked out of the window! Anyway, all that mattered to me was that they signed my form.'

In 1907 an enormously wealthy landowner named Locke King had built the Brooklands Motor Course on his own estate, and at his own expense, as much as a testing ground for the infant British motor industry as a race track. It was constructed originally as an irregularly shaped oval – two straights of unequal length joined by steeply banked turns. By the time Rob raced there thirty-two years later, various alternative track layouts were available and the concrete surface had become bumpy enough to launch the faster cars into the air at one point on the Members' Banking. 'My first race was on the outer circuit which I didn't really like very much, I suppose because I wasn't good enough. To do a good time you really had to take the bumps absolutely flat, but I had seen people go over the top there and I suppose I was a bit frightened and I used to just lift off very slightly, and so my lap times were never quite as good as they should have been. Anyway, for some inexplicable reason I was put on scratch in this handicap race alongside Ian Connell driving a 4-litre Lago-Talbot. He was the top driver that year and won more races at Brooklands than anyone else. When the flag dropped I muffed the start, Ian shot off and I never saw him again. He won and I finished as near to last as made no difference.

'My second race, on the same day, was a Mountain Handicap and I was doing rather well in it, perhaps because the handicappers had been a bit more generous to me. On the last lap I only had to pass the limit man in a little Brooklands Riley to win the race. As we came down to the last bend, which was the hairpin by the old Vickers sheds, I was right on his tail and could have gone round without any fuss and passed him perfectly easily on the straight before the finish, but in my excitement I went into the corner too fast and spun. The Delahaye was actually a very difficult car to stop spinning because the steering was so low-geared that you couldn't turn the wheel fast enough to correct it. Unless you saw it coming you were spinning before you even knew it – in fact, after the war I spun it going round Hyde Park Corner which was a bit embarrassing.

'Anyway, on this occasion I ended up halfway up the grass bank with no reverse gear, because in order to avoid making a mistake when you were changing gear quickly there was a butterfly nut which you screwed down into the gate to lock out reverse. So what I did was to run the car up the bank a couple of times, letting it roll down backwards with the clutch out, and in this way I managed to rejoin the race and finish third.

'Afterwards I was paraded in front of George Easton and Lord Howe, the stewards of the meeting, for dangerous driving. Lord Howe said he couldn't understand why I hadn't just put it into reverse instead of indulging in all that thoroughly dangerous shunting to and fro, especially as I had no chance of finishing in the money. I explained the reverse gear problem to him and pointed out that I had actually come third, which rather took the wind out of his sails, and in the end instead of taking my racing licence away they put me in the black book, which meant that I would

lose it if I misbehaved again. So I got away with it – just!'

At about this time there was much controversy – stemming from an article by John Dugdale in the *Autocar* – about which was the fastest road racing car in Britain, and it was decided to hold a special race at Brooklands to settle the matter beyond dispute. The race was to be held in two parts – the first on the Mountain Circuit and the second on the Campbell Circuit – and there was to be a prize of £100 and a painting of the winning car in action specially commissioned from Gordon Crosby. Although not as fast in terms of absolute top speed as Ian Connell's Talbot or Hugh Hunter's 2.9-litre Alfa Romeo Mille Miglia, the Delahaye's superior handling made it a serious contender for the title. But not, thought Rob, in his own inexperienced hands. Instead he invited Arthur Dobson, who was probably the best driver in the country at the time, to drive the car – a secret that was kept until the morning of the race.

On the day Hugh Hunter narrowly won the first heat from the Delahaye – by only four-fifths of a second – but was plagued by gearbox difficulties in the second heat which Dobson won easily from Connell's Talbot to emerge as the clear winner

Rob on his way to victory in a Brooklands Mountain Handicap race in 1939.

on aggregate. The controversy was not resolved, however, for there were those who claimed that the race had simply shown that Dobson was the best driver – but the Gordon Crosby painting of his Delahaye leading the Talbot on the Members' Banking which hangs in Rob's study today is proof enough for him.

In one way and another it had been a good day for Rob. Quite apart from Dobson's success, he had won his first race later in the day by beating the ERAs of Pat Fairfield, bandleader Billy Cotton and Lord Beaverbrook's son, Peter Aitken, in a Mountain Handicap. He also placed a bet on himself for the first and last time in his life, five shillings at five to one netting him twenty-five bob. Privy to inside information about the driver of the Delahaye, Count Heyden had been in a betting mood also; as a result Ian Connell entertained Rob, Doric Heyden, Arthur Dobson and a number of others to an extremely expensive celebration dinner in London. Betting on motor races was quite common in those days, and Rob can remember an occasion on which Bob Aves, his friend and personal mechanic, rented on a race-by-race basis from Delahaye, said to him before a race, 'By the way, Rob, if you see Freddie Dixon coming up behind you, move over, would you? I've got money on him to win.' Rob did, and Dixon – and Aves – duly won.

For the remainder of the spring and early summer of 1939 the Delahaye was constantly in action; once Rob lent it to Prince Bira for a race at the Crystal Palace, but mostly he drove it himself – in speed trials and, as often as possible, at Brooklands. A Cambridge friend called Ian Nicholls also raced there, in a supercharged MG. On race weekends the two of them would drive from Cambridge to London on Friday for a terrific party at a night club called the Blue Lagoon which usually ended with a recuperative session in the steam room of the Jermyn Street Turkish baths, open all night to cater for just such emergencies. Needless to say, neither of them felt much like driving when race day came.

For as long as he could remember Rob had longed to drive at Le Mans. When he was at school the Bentley Boys were his heroes and Tim Birkin's *Full Throttle* was his bible. Now the Delahaye gave him his chance to fulfil his dream.

Rob enlisted Count Heyden as his team manager and invited Ian Connell to be his co-driver. A few days before the race Rob was involved in a road accident which left him with six stitches in his left thumb, making gear changing rather difficult. At the same time Bob Aves, who was due to drive the car to Le Mans, lost his driving licence after failing to walk a straight line, the 1939 equivalent of today's breathalyser test. These were setbacks, certainly, but not insurmountable setbacks. Bob Aves replaced the Delahaye's crash gearbox with a Cotal electro-magnetic box which changed gears by the flick of a switch near the steering column, and Rob drove the car as far as the ferry at Dover. Aves took over at Calais, reasoning that he was then no longer under British legal jurisdiction.

At least Doric Heyden could be relied upon to deliver an adequate stock of champagne to the pits without mishap.

Rob flew to France in an Imperial Airways Lockheed Hudson and having somehow failed to make hotel arrangements in advance wound up in a rather sleazy establishment in the main square of Le Mans, where the continual traffic noise made it virtually impossible to sleep. As Rob was too excited to sleep anyway, that was hardly an inconvenience.

The first practice period was scheduled to begin at one o'clock in the morning, and Rob was naturally a bit nervous about driving in the dark on a circuit he had never even seen, and in really very exalted company; there were Wimille and Veyron with a special streamlined Bugatti, Sommer and Bira in a new Alfa Romeo, Brackenbury and Dobson in a twelve-cylinder Lagonda, Luigi Chinetti with no less than seven Lago Talbots – six of which he had sold, together with their entries, prior to the race – and many others, almost all of whom had con-

siderably more experience than Rob. His confidence was not improved when he encountered the aftermath of a particularly gory motor cycle accident as he drove to the circuit.

Help was at hand, however, in the shape of an Englishman named Shrubsall who lived on the Cote d'Azur and had bought one of Chinetti's Talbots. 'He reckoned that as he must have been drunk when he bought it, he might just as well be drunk when he drove it for the first time. And he was – pissed as a newt, in fact. After a few laps the organisers got the message and hung out the red flag to stop practice so that they could sort him out. Of course, everyone stopped except Shrubsall who was having the time of his life and was absolutely determined to get his money's

The Delahaye at Le Mans in 1939. Bob Aves (in the car), *Doric Heyden, and Rob.*

worth. The gendarmes were sent out into the middle of the road in front of the pits, waving red lamps in an attempt to stop him, but when he got within a few hundred yards of them and it became absolutely clear that he had no intention whatsoever of stopping, they all leapt to safety pretty smartly. Eventually he stopped to see if a corner he thought he had just gone round was really there, and they grabbed him, and that was the end of his first and last Le Mans; when he was sober they shipped him back to the Cote d'Azur.' Dawn was breaking as practice was restarted, so Rob drove his first few laps at Le Mans in daylight.

Given the vast difference in their experience, it was hardly surprising that Ian Connell was much faster than Rob in both practice sessions, and it was therefore decided that he should start the race at four o'clock on Saturday afternoon. They had agreed to do four-hour shifts, so Rob's first stint would begin at eight o'clock in the evening. As this was the fashionable hour for dinner in those days, Rob considered that a dark blue pinstriped suit would be an appropriate form of dress for the occasion; on his feet he wore a pair of comfortable rope-soled canvas shoes, and on his head a pair of goggles. A contemporary report by Gordon Wilkins, who wrote for *The Motor* and was driving a Singer in the race, said, 'I could just see the white pinstripe in Rob Walker's blue suit as my headlights caught it going down the straight at 125 mph.'

'During my first shift I was having a dice with another Delahaye driven by a Frenchman whose name I'm ashamed to say I have quite forgotten. It was great fun; first he would lead for a few laps, and then I would. As it began to get dark I thought about putting my lights on and so, obviously, did the Frenchman. The headlight switch on the Delahaye was not very well placed; you had to put your arm through the steering wheel in order to reach it. I saw this chap lean forward and put his arm through the spokes just before the kink on the Mulsanne Straight and then, of course, he couldn't turn the wheel enough to get round the corner and when I last saw him he was headed straight for a cottage beside the road at 125 mph. I never did find out what happened to him.'

Rob handed back to Ian Connell at midnight and it was now that they experienced the only mechanical problem of the race when a leaking exhaust gasket forced superheated gases into the footwell through the gaps where the pedals went through the floorboards. The Delahaye's cockpit was hot at the best of times, but now it was like an oven. By the time he brought the car in to hand over to Rob at about dawn, just when the mist rolls over the circuit to make Le Mans a driver's nightmare, Connell's feet had been so badly burned that he was unable to take any further part in the race, and Rob – dressed now in an informal Prince of Wales' checked suit to greet the new day – began what was to be a virtually uninterrupted twelve-hour shift to the finish. His rope-soled shoes saved the day. At every pit stop he would jump into a bucket of water and the soles would absorb just enough moisture to keep his feet tolerably cool until the next stop.

About two hours before the finish, Rob received an unexpected signal to stop at his pit; 'My pit crew called me in for a glass of champagne because they said they thought I might be getting a bit tired. They may have thought this because I had just been down the escape road at Mulsanne, having left my braking too late. But I

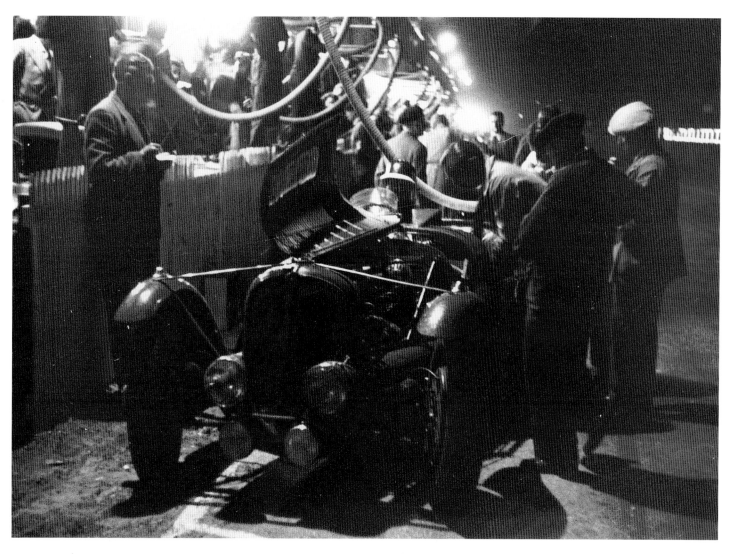

*A night pit stop for the Walker/
Connell Delahaye at Le Mans in
1939.*

Left: *Ian Connell at Arnage,
Le Mans 1939.*

Rob at Tertre Rouge, Le Mans 1939.

think the real reason for their generosity was that they had all drunk so much champagne in the pit that they were down to the last bottle and they suddenly felt terribly guilty about that poor bastard out there getting burnt to bits, and thought they ought to call him in to join the party. I don't know how much time I lost as a result of this, but I rejoined the race so refreshed that I think I must have made it all up again without any trouble.'

In the end, Rob crossed the line in eighth place overall and third in his class. The Delahaye had run for twenty-four hours without a tyre change at an average speed of 78.3 mph. After the race Rob went back to his hotel, bathed and changed, and drove to Paris where most of the British drivers – except for Arthur Dobson, who had passed out – were still celebrating in a night club at ten o'clock the following morning. By then Rob had been awake for almost forty-eight hours and had driven at racing speed for sixteen of them. He did spend an hour in bed in Paris, it is true, but rumour has it that this was not an entirely restful interlude.

As he had done so well at Le Mans Rob was invited to drive at La Baule on 3rd September 1939. This was one of the few races that paid decent starting money at the time – but there was a snag; any driver who didn't turn up or failed to start the race for any reason had to pay a fine equal to the agreed starting money. As race day approached it became clearer and clearer that war with Germany was imminent. France was in a state of chaos, troops were being mobilised, blackout regulations were in force, petrol was almost unavailable except to the military convoys which were clogging the roads everywhere, and yet the organisers of the La Baule race could not decide whether to call it off. Rob was determined not to risk being fined for non-appearance so he hung around the Automobile Club de France in Paris until, two days before war was declared, the race was cancelled. Rob caught the last ferry to sail from Calais to Dover for almost six years.

Rob with Ian Connell, Percy Maclure, Bob Aves and Doric Heyden after finishing eighth at Le Mans in 1939.

Chapter 2
A Gilded Youth

Rob Walker's passport lists his occupation as 'Gentleman'.

Robert Ramsay Campbell Walker was born on 14th August 1917, just three years after his older brother John. His father, of whom Rob has no clear memory, was orphaned as a child and subsequently elected to be brought up in Australia by his maternal grandparents, rather than to remain in Scotland. The Campbells were prominent in Australian politics at a time when the outlaw Ned Kelly was at the height of his notoriety. According to legend, Kelly's sister was employed as a house-maid at the Campbell homestead, and it was information she overheard during the course of her duties there which enabled her brother to stay one jump ahead of the authorities for so long. 'Cam' Walker was educated at Haileybury and Sydney Grammar School, and grew up to be one of Australia's most eligible bachelors – charming, gentle, generous and with, it was said, a Daimler in every State.

In 1912 he met Mary Marshal Ramsay whose father was a partner in Harrison Ramsay (now Harrison Crossfield), a company trading in tea and rubber in China, Ceylon and the Malay States. Although the family travelled extensively throughout the Far East, their principal home was in Brighton, a seaside suburb of Melbourne. It was here that Cam and Mary were married within a few months of their first meeting. Their honeymoon, which would take them around the world, had an inauspicious beginning; Mary contracted chickenpox on the first day. Later she was sufficiently recovered to be entertained by Henry Ford in Greenfield, Michigan – and he was sufficiently taken with Cam to offer him the sole Ford agency for the United Kingdom. Just why Cam turned him down remains a mystery.

Perhaps it was because work was never one of Cam's priorities. Indeed, he never worked in his entire, all too short life. Nor did he go to war; while his wife served as a junior hospital nurse and her brother was wounded on the Western Front, he was declared unfit to serve. In 1921, aged thirty-two, he died. Rob Walker was then three.

The Walker family fortune had been built upon sales of the fine Scotch whisky which bore their name. The income from Cam's considerable estate was to be enjoyed by his widow so long as she remained unmarried. In 1921 this amounted to £50,000 per annum – the equivalent of nearly £850,000 today. The capital was held in trust for Rob and John equally until they reached the age of twenty-eight.

Rob had been born at home, at Scotsbridge House in Rickmansworth. Initially looked after by his nanny and later by his governess Miss Wood ('Woody' to the boys), Rob remembers with great affection the rolling lawns of Scotsbridge leading down to the trout-filled pools and waterfalls of the river Chess a hundred yards from the house. It was a wonderful place in which to grow up.

In 1926, however, aged nine, he was required to board at Sandroyd Preparatory School near Cobham where he was initially terribly unhappy and homesick. Fortunately his first term there was disrupted by an epidemic of measles; when the school sanitorium was filled to overflowing all the pupils were sent home until the epidemic could be contained. Rob and John were disappointed to escape infection and resorted to beating each other with a stiff clothes brush in order to simulate a rash and so avoid returning to school. The ploy was unsuccessful. Rob was not a great scholar but played both cricket and soccer for the school. Friends he made at Sandroyd remain his friends today.

At about this time Rob's mother decided to register both her sons for membership of the MCC, and on visiting Lord's to do so met and fell in love with Sir Francis Eden Lacey, a man much older than she who was about to retire after twenty-nine years as secretary of the club. He had been a triple Blue at Cambridge and a prolific scorer of runs for Hampshire – of which he had been captain – and England, and had been Knighted for services to cricket. As an attractive young widow Mary Walker had had many suitors, most of whom sought to ingratiate themselves with her sons by showering them with expensive presents. Ben Lacey won their grudging respect by eschewing this obvious gambit.

In 1927 Mary Walker, now Lady Lacey, decided that Rickmansworth was becoming just a touch too suburban for her taste and determined to look for a suitable house in the country. After much reconnaissance she and Ben found a perfect early-Georgian house at Sutton Veny, near Warminster. According to the estate agent's brochure it had a hundred rooms, several staff cottages, a 270-acre tenanted home farm, decent rough shooting, excellent trout fishing on the

Sir Francis and Lady Lacey.

Sutton Veny House

Warminster, Wilts

AN IDEAL RESIDENTIAL AND SPORTING ESTATE OVER 270 ACRES

OVERLOOKING THE WILTSHIRE DOWNS

For Sale by Private Treaty.

Sole Agents:
Messrs. WILSON & CO.,
14, Mount Street, Grosvenor Square,
London, W.1.
Telephones: *Grosvenor* 1440, 1441 & 1442.

Wylye, two immaculate grass tennis courts, a squash court, greenhouses which produced peaches, nectarines and grapes in their seasons, a walled kitchen garden, and superb views of the Wiltshire Downs.

The asking price was £15,000.

The staff required to service this establishment was not inconsiderable. The most senior servant was the butler, Reid, who had deserted the Duke of Somerset in order to join the Lacey household and lived in one of the two lodges. He was assisted by two footmen/valets. May Skilton was Lady Lacey's lady's maid. Mabel, the senior housemaid, presided over two assistant housemaids, while in the kitchen the cook was assisted by a scullery maid and a kitchen maid. The head gardener, Wicks, had come from Scotsbridge House to supervise a number of under-gardeners. Finally, there were two chauffeurs. 'Bunyon, the head chauffeur, was a sweet man who had been a sniper in the war and was absolutely wonderful at everything; he looked after the bees, he did all the painting, he was a super carpenter, he worked the generator, he could turn his hand to anything – but he was a hopeless driver. Fortunately my mother liked to drive herself so his inability to drive properly was not a real handicap.' When guests came to stay at Sutton Veny they brought their own personal servants with them; the same social protocols – the same pecking order – prevailed below stairs as above.

At Scotsbridge Rob had lived in the nursery, being paraded before his mother every day for an hour after tea. For a time, however, he had slept in his mother's room; during a riding lesson, aged seven or eight, his pony had been startled by a steam traction engine and had bolted down a farm lane which culminated in a five-barred gate with a pond on each side. As he approached the gate at some speed, Rob wisely decided that it was time to disembark; alas, one foot caught in a stirrup and he was dragged behind the pony for some distance. Concussed and unconscious for more than thirty-six hours, Rob still bears the scars of this adventure. Those scars might have been worse had not his mother taped his hands together to stop him from scratching his healing wounds, and watched over him as he slept beside her bed.

At Sutton Veny Rob was allowed to eat with the grown-ups; from the age of twelve he was required to dress for dinner every evening. At seven-thirty the butler would ring the dressing bell – a retirement present from Ben Lacey's colleagues at Lord's – and Rob would struggle into his stiff dress shirt, wing collar and black tie, all of which had been laid out for him by his valet. There were many distinguished visitors to the house, among whom were Lord Hawke and Sir Stanley Jackson, each captain of England in his time; Plum Warner; Lord Harris, President of the MCC; Uncle Alec Walker, Managing Director of the family firm; Sir Eustace Fiennes, grandfather of adventurer and explorer Sir Ranulph, and, last but by no means least, Lady Thomas, who regaled the weekend house parties with choice titbits of inside information gleaned from her son, Sir Godfrey, who was Private Secretary to King Edward at the time of the Wallis Simpson episode. Entertaining though all this may have been for his parents and their guests, Rob found meal times insufferably long and tedious.

As far as he was concerned the best thing about Sutton Veny was the drive; almost a mile long from lodge to lodge, with a variety of curves and gradients leading through woods and between stone walls, it was a perfect private race track. If his mother's first mistake as a parent had been to take Rob to the Boulogne Grand Prix, then assuredly her second – committed four years later when he was eleven – was to give him and John a car for Christmas. It was a 1924 bull-nosed Morris Coupé with a Hotchkiss engine in which his brother seemed to take little interest, preferring to

listen to Louis Armstrong records on his gramophone, or to read P.G. Wodehouse. 'This left the Morris entirely at my disposal and I almost lived in it, going up and down the drive hundreds – probably thousands – of times, first of all teaching myself to drive and then going faster and faster. I could hardly wait for lunch to be over so that I could try to set yet another new record. The tradesmen making deliveries to the house were absolutely terrified, never knowing quite when they would meet me tearing round a bend on the wrong side of the road, totally out of control, and I remember getting into quite a lot of trouble one day when the baker's van was forced into the ditch. I must have used an enormous amount of petrol but as the local garage used to deliver forty gallons a week in two-gallon cans that, fortunately, was not my problem.'

Rob, aged eleven, with his first car, a 1924 bull-nosed Morris Coupé.

Rob's preoccupation with the internal combustion engine precluded an interest in hunting, shooting or fishing and, anyway, he disliked killing things, especially anything as beautiful as, say, a pheasant. Brother John, however, became a crack shot and a much respected fly fisherman.

By the time the Morris finally expired after a year or two of this treatment Rob was at Sherborne School, having failed to obtain a place at either Eton or Winchester. With a little help from his stepfather, who had been captain of cricket there many years earlier, he had just about scraped in. During his early days at Sherborne Rob, like everyone else, was restricted to pedal power but his frequent visits to the local cycle shop were prompted mostly by his interest in a car which he had discovered in the garage there, and which was for sale. This was a 1922 Belsize Bradshaw two-seater with a twin-cylinder air-cooled engine which Rob judged to have great potential as a record breaker on the drive at Sutton Veny. After a whole term of bargaining he got the price down to £3 and the deal was done. Later when John was old enough to be eligible for a driving licence Lady Lacey made him relinquish this car to his brother. Rob was not in a position to protest too vehemently since the cost of the Belsize Bradshaw had ended up on his school bill, but nor was he exactly heartbroken when John promptly broke his wrist trying to start it on the handle.

Sherborne was a tough school of the traditional cold shower variety. Perversely, cold showers there were taken at bed time; wet towels hung in a dormitory of which the windows were never shut literally froze solid during long winter nights. The school food was inedible. Rob was a patron of the tuck shop whenever funds allowed, and an enthusiastic cook when tenancy of a shared study gave him access to a small kitchen. At the beginning of each term his luggage was weighed down by cans of Heinz tomato soup and baked beans with which to augment locally acquired bacon, eggs and sausages. As at Sandroyd, Rob shone more on the playing field than in the classroom and played cricket and rugger for his house. When there were no organised games to occupy his free time he would cycle to Weymouth for tea – a round trip of fifty miles – and to see what the butler saw on the pier. Of all the repressive Sherborne institutions, Rob found the Army Cadet Force – the Corps – the most insufferable. He hated route marches, he was always the scruffiest cadet on parade, buttons undone and puttees awry, and he couldn't see the point of firing blank cartridges at nothing in particular on field days. However, he did enjoy immobilising the commanding officer's car by stuffing the uneatable sausage roll from his haversack rations up its exhaust pipe.

Risking the considerable displeasure of the school authorities, Rob kept an illegal motor bike at the local cycle shop. This was a 1924 BSA with a gear lever inconveniently placed between the petrol tank and the engine with the consequent risk to the rider of grabbing the spark plug when attempting to change gear.

The game was almost up one day when a uniformed police constable appeared during a French lesson to serve a summons on Rob for having no 'instrument of warning' on the BSA, but fortunately no one in authority realised that in addition to the law of the land school rules had been broken also. Rob was fined five shillings in the local magistrates' court – a quarter of his termly allowance – but the rise in his stock amongst his peers made it worth every penny.

Soon after his sixteenth birthday, when he had become eligible for a licence to drive a motor cycle or three-wheeler on the road, Rob had persuaded his mother to part with £30 for a 1924 Morgan with a quite potent ten-horsepower Blackburn water-cooled engine. 'It was a very quick, dangerous car with virtually no brakes. It was said to have lapped Brooklands at 84 mph and was reputed to have killed four previous owners; I can't for the life of me think how or why it hadn't killed far more – unless four previous owners were all there had been.' Rob used to climb out of his dormitory at night and go for long drives through the Dorset countryside in this car before returning it to its hiding place in the cycle shop. He came close to discovery one night when the Morgan stalled miles away from Sherborne and simply would not restart. Rob eventually got it going again just as dawn was breaking, and was never more thankful to creep back into his dormitory bed undetected.

The purchase of Rob's next Morgan, a 1922 three-wheeler with an air-cooled Anzani engine, was consummated during a Latin class. Rob passed half a crown to a friend under their desks, the friend wrote out a receipt and passed it back the same way, and the car was his. Unfortunately it was never terribly reliable; it eventually broke down once too often and Rob pushed it into a field and walked away from it.

Without fully understanding why, Rob now decided that he wanted to be a Naval officer. Perhaps he had acquired an affinity for the sea during the long voyages to Australia to visit his mother's family, or perhaps it was the glamour of the uniform which attracted him. What was crystal clear, however, was that he would never get into the Navy if he stayed at Sherborne. So he was sent to a crammer called The Old Downs at Fawkham Green, near Brands Hatch, which specialised in preparing students for service examinations.

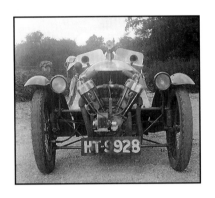

Rob's first Morgan three-wheeler.

Now seventeen, Rob was allowed to drive proper motor cars on the public highway and duly set off for Kent in the Hyper Sports Lea-Francis which his mother had given him for his birthday. Driving through Shrewton not long after leaving Sutton Veny, Rob was surprised to see a wheel overtaking him at some speed; he held his breath as the wheel narrowly missed a woman walking beside the road and then realised as the right-rear corner of the Lea-Francis began striking sparks from the tarmac that the wheel was his. Rescued by Bunyon, he completed the journey in the family Wolseley.

Rob was one of the few students at The Old Downs to have a car. On the other hand, most of the other students had plenty of money, while Rob had almost none. Thus it was agreed that he would drive the others to London every weekend in return for which he would not have to put his hand in his pocket while they were there. On Friday evenings they would check into the Mayfair Hotel before his friend Paul Warner – who styled himself 'Prince Paul' with supreme effrontery but no justification – borrowed £60 from his tailor in Savile Row and a similar amount from his shirtmaker in Conduit Street; the accounts would be settled in due course by his unsuspecting mother. Thus set up for the weekend, they never looked back.

Until now Rob had led a really very sheltered life. He had hardly encountered alcohol until one evening Paul's mother took them all to the Coconut Grove where Rob drank a great deal of champagne. He was delighted to discover that he had a very hard head. Nor did he know much about girls. He met an Austrian girl ten years his senior on a blind date and promptly fell madly in love. When he took her home to meet his parents he was surprised to find them less than wholly enthusiastic about her as a prospective daughter-in-law, and he was devastated when she ended their affair some months later. Given all these distractions it is hardly surprising that he failed the Navy entrance exam.

By now Leonard, the second chauffeur, had joined Rob in his assault on the record for the drive. They acquired two 1926 Austin Chummys at a cost of £5 and £7 respectively, underslung the chassis, lightened the flywheels, fitted twin Solex carburettors and raised the compression ratios. Both cars went really well and the record was coming down fast. The end came one Sunday morning when, as she was returning from church, Rob's mother found black skid marks on the road leading to a demolished fence with an Austin impaled on the final post. There was no corpse, fortunately, and no blood. Even so, it was decreed that the Austins must go at once, and Rob hitched them up behind his mother's Rolls and towed them to a garage in Dorking where he

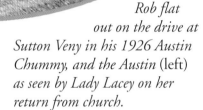

knew he would find a ready market. Instead of selling them he was persuaded to swap them for the famous Parry Thomas 'flat iron' Brooklands single-seater. The arrival of this enormous car at Sutton Veny didn't go

Rob flat out on the drive at Sutton Veny in his 1926 Austin Chummy, and the Austin (left) *as seen by Lady Lacey on her return from church.*

down at all well, and in desperation Lady Lacey offered Rob any car he wanted as long as it was not a sports car. His brains had not been entirely scrambled in his riding accident; he chose a Rolls.

His latest acquisition was a 1926 20 hp car with a very pretty Mayfair two-seater Coupé body which had been added some years later. It had only one disadvantage; it was terribly slow. Nevertheless, this was the car he took to Paris when he went there to improve his French before going up to Cambridge.

While in Paris he stayed as a paying guest with a family called Graf who had been recommended to Lady Lacey by friends. The Grafs lived in a suburb of Paris called Le Vesinet which nestles in a bend of the Seine to the north-west of the city, between the Forêt de St Germain and the Bois de Boulogne. Both Monsieur Graf and his stepson Jacques Tobler were great car enthusiasts and Rob returned to England able to discuss the most intricate automotive technicalities – but not much else – in fluent French. Jacques and Rob became great friends and travelled together to the car races at Montlhéry, to the great Champagne houses at Rheims and Epernay, and to the nearby First World War battlefields. Rob vividly remembers the lunar landscapes forged by the intense and prolonged artillery barrages of both sides, denuded of all foliage even twenty years later. He was

Below: *Leonard in the Parry Thomas 'flat iron' Brooklands single-seater.*

Rob's 1926 20 hp Rolls Royce.

Rob with his 1929 supercharged Alvis.

Rob's twentieth birthday present was this 1935 16/80 Vanden Plas Lagonda.

particularly moved by the Tranchée des Baionnettes at Verdun, where a whole company of French infantry had been interred by a German mine as they prepared to attack, their rusting rifles and bayonets projecting from the spot where they had fallen.

John Walker had preceded Rob at Cambridge and his wild behaviour had done nothing to suggest to the Master of Magdalene College that he should welcome a second Walker with anything but deep suspicion. Rob was not to disappoint him. Undisciplined, rebellious and anarchic, he was not at all keen to go up to Cambridge. He was not left-wing in a political sense; indeed politics bored him rigid. It was simply that he found the conventions of society rather unrewarding and was never happier than when he was talking to a mechanic about cars. Indeed, nothing that Cambridge had to offer could possibly interest him more than cars and racing. And any university rules which threatened these interests were made, as far as Rob was concerned, to be broken.

A second Rolls, bought on his behalf by his friend Jacques Tobler in Paris, succeeded the slow 20 hp model, but this car too had a disadvantage; delivering only 4 mpg it was very thirsty. So, by now, was its owner. As there wasn't enough money to satisfy both of them, the Rolls had to go. Next Rob paid £10 for a 1929 3-litre Lagonda which he found in a scrapyard; he and Leonard discovered two shillings in the gearbox when they were stripping it, so Rob reckoned he had got a bargain. Then came a 10 hp Talbot Coupé, a 1928 Tracta, a 1929 supercharged Alvis and, a twentieth birthday present from his mother, a 1935 Vanden Plas open four-seater Lagonda. Alas, this car was fitted with an untuned 2-litre Crossley engine which meant that it looked far better than it went. It was soon exchanged in Warren Street for another Lagonda, this time a 4½-litre pillarless saloon which went like smoke. On the way back to Cambridge the bonnet on Rob's side lifted at about 100 mph, completely blinding him. 'Drive on, Rob, drive on,' said his passenger, more than slightly plastered, 'I can see perfectly well'!

It was in the Vanden Plas Lagonda that Rob had decided to visit his friends the Grafs in Paris during the 1938 Easter vacation, and it was then that he met his future wife for the first time. Blonde and beautiful, Elizabeth Duncan was staying with the Grafs while studying painting in Paris; she and Rob were immediately attracted to each other and spent an idyllic couple of weeks driving together through the Bois de Boulogne, visiting the Louvre and the Orangerie, eating *pain au chocolat* in a little café on the Champs Elysées and drinking vodka with the White Russian emigrés who lived opposite the Grafs.

On his return to England Rob became a frequent guest at the Duncans' house in Kent. Betty's father had been called to the Bar before the First World War in which, while serving with the Lancashire Fusiliers, he had won a Military Cross and suffered wounds which had led to the loss of an eye. Her mother was half-French – pretty, artistic, musical and a marvellous hostess. The house was constantly filled with the friends of her three daughters and her son Val, and there were frequent tennis parties, and cricket matches against the local village side.

Back at Cambridge Rob, as usual, spent the summer playing cricket; he played for his college, he played occasionally for Wiltshire Colts, and he was now a playing member of the MCC as well as belonging to the exclusive I Zingari club; thus he enjoyed the company of such distinguished cricketers as the Compton twins, Bill Edrich, Gubby Allen, Nigel Haig of Middlesex, Hopper Reed and Bill Bowes, the Yorkshire bodyline bowler who had coached him at Lord's.

As well, he decided to learn to fly and applied to join the University Air Squadron. However, a disparaging remark about the RAF brought his subsequent interview to an abrupt conclusion and he found himself paying five shillings an hour for private flying lessons at Marshal's, the Cambridge aerodrome. In due course he qualified for his private pilot's licence but was not to enjoy it for long. During the lunch interval at the annual Cottenham National Hunt meeting Rob entertained the crowd by jumping the course in his Tiger Moth. The only person who was not amused was a policeman who took his number and reported him to the Civil Aviation Authority for low flying. Rob was banned from flying for life.

'We were always up to no good at Cambridge. In those days it was considered rather daring to steal a policeman's helmet and I remember persuading a couple of friends to help me acquire one on Guy Fawkes night, 1938. We selected a policeman who seemed too portly to have much hope of catching us and then the tallest of my friends knocked his helmet off into my hands, rather like a scrumhalf receiving the ball at a line-out, and I was off. Unfortunately I had reckoned without the Proctor and his Bulldogs – who were sort of campus policemen – and one of them brought me down on the pavement and knocked me cold. But I got my pass in as I fell and I still have the helmet today. I was

Elizabeth Duncan.

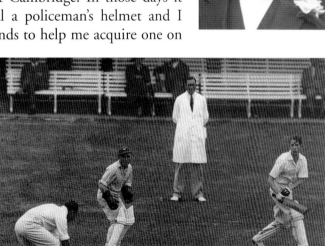

Above: *Norman and Marguerite Duncan, Betty's parents.*

Rob scoring 27 for the Young Amateurs versus the Young Professionals at Lord's.

gated for the rest of the term for this escapade and I suppose I was quite lucky not to be sent down.

'Some time later a friend of mine called Peter Miller-Munday, who was a rather good golfer, took a bet that he couldn't hit a golf ball from Piccadilly Circus to Oxford Circus in five shots. He teed off at about two o'clock in the morning when he reckoned he had a reasonable chance of getting away with it, but hooked his first shot through the plate glass window of Austin Reed in Regent Street. He was addressing a virtually unplayable lie in the wreckage of the window when the law turned up and dragged him off to Savile Row police station.'

For his twenty-first birthday Rob received a Coupe des Alpes Delahaye which had belonged to the wife of the then Minister for Transport, Lord Hore Belisha. Coincidentally, it was the twenty-first car that Rob had owned. Amongst its several eccentricities was the fact that all four gears worked in both forward and reverse. Shortly before he left Cambridge Rob was demonstrating this phenomenon after a very good dinner when, at about 60 mph in reverse, someone obscured his view through the rear window. When he could see again he found himself in imminent danger of running down a cyclist, swerved to avoid her and after several gyrations ended upside down in a ditch. Even though one of his passengers had broken a leg and Rob himself had sustained a nasty gash on his left thumb, they succeeded in righting the car and delivering the wounded to hospital in Cambridge. Next day when Rob returned to the scene of the accident to retrieve one or two things which had fallen out of the inverted car he was approached by someone who had been a witness to the events of the previous evening. 'D'you know,' said the witness, 'I could have sworn that your car was going backwards when it crashed.' Rob advised him to take more water with it in future.

Rob Walker had failed his first-year tripos in History. He had failed his second-year tripos in English. It was with great surprise that he discovered at the end of his final year at Cambridge that he had obtained a degree. The news reached him between practice sessions at Le Mans. By then it was of so little consequence to him that he failed to register his BA for more than twenty years.

Chapter 3
Fighter Pilot

Rob Walker joined the Navy on 6th December 1939.

Months earlier, only days after the declaration of war, he and some friends had enjoyed a rather bibulous lunch at the Berkeley before signing enlistment forms at the RNVR headquarters on HMS *Endeavour*, still moored even today alongside the Thames Embankment near Cleopatra's Needle. An interview at the Admiralty followed for all of them; only Rob was accepted for training as a Fleet Air Arm pilot. He attributes his success at least as much to the fact that he offered the interviewing officer a lift home in his Delahaye Coupé as to the careful concealment of his previous flying experience.

Arriving for basic training at HMS St Vincent, a shore establishment near Gosport, Ordinary Seaman Walker and his Delahaye were not, however, accorded a rapturous welcome. 'What shall I do with my car?' Rob enquired of the Guard Commander at the gate, a hoary Petty Officer of many years' service. His answer was inventive, but physically impossible. It is interesting to speculate what the Navy would have made of Rob's valet, John, quite naturally expected by Lady Lacey to enlist with her son and to look after him while he was at war. Fortunately John had a mind of his own and decided to join the Army, so the situation was never put to the test.

Sub-Lieutenant (A) R.R.C. Walker RNVR, with his Coupe des Alpes Delahaye.

Basic training lasted six weeks and consisted of reveille at crack of dawn, much scrubbing of floors and cleaning of lavatories, lessons in morse code and seamanship, and endless drilling, drilling and yet more drilling. The recruits slept in hammocks, or ''ammicks' as they were known, and there was a rather unlikely story going around at the time about Mae West – a somewhat over-endowed film actress – sending one of her bras to a sailor as a keepsake; he was supposed to have responded by writing, 'Thanks very much for the 'ammick; I sleep in one half and my mate sleeps in the other.' Rob was able to spend longer in his 'ammick than most by virtue of his ownership of an early electric razor which allowed him to shave in comfort while everyone else was scrambling for a place in the washroom. It was a situation which infuriated the Petty Officer instructors, perhaps because there was nothing much they could do about it. Rob's pay as an Ordinary Seaman was just ten shillings a week – exactly the price of a champagne cocktail in the bar of the Queen's Hotel, the best pub in Southsea.

At the end of it all Rob was elevated to the rank of Leading Seaman and given a week's leave before being posted to Elmdon near Birmingham for preliminary flight training in Tiger Moths. Here the Delahaye Coupé once again proved to be an asset. The Commanding Officer at Elmdon was quite keen on cars and rather enjoyed borrowing the Delahaye to drive up to London. In return Rob was never short of petrol or a weekend leave pass.

Rob was the star pupil at Elmdon. Still not letting on that he had held a private pilot's licence, however briefly, he went solo in only two and a half hours whereas everyone else was taking the usual seven or eight. His instructor was a hard taskmaster and a brilliant pilot who had flown in the First World War with the RFC. In due course he considered Rob competent enough to progress to advanced flying training, even though his inability to read a map and fly an aeroplane at the same time was thought to be something of a handicap.

Freddie Mills (right) *defeating Gus Lesnevitch for the World Light-Heavyweight Championship at Haringay in December 1948.*

When Rob arrived at No. 1 Flying Training School at Netheravon in April 1940 there was an immediate and unmistakable improvement to the quality of his life. As an officer candidate he was allowed to use the RAF officers' mess even though he was still technically a Naval rating. Being waited upon at table by pretty WRAFs – one of whom turned out to be an ex-girl friend – was a far cry from the rigours of HMS St Vincent, still fresh in his memory. Netheravon was then – and still is today – part of the military ghetto which borders the vast Salisbury Plain training area, and therefore quite close to Sutton Veny. Rob decided that this was a good opportunity to take his race car out of mothballs and to keep both Delahayes at the airfield.

Each day at Netheravon began with early-morning physical training under the eagle eye of Corporal Freddie Mills, who introduced himself as a professional boxer. After the war Rob was a frequent visitor to Freddie's training camp and saw him win the World Light-Heavyweight Championship by defeating the American Gus Lesnevitch at Haringay Arena in December 1948.

The principal training aircraft at Netheravon was the Rolls Royce Merlin-engined Fairey Battle which Rob enjoyed flying even though it gave him one or two nasty moments. 'One day we were practising taking off with a full five hundred pound bomb load. I was the last to go and it was quite late in the evening by the time my turn came. I suppose I was in a bit of a hurry to get the whole thing over so that I could go down to the local pub with the others and enjoy a few pints of the wonderful draught cider they had there, and I was probably not as conscientious over my cockpit checks as I should have been. Netheravon was really two grass airfields very close together and when the wind was in a certain direction, which it was on that day, you could use both of them for taking off and landing. Well, I taxied out and opened the throttle, and off I went. I used up the whole of the first airfield and it didn't feel as if it was ever going to come unstuck, and then I was bounding across the second airfield and rapidly approaching a group of aircraft which had been parked for the night on the perimeter. Somehow I just managed to ease it off the ground in time to avoid hitting them, and staggered up to five hundred feet before putting the propeller into fine pitch – only to discover to my horror that it was already in fine pitch! I suppose the person who had flown it before me must have forgotten to change back to coarse pitch before landing, and I just hadn't noticed. I reckon if the wind had been blowing in a different direction that day I would have had a big accident.

'On another occasion we were doing a night-flying test which involved making three solo landings, luckily in bright moonlight which made things rather less difficult for us. The direction in which we were landing that night took us over a small hill which stood about half a mile from the airfield. I can remember seeing the exhaust manifolds of the Merlin engine glowing bright cherry red ahead of me as I lowered the undercarriage for my third landing, then there was a bump and the aeroplane lurched upwards before I put it down on the grass, quite neatly I thought. Afterwards my instructor, Sergeant Webb, came up to me and said, 'You needn't think you got away with that, you know; I heard you hit that hilltop over there.' I reckon if he had heard the noise from that distance I must have hit it fairly hard,

Fairey Battle trainers, Netheravon 1940.

but it didn't seem to upset the old Battle too much.'

Rob Walker and Betty Duncan had become engaged to be married a few days after Rob joined up, on 11th December 1939. By mid-May 1940, with the BEF retreating in disorder towards Dunkirk, the situation looked pretty grim and the two of them decided to get married without further delay in case the widely predicted German invasion of Britain should interfere with their plans. Rob applied to the senior Naval officer at Netheravon for permission to marry and was turned down flat. He reapplied at once, this time to the senior RAF officer. 'The Group Captain asked me if I could afford to support a wife, so I told him what I was thinking of allowing Betty for housekeeping and so on and he said, "Good God, that's more than I get paid! Okay – you can have a forty-eight hour pass at the weekend."

'I was flying until midday on Saturday and then I jumped into the Delahaye Coupé, collected the family butler, chauffeur and head gardener from Sutton Veny, and drove up to London at terrific speed. They were all fairly ancient and I don't think any of them had experienced a journey quite like that before, but they bore up remarkably well.

'Betty and I were married at St Peter's Eaton Square on 25th May 1940. I was unable to provide a best man as all my friends were in the forces, so Betty supplied one for me. He was an ex-Wimbledon tennis player called Alan Collins who had been invalided out of the Army and turned up at the church looking absolutely immaculate in morning dress, complete with black silk hat. I think the vicar was rather disappointed when he discovered that the bloke in the crumpled Naval rating's bell bottoms was actually the groom.' After a brief honeymoon spent at the Dorchester Hotel in Park Lane, Rob was flying again by noon on Monday.

One consequence of Rob's marriage was to alter the direction of his life substantially in years to come, although he did not fully realise it at the time. Before consenting to marry him Betty had made him promise that there would be no more motor racing. Sprints and hillclimbs were permissible, but circuit racing was absolutely out. For a fledgling Fleet Air Arm fighter pilot about to go to war, hardly expecting to see a motor race again let alone drive in one, it was not a difficult promise to give.

Betty stayed at the George at Amesbury before finding a room in Netheravon village, at the bottom of the hill leading to the airfield, where Rob would join her for supper at the end of each day's flying. Betty was teaching herself to cook at the time and one evening she decided to try cooking her first chicken. 'On that particular day I was doing what I thought was a rather silly and irresponsible flight test which involved climbing to sixteen thousand feet without using oxygen and recording on a notepad strapped to your knee what effect oxygen deprivation was having on you. Well, of course, if you are seriously deprived of oxygen what you get is nitrogen narcosis which makes you feel rather giggly and reckless, and you take risks that you wouldn't even contemplate normally. I decided to see how fast my aircraft could go, which I suppose is something that most fighter pilots try at least once, whether or

Alan Collins, Rob's best man.

Rob and Betty Walker, St Peter's Eaton Square, 25th May 1940.

not they're suffering from nitrogen narcosis. Anyway, I pointed the nose straight down, opened the throttle and just sat there watching the airspeed indicator going off the clock. Suddenly there was a tremendous bang as an oil pipe burst, covering me with very hot and rather dirty oil. Fortunately my goggles protected my eyes but I really couldn't see very well and I found it quite hard to get the aircraft down in one piece.

'After I had made out my report of the incident – I rather think I may have left out the bit about wanting to see how fast a Battle would go – I went down the hill to see Betty, still covered in oil and feeling slightly heroic and rather pleased with myself. I found her in floods of tears because one of the village cats had eaten her precious chicken. Obviously the sheer scale of this disaster put my own little adventure into a proper perspective.'

Now qualified to wear Fleet Air Arm pilot's wings on his sleeve, Rob was commissioned as a Sub-Lieutenant RNVR. Like all newly commissioned Naval officers he was required to attend a course at the Naval college at Greenwich to learn how to hold his knife and fork properly and generally how to comport himself as an officer and a gentleman. He and Betty stayed in his brother's Sloane Street flat, being looked after by John's servant Cowell who, quite apart from his many other sterling qualities, was a superb chef, adept at making the most of meagre wartime rations. At this time, of course, the London blitz was in full swing, and Rob can clearly remember thinking how innocent the plump black bombs looked as they tumbled lazily from the bellies of the German bombers while anti-aircraft fire burst all round them and, high above, vapour trails charted the dogfights between their escorts and the defending British fighters.

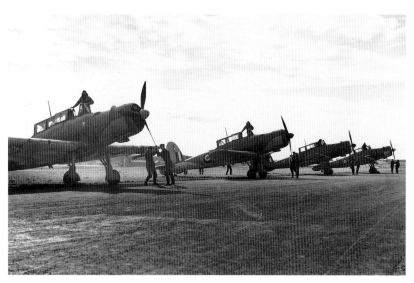

Blackburn Skuas and Rocs at Speke.

Petrol was now very scarce indeed and Rob and Betty decided to buy a small, economical car with which to eke out the petrol rations allocated to the Delahayes. They chose a 1937 Fiat Topolino with a 500 cc engine which delivered more than fifty miles per gallon as they drove from London to Eastleigh, where Rob was required to report for duty on 15th September 1940. In future years this date would be celebrated as Battle of Britain Day. During the journey they heard reports on the radio of the biggest air battle of the war; it was a last desperate gamble by the *Luftwaffe* which committed four hundred bombers and seven hundred fighters to the action, opposed by three hundred British fighters. At the end of the day fifty-six German aircraft had been shot down and at least twenty more had ditched in the Channel after running out of fuel on the way home, against the loss of twenty-six British planes. The slow Stuka dive bombers had proved particularly vulnerable and would never be used again in raids against mainland Britain.

Arriving at Eastleigh Rob found that the airfield had been badly bombed and was out of commission, so he and Betty were redirected to RNAS Yeovilton where Rob would learn to fly a number of Naval fighters including the Gloster Gladiator. 'The Gladiator was a really super little aeroplane. It could climb to ten thousand feet as fast as a Spitfire and it was incredibly manoeuvrable – just like a sports car, really – but it was lightly armed and armoured. It did have one rather nasty habit which was that when you opened the throttle for take-off you had to compensate for the torque with lots of opposite rudder or you were in real trouble.

'I remember once when my Flight was on watch a Messerschmitt 109 was spotted over Yeovil and my Gladiator was scrambled to intercept him and shoot him down. Fortunately the fighter direction wasn't up to much and I never found him, otherwise I don't know what the outcome might have been; I might have been able to out-manoeuvre him, but he would certainly have out-gunned me.'

Johnny Wakefield, who had won the 1939 San Remo Grand Prix in a privately entered Maserati, was one of Rob's contemporaries at Yeovilton. So was Peter Twiss who later became a Fairey test pilot and the first man to raise the World Air Speed Record to over 1000 mph. One day Twiss spotted an unattended fuel bowser on the airfield apron and within moments the competition Delahaye – which because of its thirty-gallon tank was used to store Rob's precious supply of petrol – was full to overflowing. Later another pilot was caught filling his car with aircraft fuel, court martialled and sent to prison for six months. Rob and Peter decided not to push their luck.

Now the Topolino showed its Achilles heel; because Italy was on the wrong side of the war, no Fiat spares were available in England.

So when the rear axle failed, that was that. The car had been such a success, however, that Rob invested in a newer one – vintage 1938 this time – which also served him well until the inconvenient and permanent loss of reverse gear. After some discussion Rob and Betty decided to replace it with a 10 hp Vauxhall; they eventually tracked one down at a rather shady used car lot near Southampton, run by a man who lived in a caravan on the lot. He obviously thought that Christmas had come early when he saw Rob and quoted an outrageous price – £60 – for the Vauxhall. This was about what the Topolino was worth complete with reverse gear; without reverse it was worth about half as much. So Rob proposed a straight swap. The dealer asked to test drive the Fiat but, as he would have had to reverse out of the lot to do so, Rob thought that was a bad idea. So he said that it was down to its last drop of petrol and whoever drove it away would certainly end up pushing it back. Rob started the engine, it sounded as sweet as a nut, and the deal was done. Alas, the Vauxhall was in worse shape than Rob and Betty had imagined, consuming oil almost more greedily than petrol.

When Rob was posted to Speke, near Liverpool, the local Vauxhall agent offered to replace the engine and repair a damaged wing for only £27. The snag was that his

The economical 1937 Fiat Topolino.

The 10 hp Vauxhall which survived the war.

workshop was located in the heart of Liverpool's dockland which the Germans plastered with bombs every night of the week. When the time came to collect the car the workshop building was the only one still standing within a radius of two hundred yards, albeit looking more than slightly second hand; the Vauxhall survived intact until long after the war was over.

Speke was an airfield with a serious fog problem. As often as not the only way the Navy pilots could find their way home was to latch on to one of the De Havilland Rapides which flew between Liverpool and the Isle of Man and were equipped with rudimentary navigational aids, and follow them in, weaving from side to side to reduce their speed to match that of the slower civilian aircraft. One day after Rob had taken off in thick fog he realised he was in a bit of trouble when he flew straight between two telegraph poles, his propeller shredding the wires and cutting off half Liverpool as he did so. The only thing to do was to try to climb above the fog and, sure enough, at about eight thousand feet he emerged into a world of brilliant sunshine and clear blue skies. Now all he had to figure out was how to get down again.

After wrestling with this problem for a while, with mounting apprehension, Rob decided that there was really no safe way down, and the only sensible thing to do was to bale out. But his gunner, Leading Seaman Nash, had other ideas. 'I don't know about you, sir,' he said, 'but I haven't the faintest idea whether we are over land or sea, and I'm buggered if I'm baling out over the middle of the Atlantic.' Rob saw his point at once.

They had been flying around for more than an hour when Rob finally spotted a tiny gap in the murk. The Roc he was flying was a dive bomber so he deployed the air brakes and plunged vertically through the hole in the fog; beneath him he could just see a small town with a football pitch in the middle of it. 'Visibility was extremely limited but I decided to try and put it down on the football pitch. As I circled to make my approach I couldn't see the pitch at all, but I had spotted two factory chimneys which sort of loomed above the fog and I thought that if I lined up on them it would probably be about right. I couldn't see the ground so I had to try and judge my height in relation to the chimneys. Of course I got it wrong and hit a rather solid brick wall which surrounded the football pitch, at which point the aeroplane simply disintegrated – both wings came off, the engine went in one direction and the fuselage in another – but thankfully Nash and I were left strapped into what remained of the cockpit, completely unhurt. Very considerably shaken, but unhurt.

'Shortly afterwards a policeman and some other people waving pitchforks and shotguns came rushing up, but once they had established that we were friendly they became less aggressive. Evidently this little town, which was called Horwich, was surrounded by highish hills and the townspeople had heard us circling above the fog for hours and had been taking bets on which of the hills we would crash into. As it was I suppose that all bets were off.'

After some time at Speke Rob received orders to join a carrier in the Mediterranean, even though he had never made a deck landing, and after a few days' embarkation leave found himself saying an emotional farewell to Betty, wondering if he would ever see her again, before joining a troopship on the Clyde for the three-month voyage round the Cape to Alexandria. Although the ship, the SS *Indrapoera*, was a requisitioned P&O liner which still retained its peacetime crew, kitchen and wine cellar, overcrowding made it uncomfortable. The more junior you were, the more you suffered from overcrowding, and Rob was very junior. Help was at hand, however; Scruffy Bromwich had been one of Rob's instructors at Yeovilton and on the strength of this earlier relationship invited Rob to share the large double cabin of which he was the sole occupant.

'Scruffy Bromwich was a most colourful character, a true adventurer. He was the son of a distinguished Admiral and had once been a professional smuggler, running cognac across the Channel from France. When that got too hot for him, he joined the RAF and became one of the stunt pilots at Hendon. He was a wonderful pilot and a real daredevil – flying through the hangar upside down and that sort of thing. He had transferred to the Fleet Air Arm before the war and used to tell a fabulous story about getting kitted up in Portsmouth. Of course, in those days you used to have to have the full works – sword, frock coat, cocked hat, telescope, the lot. By the time he got as far as the telescope, Scruffy was beginning to run out of money. In the end he settled for the cheapest telescope in the place; it looked the part – all brass and leather – but had no lenses in it, and so it was absolutely useless. Anyway, some time later Scruffy was standing watch in harbour on the battleship HMS *Malaya* when his captain borrowed this telescope for some reason or another. He was absolutely livid to discover that it had no lenses, and flung it into the sea. Next morning Lieutenant (A.) Bromwich RN was required to explain himself; "Well sir," he said, "as you know, my ancestors served with Lord Nelson, and that was one of his telescopes which had been presented to my father. Useless though it was, I'm sure you can appreciate that it had a certain sentimental value for me." Well, of course, Nelson is the Navy's idol, and the captain was absolutely mortified. "I'm terribly sorry, Bromwich," he said. "Please forgive me. I'll send the ship's divers down tomorrow to see if they can find it." Fortunately the ship received orders to put to sea that night, so Scruffy was never rumbled.' Scruffy Bromwich survived the war and now lives in Canada; he is Rob's last remaining Fleet Air Arm friend.

The voyage passed in a haze of alcohol; gin at tuppence a tot on board and generous hospitality at every port of call – Sierra Leone (where Rob spent a day in jail), Cape Town, Durban and Aden – before disembarkation at Port Taufiq and a train ride to Alexandria. Here Rob found that the goalposts had been moved; instead of joining a carrier as planned, he was to fly shore-based Fulmars from HMS Phoenix at Dekheila to supply the RAF and RNAS squadrons operating from forward airstrips in the desert.

His initiation into this role was not encouraging; on his first sortie to a forward airstrip his Fulmar, which subsequently proved to be a most unreliable aircraft, refused to lower one of its wheels. He tried winding it down manually, he tried shaking it down by thumping the aircraft onto the ground on its one extended wheel, but nothing would budge it. To make matters worse, the wheel which was deployed then refused to retract, so that Rob was left with no option but to attempt a one-wheel landing. In the event it worked out quite well; Rob came in fast, held the unsupported wing up on the opposite brake and executed a few relatively harmless spins in the sand. The aeroplane was flying again within a couple of days, but Rob was not sorry to trade it in for a more reliable Swordfish.

In April 1941 Tobruk was bypassed and besieged by the Germans during Rommel's first push towards Cairo. The siege lasted for seven months during which time Rob flew Rocs, Skuas, Hurricanes and Swordfish to transport supplies and personnel into and out of the Tobruk garrison.

On one occasion he was on his way to Tobruk when he encountered an impenetrable sand storm, reminiscent of the fog at Speke. Following the railway line at an altitude of ten feet – in visibility of not much more than ten feet – was so

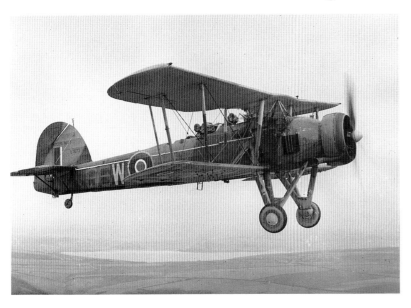

Swordfish Mk 1 torpedo bomber.

exhausting that he decided to land beside the railway tracks and wait for the storm to blow over. 'For Christ's sake don't do that,' implored his experienced navigator. 'The tracks are mined on both sides and we'll be blown to bits.' Instead they turned due north and found the coastline, which they then followed – often almost looking down the barrels of German anti-aircraft guns whose crews were too surprised to fire at them – before locating Tobruk harbour and following the road up the hill to the airstrip. Rob was the first pilot to have landed there since the sandstorm began three days earlier.

Not unshaken by this experience, Rob consoled himself with the bottle of Gordon's gin without which no self-respecting Fleet Air Arm pilot ever flew. Sheltering in their rock scrapes from the constant German bombardment, the only drinks available to the denizens of Tobruk were the rather brackish local water, and tea brewed from that same rather brackish water. Rob preferred his gin to either of these options. When the sandstorm eventually lifted, two passengers were to accompany him to Dekheila; Willy Aston, a pilot due for leave, and a Royal Marine due for court martial for selling parachute silk to the Arabs. Willy Aston took one look at Rob and reckoned that it would be safer if he flew them home, while Rob shared the back seat with the prisoner and what remained of his bottle of gin.

As they approached Dekheila Rob was smitten by a sudden attack of responsibility; he decided that he should hold on to the wing of his aircraft to prevent it from lifting in the strong wind while Willy taxied to the apron. Thus full of good intentions, Rob committed that same error of judgement which had punished countless riding mechanics at Brooklands in happier times; he got out of the car – or in this case the aeroplane – before it had stopped. The front wheels had just touched down when Rob decided to disembark, unfortunately choosing to do so on the side of the aircraft on which there were no steps. As he fell onto the runway his legs were caught by the tail wheel which ripped off his trousers and left him lying half-naked and semi-conscious on the tarmac. Luckily for Rob the duty medical officer was Doc Sheehan, with whom he had spent three months on the *Indrapoera*; thus his medical report read 'Multiple contusions and abrasions; patient partially anaesthetised at time of accident.'

In June 1942, with Rommel once again pushing towards Cairo, it became clear that it was only a matter of time before Tobruk would be overrun by the *Afrika Korps*, and Rob was determined to ensure that two particular motor bikes which he

Hawker Hurricanes over the Western Desert.

had spotted there would not fall into German hands. Despite his parlous situation the Army quartermaster in charge of the bikes seemed determined to behave by the book, and he refused to hand them over. Rob managed to distract his attention for long enough for a couple of friends to load a Norton 500 and a captured BMW into the back of a borrowed truck, and within minutes they were suspended from the torpedo rack of his Swordfish and on their way to Dekheila.

He sold the Norton, but kept the BMW. Some time later, when he was stationed in Haifa, Rob fitted a sidecar to the BMW which he found made it very difficult to drive. 'I remember one night I went out with a Palestine policeman to a Bedouin camp in the desert where we ate sheep's eyes with our fingers and drank arak, sitting cross-legged on the sand and watching the belly dancers. I'd been warned that arak was pretty potent stuff so I only had about three small glasses, but when I got on the bike to drive home things didn't seem to be going too well. After a bit we came to a corner which was just too much for us and we went absolutely arse over tit. The policeman was all right, but I cut my leg quite badly and eventually ended up in a New Zealand field hospital in Beirut with septicaemia and jaundice. On another occasion, after I'd ditched the sidecar, we were climbing Mount Carmel five up – one on the handlebars, one on the petrol tank, me on the seat and two more on the pillion – when a soldier tried to thumb a lift from us; unfortunately I couldn't for the life of me see how to take a sixth passenger on board.'

Inset: *Rob at Haifa in 1942.*

Above: *The Dido class cruiser HMS* Cleopatra *before the Sicily landings.*

HMS Victorious.

Flying from the little Haifa aerodrome, dodging the barrage balloons which protected the town, Rob towed target drogues for the Navy anti-aircraft gunners to shoot at, using live ammunition. Their aim was inaccurate enough to cause him some anxiety; on his first sortie the very first salvo exploded around his Swordfish, blowing the aircraft upside down and peppering it with shrapnel. He recalled the story of a Navy pilot who had signalled to the ship which seemed to be shooting ahead of his plane instead of at the drogue a thousand feet astern of it, *'I'm pulling this bloody drogue, not pushing it,'* but remembering also that this signal had resulted in the court martial of its author, Rob contented himself with firing off a Verey Light indicating that his was a friendly aircraft and hoping that the gunners would get the message. As it turned out this was a good decision, for he soon found himself joining the ship concerned; it was Admiral Sir Philip Vian's flagship, the Dido class cruiser HMS *Cleopatra*, to which he was posted as Fighter Direction Officer.

Cleopatra was torpedoed on the morning of 10th July 1943 while supporting the invasion of Sicily. Having been closed up at action stations all night, Rob was catnapping on the steel deck of the Gunnery Officer's cabin below the fighting bridge when the torpedo struck amidships, destroying the main engine room. Unlike others in her class which had sunk within minutes of being hit, *Cleopatra* remained obstinately afloat. After her crew had successfully extinguished a major fire she set sail for Malta, her quarterdeck awash, her maximum speed two knots, a hundred and eighty wounded – many beyond help, suffering from horrific burns – lying on her fo'c's'le.

Most of the Royal Marines on board, who traditionally man one of the after gun turrets and provide the ship's band, had been killed. However, Rob vividly recalls the few surviving bandsmen playing their hearts out on the partially submerged quarterdeck as the ship limped into Grand Harbour at Valletta, watched by the crews of all the other vessels in port, lining their rails and cheering.

Temporarily without a ship, Rob was reunited briefly with Betty and met his nine-month-old daughter Dauvergne for the first time. Before receiving new orders, he attended a routine medical which was conducted by the doctor, now a Surgeon Captain, who had sewn up his thumb in 1939. 'Good God,' he said, 'I was sure you would have killed yourself by now – I'm astonished to find you still in one piece!' Surgeon Captain Simpson's examination was to enhance the likelihood of Rob's continued survival; his night vision was found to be defective, and he was grounded. Thus he found himself posted to HMS *Victorious* as Hangar Control Officer. The ship was then refitting in Gladstone Dock at Liverpool before sailing for the Far East. First, however, came two Russian convoys and two sorties from Scapa Flow to bomb the Tirpitz in Trondheim Fjord. The Fleet Air Arm inflicted sufficient damage to prevent her from threatening the forthcoming Normandy invasion, before the RAF finished her off.

After an uneventful year in the Far East, mostly spent at Trincomalee, Rob returned to England. He arrived in London on VE night, 8th May 1945, just in time to join Betty at the gigantic street party which celebrated the end of the European war, and to see the lights turned on in Trafalgar Square for the first time since blackout regulations had been imposed almost six years earlier. He was then offered a very comfortable position as one of the Naval representatives at the Ministry of Aircraft Production. His office was in a building on the Thames Embankment, with a balcony overlooking the river. Shortly after Rob took up this appointment the atomic bombs dropped on Hiroshima and Nagasaki brought about Japan's surrender; the war was over, and Rob was free to indulge his passion for cars once again.

One of his Delahayes provided him with almost instant gratification; on his very first trip to London in the competition car Rob was fortunate enough to encounter one of the big American automobiles which were considered – at least by their American drivers – to be very much faster than anything produced in Europe, and probably superior in every other respect as well. The driver of this particular car was sweeping past everything on the road, clearly thinking he was uncatchable, when Rob took a childish delight in overtaking him at 100 mph before ostentatiously changing up into top gear. On another occasion, after a dice around Wimbledon Common with an SS Jaguar, Rob discovered that the other driver was fellow Naval officer Lance Macklin, who was involved, ten years later, in the Le Mans disaster.

At about this time Rob and Betty found a flat in a house on Chelsea Embankment where they would live for some years. Their landlady, Joan McLeod, was the widow of a

Rob and Betty in 1945.

Rob with the competition Delahaye in road trim in 1945.

Cameron Highlander who had been killed in Sicily just three weeks after the assault during which HMS *Cleopatra* had been torpedoed; one of her twin sons would later marry Rob's daughter. In due course the basement flat would become the province of the caretaker, McAllister, whose war had been spent as a Sergeant-Major in the Scots Guards; at breakfast time every morning he dispensed champagne to Mrs

Rob's 1935 Rolls Royce Continental Tourer.

McLeod's tenants in an attempt to revive them sufficiently to face the rigours of the day to come. Peter Ustinov, who later occupied the flat below Rob and Betty, was one of McAllister's most enthusiastic customers. He and Rob used to spend hours together late at night, after he had returned from the theatre, talking about cars and simulating racing car noises; Rob reckoned he did a decent ERA, while Peter could manage a passable sixteen-cylinder BRM. This was the genesis of Ustinov's hilarious monologue entitled 'The Grand Prix of Gibraltar'.

Rob used the competition Delahaye daily to drive to the office, but soon realised that this was not a terribly good idea as it made so much noise that everyone could tell when he arrived – always late, after spending the night on the town.

Meanwhile, the Coupé had lost third and fourth gears and Betty suggested that it should be replaced; Rob decided upon a Rolls Royce in which he thought he could pussyfoot into the office without disturbing anyone who was misguided enough to be working. Rob's new car was a 1935 H.R. Owen Drophead Coupé with coachwork by Gurney Nutting, usually known as a Continental Tourer. Because petrol was still rationed, Rob decided to try to run the Rolls on methanol which, albeit at a price, was more readily available. Alas the volatile methanol seemed to loosen a lot of the dirt which must have accumulated in the fuel system over the years, and the fuel filters kept blocking at inconvenient moments. Once Rob had to roll up his sleeves and wield his spanners while dressed for the Royal Enclosure at Ascot.

This apart, Rob's only complaint about the car was the usual one; it was too slow. He decided to fit an Arnolt supercharger which delivered a boost of about 8 psi and reduced the 0–60 mph acceleration time by no less than twelve seconds. It did nothing for the top speed, however, and after running flat out for about half a mile the car would suddenly stop, suffering from total fuel starvation. Rob consulted the engineer who had fitted the blower who said, 'Give me an hour to think about it and I will call you back with the answer.' Years later when Rob was writing for *Road & Track* he offered a $100 prize for the first correct diagnosis of the problem. Only a very few respondents got the answer right, amongst whom was Innes Ireland. Of course, he had knowledge gained during a five-year Rolls Royce apprenticeship to call upon.*

Robbie driving his Bugatti Type 52.

At about the same time Rob also acquired a car for his son Robbie who had been born almost a year earlier, in November 1944. It was a Bugatti Type 52, a miniature version of the Type 51 – built by Le Patron himself – which had a range of about twenty miles at a maximum speed of 6 mph and was driven by an electric motor powered by a 12-volt battery. It is not absolutely certain how many of these beautiful miniatures were produced; one theory is that each purchaser of a Bugatti Royale was given one: another that each crowned head of Europe received one for his eldest son. In any event the little Bugatti would provide much future pleasure for both Walker *père et fils*.

On 6th December 1945 Rob Walker left the Navy, six years to the day after walking through the gates of HMS St Vincent as a raw recruit. Although in many ways his had been an extremely eventful war, he had not fired a single shot in anger. He was twenty-eight. His trustees no longer controlled his inheritance. The rest of his life was about to begin.

* Hazleton Publishing will offer a similar prize to the first correct entry received. Innes Ireland need not apply.

Chapter 4
Delahaye and Delage

When the war ended, just as the competition Delahaye had been disinterred from the squash court at Sutton Veny so, across the channel in France, Rob's contemporary Maurice Trintignant unearthed his Bugatti from beneath a pile of straw which had hidden it from the occupying Germans while he fought with the Maquis. In his first post-war race Maurice was well placed until the Bugatti spluttered to a halt suffering from fuel starvation. Asked by Jean-Pierre Wimille to explain the problem he replied succinctly *'Petoulet'*, Provençale slang for rat shit. From that moment on Trintignant was known as Petoulet, and even today the excellent red wines produced by his vineyards near Vergèze are called Vins Le Petoulet.

Back in Britain, however, Rob Walker found himself the owner of a car which, in 1939, had been pronounced the fastest road racing car in the country, and circumstances suggested that it was still the fastest road racing car in the country. But, bound by his promise to Betty, Rob was not allowed to race it. So he decided to become an entrant, preparing the car for others to drive.

Guy Jason-Henry was about the same age as Rob, shared many of his interests, and was not only a very good driver but also an excellent mechanic who seemed to have both an intuitive understanding of the Delahaye and the ability to tune it to perfection. It was not long before the two of them had worked out a partnership arrangement; in return for buying a half-share in the car, Jason-Henry would become the driver and mechanic, while Rob would be the entrant and team manager. If the car was entered in sprints or hill climbs, then Rob would drive, as allowed by his agreement with Betty.

For a while the arrangement worked very well. Petrol rationing limited the number of motor races held in the immediate post-war years, but whenever and wherever the Delahaye raced, it won. When the Goodwood circuit was inaugurated on the perimeter track of a wartime airfield, the Delahaye even trounced the spectacular new Jaguar XK 120, twelve years its junior.

By 1949 racing was being organised once more on an international scale, and Rob entered the Delahaye for the first post-war Le Mans.

He chose Tony Rolt as Jason-Henry's co-driver. Before the war, as a nineteen-year-old subaltern in the Rifle Brigade, Rolt had won the British Empire Trophy

Maurice Trintignant.

race. He had then been forbidden by his Colonel to accept a works ERA drive in South Africa on the grounds that motor racing wasn't a socially acceptable pastime for a young officer in a distinguished light infantry regiment. In the fullness of time, however, Rolt was granted permission to marry that same feisty Colonel's daughter, his enthusiasm for the horseless carriage notwithstanding. Taken by the Germans during the retreat to Dunkirk, Rolt determined to spend the rest of the war making his captors' lives as difficult as possible. To this end he made a point of escaping from whichever prison camp sought to contain him, unfortunately being recaptured on each occasion – once within only fifty yards of the Swiss border and freedom. Eventually he was incarcerated with all the other bad boys in Colditz Castle, which

the Germans regarded as escape proof. Only the arrival of the liberating Americans prevented Rolt from attempting to escape from Colditz in a glider made from bedboards which he planned to launch from the castle ramparts. Had he done so, he would probably not have survived to drive at Le Mans – a race which he was to win in 1953, co-driving a C-Type Jaguar with Duncan Hamilton.

In 1949, however, he was not so fortunate; he and Jason-Henry were lying fifth at midnight, despite a minor overheating problem, when the main bearings failed. The same bearings had lasted twenty-four hours of Le Mans ten years earlier, and had not been renewed since. Luigi

Midnight at Le Mans, 1949; the Rolt/Jason-Henry Delahaye retires when lying fifth.

Chinetti and Lord Selsdon won the race in a Ferrari 166 Mille Miglia, and Rob Walker learned a lesson in team management which he would not easily forget.

Next the partners drove the Delahaye to Comminges where the French Grand Prix was to be held for sports cars. As at Le Mans, race day was extremely hot and after a while Jason-Henry drew into the pits completely exhausted. Rob, who had been nominated as reserve driver, longed to leap into the car but, honouring his promise to Betty, he contented himself with flinging buckets of cold water over his partner. This eventually had the desired effect and Jason-Henry recovered sufficiently to finish third. Pozzi won in another Delahaye after Sommer and Schell had blown up their Lago-Talbots and Luigi Chinetti had spun out of the lead at 160 mph in an attempt, thankfully successful, to avoid a lady pushing a baby carriage,

At the first corner of the British Empire Trophy race in 1951, Rob's Delahaye driven by Guy Gale is struck by a spinning Healey, while his DB2 with George Abecassis at the wheel goes round on the outside.

Eric Thompson in the Delahaye at Goodwood in 1951.

complete with baby, across the track. After the race Rob asked him how on earth he had managed to avoid a major accident; 'Never fight it, Rob,' Chinetti replied. 'Just let the car spin and you'll be all right.'

The partners were very close. They usually discussed between them which races would be entered, and then drove together in the Delahaye to the race concerned. Neither of them much liked being driven by the other; in Rob's case, he particularly disliked Jason-Henry's habit of driving flat out over blind hill crests, being certain that sooner or later they would find the road blocked on the other side. One day, sure enough, they did – but such was Jason-Henry's driving skill that he somehow managed to dodge both *camions*, and they emerged unscathed.

One afternoon soon after Rob had bought Pippbrook garage in Dorking, he was sitting in his office above the racing shop when a friend telephoned to ask if he had heard that Guy Jason-Henry had been arrested at Newhaven for trying to smuggle more than three thousand watches into the country in a false petrol tank.

'Silly bugger,' said Rob. 'Just the sort of bloody stupid stunt he would try to pull.'

'Quite right,' said his friend. 'By the way, the false petrol tank was fitted to your Delahaye.'

Next day the case was headlined in all the newspapers. Fortunately there was no suggestion that Rob had been implicated in any way; indeed, he had not known even that the car was out of the country.

It eventually emerged that in September 1949, without informing his partner, Jason-Henry had entered the car for a 1000 km race just south of Paris at Mont- lhéry. Although he didn't actually race after supposedly breaking down in practice, the event provided a perfectly valid reason for the car to be in France, and a perfect opportunity to fill the false tank with watches which would fetch a premium price in post-war England where rationing, austerity and a shortage of desirable consumer goods still prevailed. When Jason-Henry arrived at Newhaven the Customs officers focused immediately on the false tank; obviously someone had tipped them off.

It soon became clear that although they would bring him to trial Jason-Henry was regarded as small fry by the authorities, a sprat to catch a mackerel. Once this had been established Jason-Henry became a co-operative witness and was duly acquitted of complicity in the Delahaye case, but fined £25 for possession of an unlicensed pistol which the Customs officers had also discovered in the car.

Meanwhile, despite Jason-Henry's acquittal, it was beyond dispute that the Dela- haye had been carrying contraband. As such, it was forfeit. Evidently the law had it that if contraband was discovered in transit then the means of transportation was automatically sequestered; a case in which smuggled cigarettes were found in the possession of a passenger in a Bristol taxi provided the precedent under which the Delahaye was now held. Needless to say, Rob protested against this injustice, as had the innocent Bristol taxi driver before him, but to no avail. He could have the car back, certainly, but only if he paid for it.

Some pretty hard-nosed negotiations about price ensued. Rob's trump card was a letter which was leaked to the *Daily Express* asking the authorities how much Cunard paid to buy back the *Queen Elizabeth* or the *Queen Mary* every time they were confiscated because a passenger had been caught smuggling nylons. Evidently quite a few people were interested in the answer to this question and the Customs and Excise switchboard in London was jammed for days on end by callers asking, 'Well, how much do they pay?' Rob himself never did get a satisfactory answer to his query, but eventually he paid £300 to regain full ownership of the Delahaye and duly collected it from the quayside at Newhaven, much corroded after months of neglect and exposure to salt-laden sea breezes.

The Sotheby's catalogue illustration of the Delahaye for the Gleneagles sale of the estate of Major E.G. Thomson.

A few weeks after he had repurchased his car, Rob received a telephone call from Les Leston. Prior to the race at Montlhéry Jason-Henry had evidently borrowed a bonnet from Leston, and now Les wanted it back. 'I'm afraid I don't know anything about your bonnet, Les,' said Rob. 'I've just bought a car from the Customs and it came complete with a bonnet, so I think you had better get in touch with them if you have a problem.' One way and another the Customs authorities probably wished they had never heard of Rob Walker and his Delahaye.

Shortly afterwards Rob sold the Delahaye to Dan Marguiles for a few hundred pounds, and after a while it passed to an eccentric Scottish collector of classic cars who, convinced that he could improve upon the original coachwork, applied ghastly soap-box bodies to each and every one of them. Horrified, Rob tried several times to buy the Delahaye back, but was rebuffed on each occasion. When he died in 1970, Major E.G. Thomson left his entire estate to the RNLI on whose behalf the car collection was auctioned by Sotheby's at Gleneagles. The Delahaye fetched £3500. Needless to say, Rob Walker was the buyer, paying almost ten times more for what then amounted to hardly more than a waterlogged wreck than he had for the unblemished car thirty-two years earlier. Today the fully restored Delahaye may be seen at the Sparkford Museum near Yeovil, while the false petrol tank is on display in the Smuggler's Museum in Cornwall.

The restored Delahaye as it may be seen today at the Sparkford Museum.

Before retiring to Sparkford, however, the Delahaye made two more journeys to Le Mans; as part of the 1973 celebrations to mark the 50th anniversary of the Circuit Permanent de la Sarthe, two forty-five minute races were held before the start of official practice, one for Le Mans cars of the pre-war era, the other for cars which had raced there between 1949 and 1959. Stirling Moss drove the Delahaye in the first race, overcoming the handicap of a totally unsuitable axle ratio to finish fourth. The second race was won by the Ferrari 250GT with which Stirling had won the 1960 Tourist Trophy for Rob, and which he and Graham Hill had driven at Le Mans in 1961, leading their class until the fanbelt broke. Although owned and entered by Sir Anthony Bamford, the car still sported the dark blue and white Walker livery. Victory celebrations were curtailed, however, when the organisers realised it was not eligible for the race and declared Willie Green driving a JCB D-Type Jaguar the new winner.

Then in 1979, forty years after racing there, Rob returned for a photo session to illustrate a feature in the American magazine *Road & Track*, to which he was then a contributor. Driving the old car around the circuit before the modern racers were allowed to practise, to the great delight of the French gendarmes, marshals and spectators, Rob was surprised how much it had changed; the road was much wider – at least twice as wide, in his judgement – than in 1939, the corners were much more open, the spectators further away from the action, and the pine trees which lined the track protected by double Armco crash barriers. But then the cars were different

Rob driving the Delahaye beneath the Dunlop Bridge at Le Mans in 1979.

too. In 1939, Rob and his co-driver Ian Connell had agreed upon a rev limit which delivered some 125 mph on the Mulsanne Straight; forty years later the fastest cars were slipstreaming each other at speeds in excess of 220 mph at the same point on the circuit.

Rob's son drove the Delahaye back to England after this excursion. At Newhaven he was stopped by a Customs officer who said, 'I suppose you know why I'm stopping you, don't you?' Robbie replied, 'Surely you can't expect to find another three thousand watches in the petrol tank?' and they parted company with much good humour.

'After I had sold the Delahaye to Dan Marguiles I bought an ex-works Aston Martin DB2 – VMF 65 – for Tony Rolt to drive in sports car races. We had entered it for the Tourist Trophy race at Dundrod in 1951 when, only about a week before the race, Tony was offered a drive by the Jaguar factory team. He told me that he would very much like to accept, and asked if I would mind if he did so. Actually I minded very much but I wasn't going to be dog in the manger about it and prevent Tony from taking up this wonderful opportunity, so I told him to go ahead and I got Eric Thompson to drive my car instead – and he drove it jolly well to finish eighth overall and third in his class.

'The night before the first practice day Tony and I were at a party in our hotel

Eric Thompson in Rob's ex-works Aston Martin DB2, Easter Goodwood 1954.

until about five o'clock in the morning, and we only had a few hours' sleep before we drove out to the circuit. Tony seemed to be as fresh as a daisy, but I have to say that I wasn't feeling any too good. Anyway, I had noticed that when Tony signed autographs he just scribbled his name and never looked at the person for whom he was signing. So I strolled into the Jaguar pit armed with a piece of paper which I thrust under his nose, and he duly autographed it without looking at me. Then I said, "Right, that's got you signed up for next year." Lofty England and Bill Lyons who were standing nearby turned pale, and I thought for a moment that Lofty was going to pass out. It took quite a while before he saw the funny side of it.'

Back in 1949, however, just as Rob had introduced Tony Rolt to sports cars, so Rolt now persuaded Rob to enter the world of single-seater racing. But it was not easy to find a competitive car. Their first choice was one of the supercharged $1\frac{1}{2}$-litre W165 Mercedes which had been specially built for the Tripoli Grand Prix in 1939 and sent for safe keeping to the concessionaire in Switzerland at the outbreak of war. Rudi Caracciola who, of course, had been a Mercedes team driver in those far-off days, somehow felt that the car was his to sell but, alas, military red tape prevented Rob from buying it. Civilian red tape thwarted his next attempt to acquire a race winner; immediately after the war exchange-control regulations stipulated that the only foreign cars which could be sold in Britain were those which had been granted a special import licence for exhibition at the Earl's Court Motor Show. Rob visited Tony Lago in Paris and persuaded him to allow the French coachbuilders Figoni et Falaschi to exhibit one of the new $4\frac{1}{2}$-litre Grand Prix Lago-Talbots on their stand so that he could buy it for Rolt to drive in the coming 1950 season. On the eve of the show, during the Society of Motor Manufacturers and Traders' final inspection, the car was declared ineligible for an exhibition devoted to road cars and removed from the stand – and from Rob's shopping list.

In the end it was more or less Hobson's choice, and with the help of Reg Parnell Rob bought a 1927 Delage with a 1½-litre supercharged straight-eight engine. Actually, he bought two; one was a runner acquired from Richard Habershon while

Chiron with the Seaman Delage at Indianapolis in 1929.

the other, which came in a state of advanced decay from David Hampshire, would be cannibalised for spares for the race car. This plan was soon discarded, however, when it was discovered that the second car had a most distinguished history.

It had originally been a Delage team car but had disappeared for a couple of years following the withdrawal of the factory team at the end of their triumphant 1927 season. Then in 1929 it resurfaced in the hands of Louis Chiron, who took it to America to finish seventh in the Indianapolis 500, winning $1800 prize money in the process. The car reappeared in Europe driven by one of the original Delage team drivers, Robert Sénéchal, and came to England in early 1933 as the property of Lord Howe, who then sold it in 1936 to young Richard Seaman, rapidly becoming established as a star driver.

Giulio Ramponi, ex-Alfa Romeo Grand Prix driver and Scuderia Ferrari mechanic, worked hard to improve the Delage; the cable-operated brakes were discarded in favour of a Lockheed hydraulic system, and the heavy eight-speed Wilson preselector gearbox which had been installed by Lord Howe was exchanged for a lighter crash box during a slimming programme of which even Weight Watchers would have been proud. Ramponi did his work well, and Seaman scored four spectacular victories – in the 200-mile RAC light car race on the Isle of Man, the Coppa Acerbo at Pescara, the Prix de Berne, and the JCC 200-mile race at Donington Park – before being offered a Mercedes-Benz factory drive for the following season. The Delage was sold to Prince Chula of Siam for his cousin Prince Bira to drive and then, via Reg Parnell and David Hampshire, to Rob Walker.

Clearly it would have been sacrilege to break up this marvellous car for spares and, since he had a small mountain of spares with the two cars anyway, Rob decided to restore it to as near as possible Seaman condition. Racing commitments relegated the restoration project to a humble position in Rob's order of priorities for many years, and it was not until 1964 that John Chisman, one of Rob's race mechanics who had been involved from the beginning, could see light at the end of the tunnel. Finally, the car was complete but for the badge on the radiator grille. John turned to a local gunsmith in the hope that he could manufacture a reasonable facsimile of the original; it turned out that the gunsmith's French wife had worked at the Delage factory as a girl and could describe the badge in her sleep. When produced it was

Rob in the ERA-Delage, Brighton Speed Trials 1951.

Rob and the ERA-Delage at Brighton in 1952.

perfect in every minute detail.

Only a few years later, disaster struck. In 1968 Colin Chapman sold Rob the Lotus 49 in which Jim Clark had won the South African Grand Prix earlier in the year. Jo Siffert was to have his first competitive drive in their new car at Brands Hatch in March, at The Race of Champions. Eager to get to work, first out in the first practice period, Seppi powered through the long left-hander behind the pits and disappeared under the bridge on his second lap when suddenly everything went very quiet. Moments later he appeared running down the track towards the pits; Rob ran to meet him. He had slid on a damp patch, got on the marbles, collected a concrete marshals' post and bent the car beyond immediate repair. Although unhurt he was immensely depressed – but his sense of humour remained intact. 'His Porsche anorak had a little note pad attached by elastic to the front pocket; you could pull it out, and when you let go it would pop back into the pocket again. Whenever anyone asked him what had happened Seppi would show them this little pad on which he had written *"Merde, alors"* and then let it flick back into his pocket, like a conjuring trick.' Later that day Siffert flew home to Switzerland, while Rob and Betty decided to watch the following day's practice before going home themselves. Halfway through the afternoon, Rob was called to the telephone.

'Bad news, Guv'nor,' said the voice of his garage manager, Stan Jolliffe. 'There's been a fire in the racing shop.'

'How bad is it?' asked Rob.

'Couldn't be much worse – everything's gone,' was the reply.

Indeed, it could hardly have been much worse. The mechanics had been stripping the damaged Lotus, emptying the last of the fuel from the bags, when someone had worked an electric drill which had arced and triggered an horrendous inferno. Rob's chief mechanic, Tony Cleverley, his escape through the main doors blocked by the flames, fled to the office, slammed the door behind him and dived through the window into the river below. Everything in the racing shop was consumed – the remains of the Lotus, two brand new Ford DFV engines, a Cooper-Maserati and more than thirty years' worth of treasured racing souvenirs, including Rob's scrapbooks containing irreplaceable photographs and press clippings from his pre-war days, one of the worn tyres on which Stirling Moss had won the Argentine Grand Prix in 1958, Robbie's Type 52 Bugatti – and the Delage.

His mechanics realised just how much this car meant to Rob and had thoughtfully hidden it away when he first came to view the damage to the racing shop. The Delage was deemed to be a total loss, the insurance company paid up in full, and that seemed to be the end of that. Until, visiting his old charge one day, John Chisman discovered that, almost miraculously, the engine would still turn over on the starting handle. Brushing away the melted cam covers, supercharger casting and other detritus from the lower half of the engine, John realised that the block and sump were more or less intact. The bodywork had disappeared completely, the iron girder-frame chassis had melted and was sagging to the ground, all four wheels had been totally destroyed, and only one brake drum was more or less intact. And yet John felt that restoration would not be impossible – not easy, but not impossible.

Naturally Rob lent his enthusiastic support to the project, and so did countless others. The partially melted and sagging chassis was sent to Blakers in the hope that they might be able to help; no problem – they still had blueprints dating from 1930 when they had repaired the very same car after a racing accident. They also remembered that the chassis had been stove-enamelled in black and not engine-turned and polished as Rob had thought. As well, they produced new wire wheels off a shelf on which they had been gathering dust for nearly forty years (at a fraction of the price of a wheel for a contemporary Grand Prix car) and John Chisman refurbished the hubs and hubcaps, though not without considerable difficulty.

Paul Jamieson made new brake drums and backing plates, using the damaged parts to generate patterns. Ferodo provided new brake linings which were fitted to the original brake shoes after they had been restored. Edmunds Walker located an original 1937 Lockheed master cylinder and also provided flexible hydraulic pipes of exactly the same specification as those used by Giulio Ramponi when he installed the new braking system thirty-two years earlier. Girling were able to unearth two pre-war rear dampers, but John Chisman painstakingly made the front friction-type shock absorbers by hand.

The chassis was now complete but for one important detail; when Ramponi had reworked the car in 1936 he had put two baulks of timber between the dumb irons in order to strengthen the chassis and reduce flexing. It was these pieces of timber, in fact, which had enabled George Monkhouse to verify the authenticity of the car during the first restoration. Now the local Dorking undertakers, Sherlocks, replaced them with finest coffin oak.

The restored Delage showing one of the front friction-type shock absorbers made by John Chisman.

Inset: *The dumb irons await baulks of coffin oak from Sherlocks.*

After Dick Seaman had sold the Delage to Prince Chula, Lord Howe's preselector gearbox had somehow found its way back onto the car; now it was a sorry sight. In the fire the casing had partially melted and the gears and bearings were welded together. Fortunately Major Wilson, who had designed the gearbox fitted to the Delage, had also designed the epicyclic gearboxes with which even modern battle tanks are equipped, so Rob turned for help to a Midlands engineering firm specialising in military hardware. Nothing official, you understand, but if you knew the password and the right person to approach – and Rob knew both – then no gearbox problem was too difficult. Strictly cash and no questions asked.

The engine was next on the agenda; Paul Jamieson straightened and rehardened the camshafts and fabricated new cam covers, Terrys made new valve springs – no less than three springs per valve being required – and Rob managed to buy back a spare supercharger which he had sold years earlier. All the gaskets were specially made by J. Walker & Sons, and John Chisman made up the oil seals from felt provided by a local saddler. SU found an original carburettor and supplied the special needles required to convert it from alcohol to petrol. Blumels were able to supply a steering wheel similar to one of those used by Seaman – he had used three different kinds of wheel depending upon the type of circuit at which he was racing – at the price Seaman had paid when he bought his in 1936. But the Bosch magneto was altogether more difficult.

The 1½-litre supercharged straight-eight engine of the restored Delage.

Fortunately the Bosch competitions manager, Fritz Juttner, had worked for Rob at an earlier stage of his career and, knowing that Fritz would be there, Rob took the charred magneto to the Nürburgring for the 1968 German Grand Prix. When he saw the remains Fritz shook his head gloomily and said, 'Mr Walker, I don't think anything can be done with this, but I'll take it back to the factory and see what they have to say.' A week later Rob received a cable confirming that the magneto was beyond repair. Almost before he had digested this depressing news a second cable arrived: 'MAGNETO SIMILAR TO YOURS FOUND IN OUR MUSEUM. PLEASE ACCEPT IT COMPLIMENTS OF BOSCH. FRITZ JUTTNER.' The magneto was delivered at the next race by Seppi Siffert and not only fitted perfectly, but also worked perfectly.

Where the radiator was concerned, John Chisman turned for help to Gallays who had made the original, only to be told that they would be interested in nothing less than an order of a thousand units. Following this unproductive encounter, a stroke

The restored Delage in all its glory.

of good fortune placed one of the works foremen in the car park as John was loading the lump of melted brass which was all that remained of the Delage radiator into the boot of his car. 'That looks like one of the diamond radiators that old Bob used to make in the thirties,' he said. 'I'll go and fetch him and we'll see if I'm right.' Within three weeks old Bob had made an exact replica of his original masterpiece.

Now only the reconstruction of the body remained. Wakefields of Byfleet had done the job once before during the earlier restoration, and still employed two panel beaters who had worked on the car in its Brooklands days. The finished product was authentic down to the last rivet. This time the badge on the bonnet was supplied by Peter Graham of the Delage Owners' Club and – the finishing touch – the unusual counter-clockwise tachometer was donated by Lord Howe, son of the previous owner.

The first public appearance of the resurrected Delage was at the 1970 Jacky Ickx Racing Car Show in Brussels. As the climax of the show's closing ceremony the car was started, the blood curdling screech of its exhaust emptying the exhibition hall of all but the most dedicated fans in short order. In Rob's opinion only the exhaust noise of the pre-war Auto Unions and Mercedes, the sixteen-cylinder BRM and maybe, just maybe, the vee-twelve Matra have the same visceral, goose-pimpling effect as that of the Delage. Some time later Rob and John Chisman took the car to

Goodwood where they were initially refused permission to fire it up for fear of complaints from the neighbours, even though Denny Hulme's CanAm McLaren was thundering around the track on test. Eventually John Surtees was allowed one lap just to show that the old lady was back in business.

In due course the Delage became an important exhibit in Tom Wheatcroft's museum at Donington, driven occasionally by Rob in events organised by the Club des Anciens Pilotes. In 1984, however, Rob sold it for £130,000 to a private collector in France. Had his timing been slightly better it might have fetched more than a million.

In its heyday the Delage was a most remarkable racing car. In more recent times a panel of experts including Rudi Uhlenhaut, Stirling Moss, Mauro Forghieri, John Wyer and Denis Jenkinson was asked to nominate the five best racing cars of all time, and three of them included the Delage in their list. It exists in its pristine form today, risen Phoenix-like from the ashes of the 1968 fire, thanks not only to Rob's personal commitment, important though that certainly was, but also to John Chisman's immense skill, initiative, and dogged perseverance. Alas, John died of a sudden and massive heart attack in 1987, still a young man. In a sense, the restored Delage is a most fitting memorial to one of nature's gentlemen, and to a life modestly devoted to the pursuit of excellence.

John Chisman.

Rob driving the Delage on the Promenade des Anglais at Nice in 1982.

Chapter 5
Early European Adventures

Meanwhile the other Delage, which had been fitted with independent front suspension by Prince Bira, was enjoying considerably less success than Rob had hoped despite the capable driving of Tony Rolt. Rolt had persuaded the legendary Freddie Dixon to assist with the preparation of the car and a large part of the trouble was that while Freddie was a wizard with carburettors he was completely dyslexic – although, of course, he wouldn't admit it – about superchargers. The installation of a Wade blower giving 17 psi boost resulted in a number of unfinished races as well as the complete destruction of no less than four expensive engines in a single season.

Another significant part of the problem was that Freddie spent much of his time feeling rather tired and over-emotional; his standard response to the demise of yet another engine was 'Oh well, let's all go and have another drink'. Stan Jolliffe, who left Connaught to become Rob's first full-time racing mechanic, recalls arriving at Freddie's house to be interviewed for the job; as he could obtain no reply to his knock, he opened the unlocked front door to discover Freddie in a state of collapse in the living room. All Stan's efforts to revive him failed until, just as he was about to call an ambulance, Freddie suddenly sat up and demanded to be driven to the local pub – whereupon a renewed state of collapse was rapidly induced. This ritual continued for several days without the subject of Jolliffe's employment being seriously broached – until one day Freddie emerged from a period of oblivion to say not 'Right, let's go to the pub' but 'Right, let's go to work'. He threw himself into his work with at least as much enthusiasm as he devoted to his other interests and Stan Jolliffe had lived night and day with the Delage for almost three weeks before he found time to go home and tell his wife that he was still a racing mechanic.

Tony Rolt driving the ex-Richard Habershon Delage at Silverstone in 1950.

With only one Delage block and head remaining – still unmachined – Rob decided to try an E-Type ERA engine in the Delage chassis, an experiment which produced an ugly, fast and fragile racing car which seldom lasted more than a few laps. After the Formula changed from 1½ litres supercharged to 2 litres atmospheric in 1952 Rob disposed of the ERA-Delage with few regrets.

In its place he bought a nearly new A-Type Connaught with a Lea-Francis

Tony Rolt chasing Duncan Hamilton's Lago Talbot in Rob's ERA-Delage at Goodwood in 1951.

engine; although rather under-powered, the car handled beautifully and, best of all, it was as reliable as its predecessor had been fallible. In 1953 the Connaught appeared at twenty-four meetings, winning sixteen races, including Rob's first international victory in the Coronation Trophy at Crystal Palace, and finishing second seven times and third five times. The only occasion on which it retired because of mechanical failure was in the British Grand Prix at Silverstone, when Rolt stripped a

Prescott 1953 – Tony Rolt hill-climbing Rob's A-Type Connaught.

Tony Rolt driving the Connaught in the 1953 British Grand Prix at Silverstone.

Right: *Rob's first international victory: Rolt leads Ken Wharton's Cooper-Bristol to win the 1953 Coronation Trophy at Crystal Palace.*

driveshaft key while reversing at high speed after overshooting his pit during a refu-elling stop. He was in fourth place at the time, with only ten laps to go. Later the broken key was replaced by a screwdriver blade from a mechanic's tool box and Rob drove the car to victory in the Ramsgate Speed Trials the next day.

Tony Rolt.

Following his victory at Le Mans, and his very successful season in single-seaters, Tony Rolt decided that the time had come for him to retire from motor racing, and Peter Collins replaced him in the Walker team for the 1954 Formula Two series. 'Tony was a gentleman driver, and he drove like a gentleman; if someone who was obviously faster wanted to pass him, Tony would move over to let him through. Peter was quite different. He was my first professional driver, and he really opened my eyes to what the cut and thrust of truly competitive race driving was like. I remember one race at Crystal Palace which was run in two ten-lap heats; in the first heat Horace Gould in a Cooper-Bristol got the drop on Peter at the start and then blocked him for the whole ten laps. During the interval I heard Peter saying to Horace, "If you do that to me again, Horace, I'll push you off." Horace did, and Peter pushed him off. And won. Peter had the most incredible will to win.'

Peter Collins.

It was this will to win which later endeared Peter Collins to Enzo Ferrari who, after the death of Dino, treated him like a surrogate son. And in all probability it was this will to win which killed him at the Nürburgring in August 1958.

Back in 1954 the Formula had changed yet again and Rob acquired a 2½-litre B-Type Connaught with which to compete in Formula One races. It was not a great success; it did not share the reliability of the earlier Connaught – indeed Rob's mechanics seemed to rebuild it completely after every race, and often after every practice session also. In addition the tremendous torque delivered by the Alta engine was very difficult to handle, particularly at the start; in one of Reg Parnell's first races for Rob he was on the front row of the grid alongside Stirling Moss's Maserati 250F at Crystal Palace when the torque got the better of him and he made a rotten start. Determined to overtake Stirling, Reg left his braking too late at the end of the first lap, locked up and went off the road. The car was a complete write-off and Reg broke his collarbone; he never raced seriously again. On another occasion Rob spun at the Brighton Speed Trials, pinning a marshal against the wall on Madeira Drive,

A mixed bunch at Crystal Palace in June 1954. Peter Collins (number 4) in Rob's A-Type Connaught chases the rear-engined Cooper-JAP of Les Leston and Rodney Nuckey's Cooper-Bristol, with Jack Fairman (Turner) taking a wide line and the Cooper-Bristol of Horace Gould leading the rest.

Jack Fairman about to drive Rob's B-Type Connaught at Crystal Palace in July 1955.

Peter Walker winning at Snetterton in the Connaught B-Type, August 1955.

fortunately without injury, in the process. The officials were so disorientated by this performance that they allowed him an immediate second run.

The car won only one race in its entire history when Peter Walker fought tooth and nail with Roy Salvadori's Maserati 250F for twenty laps of the Snetterton circuit. Rob felt that there was a certain piquancy to Salvadori's post-race complaint about Walker's robust driving.

'In mid-1956, soon after the Crystal Palace accident, John Cooper brought out the first of his cars to be powered by the 1100 cc Coventry-Climax fire pump engine. It was an immediate success and the engine was enlarged to 1500 cc to make it competitive in Formula Two racing. As soon as I saw it I felt that it would be a winner and I rang Reg Parnell, who was still recuperating from his injuries, to ask his opinion. He agreed with me and also told me that Alf Francis, Stirling Moss's famous mechanic, had had a row with Stirling and was on the market. I was the first person to order a Formula Two Cooper-Climax from John, and I lost no time in contacting Alf and persuading him to join me. I suppose that those were the two most important decisions I ever made in my entire racing career.'

Of course it wasn't quite as easy as Rob makes it sound. At first he was unable to contact Alf who was on holiday with his wife and daughter. And when they finally made contact Rob discovered that Alf was far from sure that he wanted another job in motor racing. His dispute with Stirling had not been personal; the two men liked each other, but they could not agree professionally. Alf felt, perhaps with some justice, that he was the better engineer of the two and he resented what he regarded as Stirling's interference in the preparation of the race cars. He wanted to be his own master and his recent experiences made him deeply suspicious of Rob's assurances that he would have freedom of action at Pippbrook.

However, after seven weeks on the dole Alf agreed to join Equipe Walker, intrigued by the prospect of working on the Cooper-Climax Formula Two car, and seduced by the prospect of living in a cottage which Rob had found for him on the outskirts of Dorking.

Alf spent his first two weeks as a member of Rob Walker's team helping to build their Cooper chassis at the factory in Surbiton. It was planned to run the car in the Gold Cup race at Oulton Park where the unusually generous prize money would go a long way towards recouping its cost. Predictably enough the engine was not delivered by Coventry-Climax until a few days before the race, and installation was not completed until the eve of the first practice day. Alf set off from Surbiton at

Tony Brooks drives Rob's 300SL Mercedes to victory at Oulton Park in 1956.

Tony Brooks leads Roy Salvadori at Brands Hatch in 1957.

midnight for the six-hour drive to Oulton Park in a transporter carrying a racing car which had not so much as turned a wheel.

All this notwithstanding Tony Brooks – who was driving for Rob at the suggestion of the injured Reg Parnell – was fastest in practice ahead of Roy Salvadori's works Cooper and young Jack Brabham, then virtually unknown in Europe, driving a Cooper which he had built alongside Alf at Surbiton but had not even had time to paint. Alas, on race day Alf made one of his rare mistakes; he fitted new, barely scrubbed tyres which so upset the handling of the Cooper that Brooks was distraught as he took his position on the grid after the warming-up lap. 'What's wrong with the car, Alf?' he said. 'What have you done to it?' It was too late to change the wheels and Rob, Tony and Alf had to endure the frustration of seeing Roy Salvadori run away with the race and with the prize money. Brooks finished second after Jack Brabham had fallen back with fuel pump problems. 'Tony Brooks was a fabulous driver – quite brilliant – but he was careful. He always drove on the safe side and I don't think he ever went anywhere near his absolute limit. I can remember that whenever Tony sat in a new car his first question was always "Is it safe?" On the other hand, as I was to discover later, Stirling's first question was always "Is it fast?" '

Mollified slightly by Tony Brooks' success in the GT race at Oulton Park, in which he drove Rob's lightweight gullwing 300SL to victory, the Walker team took their full revenge at Brands Hatch a month later; although there had not been time enough to attempt serious development of the Climax engine, Alf had fitted a Tipo Mona mechanical fuel pump which improved the performance a little and, his car shod with well-scrubbed tyres, Brooks had no difficulty in trouncing both Salvadori and Brabham.

His Formula Two car had been so successful that John Cooper now began to fancy his chances in Formula One; Coventry-Climax agreed to enlarge their engine to 1960 cc so long as Cooper would fund the development cost. But 1956 was the year of the Suez crisis, when the invasion of Egypt by combined British and French forces was followed in Europe by petrol rationing and considerable uncertainty about the forthcoming motor racing season. Under the circumstances John Cooper understandably got cold feet about the project, but Rob took a more optimistic view and offered to bankroll the development on condition that he could buy the first of the bigger engines. He also asked John Cooper to build him a stronger chassis to accommodate it.

Alf Francis warms up the B-Type Connaught in the paddock at Brands Hatch.

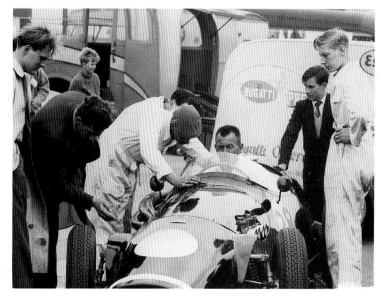

By now Alf Francis felt completely at home in the Walker team and had realised that Rob truly intended him to have total autonomy in the engineering department. It was the first time in his racing career that Alf had enjoyed both responsibility and authority, and he revelled in his new-found freedom of action. His contribution to the team was not confined to his engineering skill, however; the vast experience of motor racing in Europe which his new chief mechanic had gained first with HWM and later with Stirling Moss gave Rob the confidence to venture across the Channel, initially with the Formula Two Cooper.

In 1957 Tony Brooks continued to drive for Rob from time to time but, as he was contracted to Vanwall for Formula One racing, Jack Brabham became the regular team driver. His first appearance in Walker colours was at Syracuse in March. It was hardly an auspicious beginning; Jack and Harry Schell were travelling together from Rome to the port of Reggio di Calabria on the toe of Italy when their train broke down in the middle of the night, in the middle of nowhere. Climbing out of their compartment onto the track, the two of them ran several miles to the next station where they hired a taxi which delivered them to the quayside just in time to catch the last ferry to Messina. Even though they bribed the ship's captain to make all possible speed it was daylight when they landed in Sicily and rented a battered

Fiat which Harry drove to Syracuse faster than Jack believed possible, only to arrive at the circuit after the start of practice. Quite undaunted, Jack jogged more than a mile to the pits, carrying his helmet and overalls and dodging Carabinieri and course marshals, before leaping – hot, sweaty, tired and short of sleep – into the Cooper to qualify faster than any other Formula Two car. He finished sixth in the race, having lapped Peter Walker in Rob's Formula One Connaught.

Jack Brabham lying third in the 1957 Monaco Grand Prix.

Brabham's punctuality had improved hardly at all by the time of the Monaco Grand Prix in May. The new 1960 cc Formula One Cooper-Climax was ready and waiting at the start of the first practice session, but there was no sign of the driver. At Rob's request Peter Collins, now a works Ferrari driver, tried the car and pronounced it interesting, but this hardly helped to qualify it for one of only sixteen positions on the starting grid. In those days of stringent exchange-control regulations, starting money made all the difference between paying the hotel bill and washing the dishes. Eventually Jack turned up, having lost his way to Monaco *en route* from Modena, full of apologies and too late to practise.

On the second day of practice Jack was out early. He soon realised that his brake balance required adjustment but decided to do one more lap before stopping at his pit; he overcooked it on the approach to Casino Square, locked up and wrote the car off as he crashed through the telegraph poles which protected the stone balustrades leading to the side door of the casino.

Jack Brabham pushing Rob's Cooper into sixth place at Monaco in 1957.

Happily the 1960 cc engine – like the driver – was undamaged, and it was decided to shoe-horn it into a works Formula Two Cooper chassis which had been intended for Les Leston to drive. It was an all-night job involving Alf and Rob's mechanics, the Cooper mechanics and a host of volunteer helpers.

During the final practice period next day there was inevitably a certain tension in the Walker pit which was exacerbated when Masten Gregory deposited a puddle of oil from the blown engine of his 250F Maserati at Ste Devote. Fortunately the chief marshal at Ste Devote was also the head barman at the Hotel de Paris and it goes without saying that he and Rob were old friends. The two colluded to stop practice while the oil was cleared, and three minutes before the end of the extended session Jack did a lap which ensured that Rob would not have to wash up after the race.

The 1957 Monaco Grand Prix is chiefly remembered for the triple accident at the chicane which eliminated Moss, Hawthorn and Collins.

However the demise of those three star drivers cannot obscure the fact that Jack Brabham drove a brilliant race; after 100 of the 105 laps the little Cooper was lying third behind Fangio's Maserati and Brooks' Vanwall – each of which, of course, was a full-blown Grand Prix car. Then the Tipo Mona fuel pump broke loose from its mounting and the engine spluttered and died at the Station Hairpin. Jack coasted down the hill to rejoin the promenade, and then pushed the car through the tunnel – with the others blasting past him in semi-darkness at 120 mph – down the hill to the chicane and round Tobacconist's Corner to the finish, the crowd cheering every step he took. He was sixth, and utterly exhausted.

Had he finished in third place there was a good chance that Brabham might have been disqualified, as the Ferrari team were ready to lodge a protest with the stewards of the meeting after an incident at the Walker pit. The smaller tank capacity of the Formula Two Cooper chassis meant that Brabham had had to make a stop for additional fuel, and his mechanics had been so anxious to get him back into the race with the least possible delay that they had infringed regulations by giving him a push-start. Realising their mistake, they had invented an alibi of sorts; they had not in fact been pushing the car, as it must have seemed – rather they were chasing after it in an attempt to release Alf Francis' fingers which had become trapped in the rear transverse leaf spring! Luckily this alibi was not exposed to scrutiny as Trintignant's sole surviving Ferrari finished ahead of Brabham, and no protest was therefore made by the Italian team.

Juan Manuel Fangio inspecting Rob's Cooper at Rouen in 1957.

Rob could hardly believe that his team had been within minutes of finishing third in a World Championship race and he was devastated by the trivial nature of the mechanical failure which had snatched success from them. Later that evening, as they dined together at Cap Estel in Eze-sur-Mer, Betty consoled him with the prophecy that they would do even better next year. Rob was not entirely convinced, but at least they could agree that Jack Brabham's incredible determination alone would be enough to lead him to the World Drivers' Championship in due course.

The Cooper was rebuilt in time for the French Grand Prix at Rouen-les-Essarts. Brabham's luck was no better there; on the second lap the gearbox on Horace Gould's Maserati 250F seized and he pulled off the road without warning, forcing Jack to crash in order to avoid hitting him, and confronting the mechanics with yet another total rebuild. Prior to this disaster, however, Juan Manuel Fangio had visited the Walker pit and shown great interest in the Cooper, then the only rear-engined car competing at the highest level. Then and always the language barrier – Rob speaks English, of course, and French; Fangio speaks Spanish and Italian, but no French or English – prevented him from getting to know the great Argentine driver as well as he would have liked.

As the season wore on, disappointment followed upon disappointment; Brooks wrote off the Formula Two car at Brands Hatch, Brabham retired from the British Grand Prix at Aintree with clutch failure when he was lying seventh, the clutch failed on Brooks' Formula Two car at Caen, and at both Oulton Park and Silverstone Brooks' gearbox failed on the line, to Rob's intense frustration, after he had won pole position.

For some time it was uncertain whether or not the Walker team would appear at the Nürburgring for the German Grand Prix; the issue of starting money was not resolved until Rob called the bluff of the principal organiser, Herr Schmidt, at Aintree. 'John Cooper and I met this person, who looked as if he must once have been at least a Colonel in the SS – and had been, in fact – in one of the rooms above the stands to discuss starting money. He made a decent offer for Roy Salvadori in the works car but offered a pitiful amount for Jack in my car because he claimed that no one had ever heard of us. So I said, "Unless I get the same money for Jack as John is getting for Roy, I'm not going to race. I don't like the Germans and I don't like Germany, and nothing but decent starting money will persuade me to go there." John Cooper kept trying to placate me by saying, "Don't upset him, Rob, you can have a share of our starting money," and I said, "I don't give a bugger if I upset him, I'm not going to race unless he pays me properly." And of course the Germans love to

Jack Brabham leads Tony Brooks' Vanwall in the 1957 British Grand Prix at Aintree.

know who is boss, and he came up with the money.' In the event Brabham's race lasted for only six laps before the gearbox broke. Rob was then free to observe other teams in action and he was fortunate enough to be in the Maserati pit at a time of high drama.

Fangio had been fastest in practice in his Maserati 250F, followed hotly by Hawthorn, Collins and Musso in their Ferraris. The Ferraris were expected to complete the race on a single set of Englebert tyres, whereas the Maseratis on their softer Pirellis would certainly have to stop for fresh rear tyres. Fangio started with half-empty tanks in the hope that the lighter fuel load would enable him to build a lead over the Ferraris which would give him time to accommodate his tyre stop. On lap twelve, in the lead by thirty-one seconds, Fangio swept into the pits for new tyres. One of the rear wheels stuck on its splines – half on and half off the hub – and Fangio was stationary for almost a minute while his mechan-

ics struggled with the recalcitrant wheel and Collins and Hawthorn moved into a commanding lead. Rob recalls that Fangio, taking an occasional drink from a bottle of cold mineral water, remained absolutely calm and relaxed while surrounded by the sort of total panic that only Italian pit crews seem able to generate.

Juan Manuel Fangio during his celebrated drive to victory in the 1957 German Grand Prix.

But it was a different story when he rejoined the race. After a couple of slowish laps designed to warm up the new tyres and lull the Ferrari team into a false sense of security, Fangio set out on the pursuit of his life. Driving like a man possessed, braking impossibly late and controlling a seemingly endless series of opposite-lock slides, bouncing the Maserati off banks and kerbs, occasionally putting two wheels on the grass, Fangio broke the lap record on ten consecutive laps; his average speed for the 312-mile race, including his fifty-six-second pit stop, was faster than the record he had set for a single lap a year earlier. On the penultimate lap, Fangio was a mere six seconds behind the Ferraris as they passed the pits, and Rob asked how far behind Alf thought he would be at the finish. Alf replied, 'He won't be behind; he'll be in front.' And he was. After this victory, which assured him of his fifth World Championship, Fangio said, 'I did things today that I've never done before, and I never want to drive like that again.' Rob believes that there has never been – and never will be – a more exciting sight in motor racing than Fangio in a full four-wheel drift at, say, 150 mph, and no one who saw Fangio in action at the Nürburgring on 4th August 1957 could fail to agree that he had been privileged to witness one of the greatest Grand Prix drivers of all time doing his very best work.

The final Formula One race of the 1957 season, the Moroccan Grand Prix, was a non-championship event to be held on the corniche circuit at Casablanca. It was conducted in a carefree, almost festive atmosphere; there was nothing very much at stake, and everyone was anxious to enjoy themselves as much as possible at the end of a long and arduous season of racing. It was generally agreed that by far the most spectacular of the numerous parties was given by King Mohamed at his palace at Rabat, even though his guests – whose reputation, perhaps, had preceded them – were only permitted to inspect the Royal harem from the outside.

It soon became clear, however, that quite the most fun in Casablanca was provided by Le Sphynx, an establishment which catered for every conceivable taste. In the basement there was an extremely comfortable cinema which showed movies which were not exactly designed for family viewing, while on the ground floor both the bar and the dance floor were crowded with glamorous and co-operative ladies of every nationality and hue. Upstairs were luxurious bedrooms in which the ladies entertained their guests with infinite ingenuity and great enthusiasm; some of these rooms were equipped with secret two-way mirrors for those who preferred to observe rather than to participate. Rob claims to have indulged in nothing more sinful than a beer or two at the bar, but the size of his bill suggested that the rest of the team had not been wasting their time. Rob was hardly surprised when Alf fell off the team motor bike on his way back to the hotel.

Race day dawned hot as hell with a stiff breeze blowing sand across the track, making it difficult to identify the cars as they passed the pits. After only four laps the Cooper gearbox packed up yet again, and Rob's disconsolate mechanics wheeled the car into the dead car park. Soon afterwards further mechanical failure began to decimate the field and Alf suddenly said, 'Come on, let's change the gearbox and get back in the race to see if we can break the lap record.' Thirty-five minutes later, Jack Brabham was back in action.

The Clerk of the Course at Casablanca was Toto Roche, a florid, rotund and irascible Frenchman running on a very short fuse. 'It took a lap or two for Toto to realise that Jack had rejoined the race, but once he did so he flew into one of his spectacular rages and announced that he was going to black-flag Jack immediately. For three laps or so Toto forgot to show the number of the car with the black flag so, of course, no one took the slightest notice. Then I realised that it was very difficult for him to recognise the cars as they approached him at high speed through the flying sand, whereas it was very easy for me to predict when Jack would appear because I had a watch on him.

'Each time Jack was due to come round I would tap Toto on the shoulder and suggest in very laboured and faltering French that he should be allowed to go on entertaining the crowd until the end of the race and then disqualified, and by then of course Jack was past and off on another lap. Toto was not completely stupid and after about three or four laps of this when I tapped him on the shoulder he leaped into the air expecting to flourish his black flag at Brabham but actually waving it at Fangio. The great man was feeling slightly guilty as he had earlier received an illegal push-start after spinning and stalling his engine, so he stopped at once. By now the crowd was beginning to give Toto the bird which of course made him madder than ever and in the end he said that if I didn't call Jack in at once he would see to it that my entrant's licence was revoked, so I had no alternative but to obey. No doubt the applause which greeted Jack as he stopped at our pit did nothing to assuage Toto's anger.'

Rob's 1957 F2 Cooper-Climax.

Rob's 1957 season had promised much but in the end delivered very little, although it did end on a high note; at the Boxing Day meeting at Brands Hatch Jack won the Formula Libre race in the 1960 cc Cooper-Climax, the gearbox specially strengthened by Alf Francis, and set a new lap record in the process. Maybe this augured well for 1958.

Jack Brabham after winning the Formula Libre race at Brands Hatch on Boxing Day 1957 in Rob's 1960 cc Cooper-Climax.

Chapter 6
The Giantkillers

Long before that encouraging end-of-season result at Brands Hatch, however, Jack Brabham had decided that he would not drive for Rob Walker in 1958. When the two of them had met in Paris in October to fly together to Casablanca Jack had announced, as Rob had feared he might, that he intended to sign for the Cooper works team for the following year. Rob had offered him a retainer of £5000 for the season – good money at the time – but Brabham was a talented engineer who wanted to prepare and develop his own cars, and he took the view that there was not room for both him and Alf Francis in the same team. Or, as Rob put it, 'You couldn't have two chief mechanics working on the same car – especially if one of them was Alf Francis. Or Jack Brabham.'

Rob and Stirling Moss were occupying adjoining suites in their hotel at Casablanca, and the night before the race Stirling asked if they could meet for a chat in the privacy of Rob's room. Over a drink Stirling explained that he had been thinking of buying a Formula Two Cooper to enter privately in the coming season; in fact Stirling had asked Alf if he could try out the Walker Formula Two car after practice for the Goodwood meeting a month earlier and, dodging MG and Triumph sports cars during the free-for-all at the end of the day, he had recorded some pretty impressive lap times. Stirling now said that he considered Rob's Cooper to be the quickest Formula Two car he had ever driven; this hardly surprised Rob since he knew – although Stirling didn't – that Alf had sent him out in the car with the 1960 cc engine. Stirling had contracted to drive Formula One for Vanwall during 1958 but asked if he could drive in selected Formula Two races for Rob. Coming so soon after Jack Brabham's defection, Rob could hardly have received better news; the deal was done on the spot, and so started a relationship which would in time prosper beyond Rob's most optimistic expectations.

There is a fundamental difference of opinion within the Walker family about the merits of snow and skiing. Betty comes from a skiing family; her grandparents were amongst the first British skiers to venture to Switzerland soon after the turn of the century, staying at the Hotel Fluella in Davos and climbing the Parsenn before skiing down the valley to Klosters. In those days skiers literally had to climb up any mountain they might wish to ski down; a little later the Ski Club of Great Britain persuaded the Swiss to open their mountain railways – built for the convenience of summer walkers – in winter also, and so laid the foundations of modern recreational downhill skiing. Robbie shares Betty's enthusiasm for the slopes but Rob, used to spending the European winter months with his mother's family in the warmth of

Stirling Moss on his way to victory in the 1958 Argentine Grand Prix at the wheel of the Walker Cooper.

the Australian summer, can't stand the cold. His daughter Dauvergne is on his side.

At Betty's instigation, however, all four of them found themselves spending two weeks in a little-known Swiss ski resort called Rigikulm in early January 1958. 'To my absolute horror I found that we were staying in a hotel which was all by itself at the very top of an alp; there was hardly anyone else staying there, which didn't surprise me a bit. For me, it was a fortnight of sheer hell; it was bitterly cold, the sun never shone, the food was rotten – but at least I managed to avoid actually skiing. Instead, Dauvergne and I played cricket for two weeks, using a ski pole as a bat and bowling with a snowball.

'However, there was one interesting diversion when Stirling's manager, Ken Gregory, called me to say that Vanwall could not convert their engines from alcohol to petrol to meet the new regulations for the Argentine Grand Prix in under two weeks' time, and asked if I would allow Stirling to drive my 1960 cc Cooper there. My first reaction was to wonder how on earth we could get the car there in time as I couldn't possibly have afforded the cost of air freight. However, Ken told me that the Argentines were so keen to have Stirling in the race that they had offered to pay for the car and two passengers to fly to Buenos Aires, and so I agreed to go ahead. I decided not to travel to Argentina myself as Robbie's first half at Eton started just before the race and I naturally wanted to be with him then. Anyway, it was important to have two mechanics available to prepare the car properly, so Alf and Tim Wall used the two free tickets.

'When they rolled the car out of the aeroplane at Buenos Aires the Argentines were absolutely furious to discover that they had paid so much money to fly such an insignificant-looking little beetle halfway across the world, even if Stirling Moss was going to drive it, and the other teams – particularly Ferrari – dismissed it out of hand. However, when Stirling set the third fastest time in the first practice period they began to sit up and take notice.'

The Cooper had had a longer though less eventful journey than its driver; flying from his home in Nassau via Miami and Lima Stirling had discovered *en route* that he was not equipped with the visa required for entry to Argentina. Only some smart work by PanAm and the Argentine Embassy in Lima saved the day.

Practice went hardly better. On the first day it was fortunate that Stirling had set a good time early on as he completed only fifteen laps before the transmission seized after the gearbox drain plug fell out. In subsequent practice periods Stirling was handicapped by blurred vision after his new wife, Katie Molson, had accidentally poked her finger into his eye while they were fooling around in their hotel. Indeed, Stirling's eye was heavily bandaged until only half an hour before the start of the race.

In the end the Cooper was seventh fastest in a field of ten; three new Dino 246 Ferraris for Mike Hawthorn, Peter Collins and Luigi Musso, and six Maseratis (none of them works cars, for Maserati had now withdrawn from Formula One racing) for reigning World Champion Juan Manuel Fangio, Menditeguy, Behra, Godia,

Harry Schell and Horace Gould.

It had been clear during practice that the track surface was extremely abrasive and that therefore tyre wear would be critical. This placed the Cooper at a considerable disadvantage, for while the knock-on Borrani wire wheels of the Ferraris and Maseratis could be changed reasonably quickly, even by Italian mechanics, the four-stud wheels on the Cooper could not. Stirling quite simply could not afford to stop for fresh rubber and expect to finish in the money; he had to gamble on completing the entire race on one set of tyres.

He made an absolutely magnificent start and was running third behind Hawthorn and Behra early in the race until, on the fourth lap, his gearbox stuck in second gear. What had happened – although this was not established until the race was over – was that the clutch had broken. The Cooper had a clutch-operated locking device on the gearbox to prevent it from jumping out of gear, and this mechanism was normally released by the depression of the clutch pedal. Thus when the clutch broke, gearchanging became totally impossible. Stirling had completed almost an entire lap in second gear, losing a couple of places in the process, and was about to stop at his pit for repairs when, almost miraculously, a small stone chipping

Stirling Moss in Rob's 1960 cc Cooper-Climax follows Jean Behra's 250F Maserati and Mike Hawthorn's Dino 246 Ferrari in the early stages of the 1958 Argentine Grand Prix.

89

*Hawthorn's Ferrari closely
followed by Stirling Moss in the
clutchless Cooper.*

*Moss slips inside Hawthorn to
take second place behind Fangio.*

lodged beneath the locking mechanism and jammed it in the open position for the rest of the race.

Once he had settled into the rhythm of making clutchless gearchanges Stirling rapidly overhauled Behra's Maserati and then set about Hawthorn's Ferrari. Mike was not at all keen to be passed and there was much waving of blue flags by the marshals – and fist waving by Stirling – before he finally got by to run second behind Fangio. When Fangio pitted for new tyres on lap thirty-five Stirling went into a lead which he was never to lose. He was helped by the fact that the rival teams expected him to make a tyre stop which they knew would put him out of contention, and Alf confirmed these expectations by making noisy and obvious preparations for a tyre change, showing Stirling a wheel as he passed the pits. Adapting his driving style to the circumstances, running on the oily parts of the track whenever possible and keeping a very careful eye in his mirrors on the white canvas strips showing on both his rear tyres, Stirling resisted a late challenge from Musso to take the chequered flag, with Fangio and Hawthorn in third and fourth places. After the race, the Cooper's Continental tyres were found to have worn through three of their five layers of canvas. They may not have had more than a lap left in them.

Ken Gregory called Rob late at night to tell him of the team's success. Until the reality of the following day, when his home was besieged by journalists and photographers anxious to join in the celebration of a famous victory, Rob half thought that Ken had been pulling his leg. Everything Stirling did in those days hit the headlines; even when he blew his nose it was news. Now, suddenly, Rob was famous too – as the first private entrant to defeat the factory teams, the first to provide a Grand Prix winner for Cooper, and for Coventry-Climax. The magnitude of his team's achievement, when it finally dawned upon him fully, gave Rob far more pleasure than the attention of the press, flattering though that was. But there were still those who derided the Cooper and claimed that only the genius of Stirling Moss could have combined with the absence of BRM and Vanwall to attain that astonishing result in Buenos Aires.

In fact the World Championship status of the race would remain in doubt for some time as both BRM and Vanwall had lodged protests with the FIA on the grounds that they had received insufficient notice of the race regulations. Although both protests were withdrawn following Stirling's victory, the FIA kept everyone in suspense for several weeks before confirming that the race would indeed count towards the outcome of the Drivers' Championship.

One of the rear tyres from the Cooper showing three of the five layers of canvas worn away.

The Argentine Temporada concluded with a Formula Libre race at the Autodromo in Buenos Aires which was contested by the Grand Prix field augmented by a number of local drivers in assorted, mostly hybrid machinery. Stirling's luck deserted him in this race and he was punted off the track soon after the start by Jesus Iglesias driving a Chevrolet Special. The race was won by Fangio's Maserati with Luigi Musso's Ferrari second.

Although the reunion between Stirling and Alf had got off to an auspicious beginning, it soon became clear to Rob that his principal function in the team would be to act as a mediator between them. 'I think that they had missed working together, although of course neither of them would admit it. I think they admired and respected each other but they often disagreed about the preparation of the car and the trick was, really, to keep them apart as much as possible. They both knew that in the end the final decision would be mine, and I think they respected me for making a clear decision whenever I had to, and then sticking to it.

'I can only recall one serious confrontation between me and Stirling during all the time we raced together, and that took place at Riverside in 1960. Our crown-

Stirling considers Lotus gear ratios at Riverside in 1960.

wheel and pinion was pretty worn, having done several races, and after the final practice period Stirling said he wanted to fit one of the new ones which Colin Chapman had brought out with him from England. That evening I went down to the garage at about eleven o'clock to find the mechanics burning the midnight oil as usual and Alf said, "Look, sir, if I have to change the crownwheel and pinion it's going to take all night and I won't have time to prepare the car properly; I really think it would be best if we leave the old one in. I'm sure it will last the race." I said, "If that's what you think, Alf, go ahead."

'About fifteen minutes later Stirling turned up, having been

Stirling and Alf.

to the cinema, and asked how the crownwheel and pinion was coming along. I said, "It's not going to be done; Alf hasn't got time to do it." Stirling looked at me for a moment and then without saying a word he just turned on his heel and walked out.

'At about one o'clock in the morning, just as I was about to turn my light out and try to get some sleep, I saw that a note was being pushed underneath my bedroom door. It was written on hotel writing paper, and it was from Stirling; in it he apologised for the incident at the garage, said that he still believed that the crownwheel and pinion should have been changed, but that even so he would do his utmost to win the race for us. As if I had ever doubted it! In the event he won quite easily and as he took the chequered flag Alf was standing on the pit counter and waving a crownwheel and pinion at him.

'In this particular race there was a special prize of $1000 for the driver who made the fastest lap, and a few laps from the end Jack Brabham improved marginally on Stirling's best time. Alf and I decided that we would not tell Stirling this in case he decided to go for a better time, overtax our old crownwheel and pinion in the process and lose the race. After it was all over Stirling was a bit miffed to discover that Jack had won the thousand dollars. "Why didn't you give me a signal?" he asked. "I could easily have gone faster." After I had explained our position Stirling thought for a moment and then he said, "When I go faster, I don't take anything more out of the car – I take it out of myself." '

Maurice Trintignant (above) *leads the 1958 Monaco Grand Prix in Rob's 1960 cc Cooper-Climax.*

Right: *Maurice with Princess Grace and Prince Rainier of Monaco after his victory.*

Back in 1958, however, still basking in the glory of their giant-killing act in Argentina, the team headed for Pau in the foothills of the Pyrenees. Here Maurice Trintignant, who had been signed up for all but a few Formula One races, would drive the Formula Two car while Stirling was engaged elsewhere. Racing on the Pau street circuit is the ideal dress rehearsal for the Monaco Grand Prix, and Petoulet's style of driving – careful, conservative, extremely precise – was ideally suited to it. He won and set a new lap record.

'Maurice spoke no English at all and if he understood any he certainly wasn't letting on. He used to rely upon Harry Schell to teach him phrases suitable for various social occasions, one of which was important enough for Harry to write down in Maurice's diary so that there could be no mistake about it. From that moment on, whenever he was introduced to an English-speaking lady, Maurice would thumb through his diary and then, with a dazzling smile, he would recite, "Ow do you do; weel you slip wiz me tonight?" I believe that this direct approach had almost as many successes as failures.' Maurice spoke French to Rob and Italian to Alf. Rob and Alf spoke English to each other, and to the mechanics. Somehow it worked.

Rob and Betty drove to Monte Carlo in their gullwing 300SL after mixed fortunes in the early-season meetings at Goodwood, Aintree and Silverstone. As they discussed the forthcoming Monaco Grand Prix over dinner at Cap Estel, neither of them truly believed that the prophecy made by Betty a year earlier would be fulfilled, even though Maurice had won the race in 1955 for Ferrari. Ranged against him in Rob's 1960 cc Cooper this year were the works Ferraris of Hawthorn, Collins, Musso and von Trips, the Vanwalls of Moss, Brooks and Lewis-Evans, the BRMs of Behra and Schell, and the works Coopers of Brabham and Salvadori. It was formidable opposition.

Although Brooks won pole position on the grid, the Vanwalls proved to be a handful at Monaco. Stirling tried Rob's Cooper during practice and was in no doubt which car he would prefer to drive. In the race all three Vanwalls retired and Maurice won from the Ferraris of Luigi Musso and Peter Collins. 'It was absolute hell for me. It was the first time I had ever seen one of my cars leading a Grand Prix, and I couldn't really believe it was happening. I think Maurice took the lead when Mike Hawthorn retired on lap forty-six, and I agonised for the next fifty-four laps. Towards the end Musso looked as if he was beginning a charge and without my knowledge or permission Alf gave Maurice the signal to hurry up, and he immediately put in a quicker lap which showed that he was in total control of the situation. At the end the crowd swarmed over the track and surrounded us in the pits and had we not

Maurice leading George Wicken (Cooper) in the Kentish 100 Formula Two race at Brands Hatch in 1958.

been protected by Ettore Bugatti, a big strong man who was a close friend of Trintignant's, I think we might have been hurt – quite unintentionally, of course – in the crush.' Now the little Cooper's critics were silent; no longer could anyone doubt that it was a serious Grand Prix contender, whether or not Stirling Moss was driving it.

The Dutch, however, had been amongst the sceptics and had not invited Rob to take part in their Grand Prix at Zandvoort, his success in Argentina notwithstanding. Lengthy post-race discussions took place at the Hotel de Paris which finally arrived at a formula which would allow the Dutch to save face, enable Trintignant to race in Holland, and contribute substantially to Rob's bank balance. In the event Maurice would finish a lowly ninth there; the race was won by Stirling in his Vanwall, followed by the BRMs of Harry Schell and Jean Behra.

Maurice Trintignant was anxious to do well, understandably enough, in the French Grand Prix at Rheims in which he was to have a one-off drive in a BRM, but his plans went awry when his Rob Walker Cooper caught fire as he accelerated down the long straight towards Thillois during practice for the supporting Formula Two race. After braking hard he was forced to abandon the car while it was still travelling at some 35 mph and was unlucky to find that the first fire extinguisher with which he tried to douse the flames was empty. Trintignant continued to practise and race with quite severe neck burns, but to no avail. Both he and Stirling Moss retired in the Formula Two race, although Stirling won a hundred bottles of champagne for the fastest Formula Two practice lap. In the main event Trintignant fared no better and retired his borrowed BRM, while Stirling's Vanwall finished second to Mike Hawthorn's Ferrari.

For the next race, the British Grand Prix at Silverstone, Maurice was back behind the wheel of Rob Walker's Cooper, its Coventry Climax engine enlarged to 2014 cc. Alas, the new engine soon developed a serious oil leak and Maurice struggled to finish eighth in a race which was dominated by the Ferraris of Collins and Hawthorn after the demise of Stirling's Vanwall.

Stirling Moss had won in Argentina in Rob's Cooper, and then in the Vanwall at Zandvoort. He had finished second at Rheims, but in the other races the Vanwall had failed him, and by the time of the German Grand Prix at the Nürburgring he

Stirling on the grid at Brands Hatch in Rob's Formula Two Cooper. Taking a keen interest is Charles Cooper, the father of the car's creator.

and Mike Hawthorn were level on points for the World Championship. Stirling was very disillusioned by the unreliability of the Vanwall, and his retirement in the British Grand Prix was almost the last straw. By the time the circus assembled in the Eifel Mountains he was beginning to consider his options very seriously.

Mike Hawthorn qualified for pole position at the 'Ring with Collins, Brooks and Moss alongside him on the front row of the grid, but it was Stirling who shot into an immediate lead only for his Vanwall to let him down yet again when the magneto failed after four laps. Collins now led from Hawthorn with Tony Brooks on the attack in third place; on lap eleven the Vanwall passed both Ferraris to take the lead. Hawthorn, nursing a slipping clutch which he had overheated at the start, could do little but sit back and watch Peter Collins fighting to stay on terms with Tony Brooks. Then Collins made a small error of judgement and ran slightly off the racing line at the entry to a right-hand bend soon after the Karussel. Sliding to the left, the car struck a low grassy bank beside the road and turned over, throwing Collins clear. He was rushed to Adenau hospital, then transferred by helicopter to a clinic in Bonn where he succumbed to serious head injuries.

Meanwhile the clutch on Mike Hawthorn's Ferrari had finally failed out on the circuit and he was left in suspense about the fate of his friend – 'Mon ami mate' – until the race ended and he could return to the pits. As far as Stirling Moss was concerned his frustration with the Vanwall was heightened by Maurice Trintignant's fine drive into third place in Rob Walker's Cooper, even though the position between himself and Mike Hawthorn was unchanged in terms of the World Championship.

Stirling won in Portugal with Hawthorn in second place. This time Trintignant could do no better than eighth in Rob's car. Starting from pole position at Monza, Stirling's gearbox broke on lap eighteen; the Moss jinx had struck again. Tony

Brooks drove brilliantly to win the Italian Grand Prix at record speed with Mike Hawthorn once again in second place twenty-four seconds adrift. For once Trintignant failed to finish in Rob Walker's Cooper, retiring on lap twenty-five.

The system of computing the final points standing for the World Championship in 1958 meant that if he was to win the title Stirling had to climb a mountain in Morocco; although he did so, as we shall see, even that was not enough.

Trintignant retired once again at Casablanca but even so the Walker team could look back on the 1958 season with some pride. They had won a total of ten major races, including two Grandes Epreuves, and Maurice had finished sixth in the World Championship. As well, he had defeated Jean Behra for the Championship of France with his victories at Monaco and Pau, Caen and Clermont-Ferrand, and his third place at the Nürburgring. The team had also contributed substantially to Cooper's third place in the Constructors' Championship.

As the Tasman series unfolded Down Under – with Stirling winning both the Melbourne Grand Prix and the New Zealand Grand Prix at Ardmore in Rob's Cooper – it became clear that Vanwall would not be racing in 1959. 'We had got to know Stirling quite well during 1958 although as he was driving for three teams – Vanwall, Aston Martin and ourselves – we didn't see as much of him between his drives for us as we would have liked. This was because Stirling had such total commitment and such a fantastic sense of priorities. When he was driving for us, he devoted himself one hundred per cent to our team; he wouldn't allow himself to be distracted by the other teams, he wouldn't talk shop to them, he wouldn't socialise with them – as far as he was concerned they simply didn't exist. And quite rightly he behaved in exactly the same way towards us when he was driving for Vanwall or Aston Martin. But I think he rather enjoyed the life we led when we were racing. By this time the team had become a very close little family; Stirling had become a part of that family, and I think he really rather enjoyed it. Anyway when the time came for him to choose between the various options which were open to him for 1959, he chose to sign with us for both Formula One and Formula Two. I think he just wanted to escape from the size and formality of a factory team and to do his own thing again. It was the best thing that ever happened to me, and I think and hope that Stirling has never regretted it.'

Chapter 7
Death of a Champion

Rob Walker first met John Wyer when he was running Monaco Motors in Watford; it was an engineering firm to which Rob used to send various bits and pieces of the Delage for repair or restoration. Later, when Wyer became established as manager of the Aston Martin works sports car team, Rob went to work for him as a timekeeper, gladly sitting at the feet of the man he regarded as the most efficient team manager since the legendary Alfred Neubauer had ruled the pre-war Mercedes factory team with a rod of iron.

John Wyer.

'I did it because I wanted to learn as much as I could from John about timekeeping and about team management. He was absolutely meticulous about timekeeping which he regarded as an essential race management tool. At Aston Martin we had one timekeeper per car and I remember that at every race all the timekeepers' watches – we had two each – were laid out on the pit counter and set going half an hour or so before the start so that they would be warmed up and settled down by the time they were needed. It was this sort of attention to detail which made John the great team manager he undoubtedly was.

'Luckily for me John didn't require us to use stop watches with a split second hand because my mental arithmetic wouldn't have been up to it. Betty could cope very easily and people like Bette Hill and Patty McLaren could time a whole field of Grand Prix cars with just one watch; but it was too much for me.

'In the fullness of time, I think I became quite a good and accurate timekeeper. John always used to say that he thought that women made the best timekeepers because they were less easily distracted than men, but I think he made an exception in my case. I believe that in his book *Motor Racing Management* John wrote about the 1952 Goodwood nine-hour race during which one of the Astons caught fire as it was being refuelled in the pits. It was all pretty frightening at the time, and John and two of the mechanics were really quite badly burned. Months afterwards

when he emerged from hospital John examined my time sheet and was astonished to discover that I had gone on timing my car as if nothing had happened, simply making a note in the margin which said 'No. 15 caught fire.' Of course I never told him that in all the excitement I had missed a lap and then divided the time for two

Rob concentrating on his time sheet.

laps by two to make it look right. Even my mental arithmetic could handle that!'

On another occasion Rob's equanimity was put to a different kind of test; he paid his first visit to the United States with the Aston Martin team for the Sebring twelve-hour race in March 1954, crossing the Atlantic in a PanAm Boeing Stratocruiser which was equipped with bunks in First Class. 'I remember waking up and looking out of the window at the position of the sun and thinking, 'I wonder if the pilot knows he is going the wrong way?' Luckily he did; he was taking us back to the Azores because the weather had closed in on the east coast of America. When we made it to Idlewild at the second attempt we couldn't land there because of snow on the runway and we were diverted to Washington DC where we finally touched down twenty-six hours after taking off from London.

'For some reason I was timing all three works cars at Sebring, which kept me pretty busy. Fortunately they all retired within the first hour or two so my inability to juggle six watches and three time sheets was not unduly exposed. After the race we all flew up to New York and spent a night there before flying home to England next day. I don't remember much about New York except, after a very long and liquid evening at The Gay Nineties, being rolled down 46th Street in a wire litter basket by Peter Collins, Roy Salvadori and Pat Griffith. No doubt they hoped that the trash wagon would come along and dispose of me. The next morning, feeling very much the worse for wear, I staggered down Fifth Avenue looking for a pair of crocodile shoes to take home to Betty, and by the time I got back to the hotel all the others had left for the airport. I realised that I was going to miss the plane unless I got a move on so I gave the hotel doorman a large tip to find me a taxi while I had a quick hair of the dog in the bar, and then I promised the driver all the money I had – he wasn't to know it was only five dollars – if he could get me to the airport in time. After an absolutely terrifying drive I arrived at Idlewild a quarter of an hour after the scheduled departure time of our flight to London, but fortunately the others had persuaded PanAm to hold the flight for me and they had even arranged for my own personal Immigration and Customs officers to be waiting on the steps to stamp my passport and check my baggage. Those were the days!

'I'm afraid that after all this excitement I may have relaxed and enjoyed rather too much of PanAm's very generous hospitality during the flight; it was a long flight with stops for refuelling at Gander and Shannon and I was having a very good time indeed until I looked out of the window and recognised Windsor Castle below us, and realised to my horror that in only a few minutes I would have to face my wife. After we landed Betty drove the car right up to the aeroplane, which was allowed in those days, and was waiting for me at the bottom of the steps. Reg Parnell very kindly went ahead to prepare her for my appearance; he explained that the flight had been a particularly bumpy and unpleasant one and as a result I was not feeling at all well. Of course the moment Betty saw me she knew that Reg had lied through his teeth!'

Rob was a timekeeper for the Aston Martin team at Le Mans for many years. By

tradition the team always stayed at the Hotel de France at La Chartre-sur-le-Loir about fifty kilometres south-east of Le Mans along the D304. Rob, however, preferred to be in Le Mans itself, staying with James Tilling, Jaguar team drivers Tony Rolt and Duncan Hamilton, and Gerald Lascelles – who was also an Aston Martin timekeeper – in a house owned by a certain Madame Lamothe. 'We always had terrific fun together. Duncan Hamilton was very good value. He had an extremely fertile and vivid imagination and used to tell the most marvellous stories, one or two of which were actually true. He also had a curious habit of dressing up in women's clothes or, as the mood took him, undressing altogether. One evening before dinner he appeared dressed in Lois Rolt's nightie which fairly brought the house down – only Madame Lamothe was a bit uncertain about it all. On an earlier occasion – I think it was after the christening of one of Tony and Lois's children – he disappeared into the kitchen of the rather smart restaurant near Stratford-upon-Avon in which we were having dinner to re-emerge dressed in nothing but a chef's hat and a loincloth made out of a folded napkin.

'The year Mercedes-Benz first came out with the air brake on their 300SLR I remember that when we drove home after a very jolly dinner in a restaurant not far from Le Mans Duncan would open the car door every time we came to a corner to demonstrate how the air brake worked, just in case any of us had missed the point.' That was in 1955 when, for a variety of reasons, Rob was not occupying his usual timekeeper's position in the Aston Martin pit.

Mercedes-Benz came to Le Mans full of confidence; a few weeks earlier Stirling Moss and his navigator, Denis Jenkinson of *Motor Sport*, had won the Mille Miglia in record time with Fangio in second place, albeit some distance behind. At Le Mans Moss and Fangio were to share a 300SLR supported by two further Mercedes to be driven respectively by Karl Kling and André Simon, and John Fitch and French idol Pierre Levegh. Three 4.4-litre 121LM Ferraris were entered for Eugenio Castellotti and Paolo Marzotto, Harry Schell and Maurice Trintignant, and Phil Hill and Umberto Maglioli. There were also three D-Type Jaguars for past winners Tony Rolt and Duncan Hamilton, Bob Beauman and Jaguar test driver Norman Dewis, and Ivor Bueb and Mike Hawthorn. Although it seemed certain that the issue would be settled between these three teams, the field of sixty cars was completed by the factory teams of Aston Martin and Maserati, various privately entered Ferraris and Jaguars, the usual gaggle of small-capacity French cars competing for the Index of Performance, that unique Gallic eccentricity, together with representatives of such famous marques as Lagonda, Talbot, Gordini, Frazer-Nash, Bristol, Triumph, Porsche – and the single Austin Healey which Lance Macklin was to share with Les Leston.

Castellotti's Ferrari was fastest in practice, and when the flag fell at four o'clock on the warm, sunny afternoon of 11th June 1955 it was he who shot into an immediate lead, hotly pursued by Maglioli and Hawthorn. Fangio had made a slow and careful start but was soon carving his way through the field, breaking the lap record time and again despite the traffic on the circuit until, on lap twelve, he passed Hawthorn in front of the pits to take second place. After an hour only five seconds separated the first three cars, but soon Castellotti's Ferrari began to fall back, leaving Fangio and Hawthorn to duel for the lead. And duel they did. The next hour was more like the opening stages of a Grand Prix than the early part of a twenty-four-hour endurance race, with first Fangio and then Hawthorn setting a new lap record, first Hawthorn and then Fangio taking the lead; more often than not they were side by side as they hurtled past the pits and into the right-hander before the Dunlop bridge and the Esses, or raced at over 180 mph down the Mulsanne Straight. It was a motor racing spectacle such as most people would never have the good fortune to see in their entire lives.

Soon after six o'clock in the evening the faster cars began to make routine refuelling stops accompanied by driver changes. On lap thirty-four Castellotti brought the Ferrari in to hand over to Marzotto; Hawthorn was due to stop on lap thirty-five. Now some eight seconds ahead of Fangio, he caught Levegh's 300SLR at Arnage Corner and passed Macklin's Austin Healey moments later, soon after White House. Then he pulled over to the right-hand side of the road and slowed for his pit stop, being caught by the drivers he had just passed as he did so. Macklin's Healey moved to the left to overtake the Jaguar just as Levegh, travelling at almost 160 mph, tried to squeeze past him at the right-hand kink in front of the pits. The two cars brushed together, barely touching, and in the blink of an eyelid the situation was beyond the control of either driver. The Mercedes hurdled the Austin Healey, leaving a tyre mark on Macklin's helmet, and landed beyond the earth embankment protecting the packed tribunes opposite the pits to bounce, disintegrate and burst into flames, killing poor Levegh and eighty-three spectators. Back on the track Hawthorn, understandably distracted by what was going on behind him, had overshot his pit and was sent round to complete another lap, while Macklin scythed down a gendarme and a pit marshal before spinning to a halt in the centre of the road. Fangio, warned it is said by Levegh's raised arm signalling danger even as he

Partnered by Ivor Bueb, Mike Hawthorn won the 1955 Le Mans 24 Hours for Jaguar but their victory was rendered meaningless by the terrible tragedy that claimed more than eighty lives.

faced death, relied upon his superb reflexes to dodge the spinning Healey and continue the race. Afterwards Fangio said he thought that Levegh had probably saved his life.

Rob had watched the early part of the race from a pit set aside for Anciens Pilotes du Mans, but shortly before the accident he had moved to the Jaguar pit to talk to Lois Rolt and Duncan Hamilton, ready and waiting to take over the D-Type he was sharing with Tony. He was there when Mike stopped at the end of his extra lap. 'Although we didn't know the full extent of the accident then – I don't think anybody did – it was obvious that something pretty bad had happened. When Mike got out of the car he was absolutely distraught, shocked beyond words, hardly knowing what he was doing or saying. What he did say was "It was all my fault; I wanted to get into the pit before Fangio came past. It was all my fault." I have absolutely no doubt in my mind that Mike truly thought that he had caused the accident; I was there at the time and I remember it perfectly clearly, just as I remember Lois pouring a tumbler full of brandy down his throat and telling him to shut up.'

While the doctors, nurses and ambulancemen treated the injured, and priests moved among the dead and the dying, the race went on. Moss had taken over from Fangio as had Ivor Bueb from Hawthorn. The Mercedes held a commanding lead when at two o'clock on the morning of 12th June both surviving cars were withdrawn as a gesture of mourning. All three Ferraris had already succumbed to various mechanical disorders. Fourteen hours later Mike Hawthorn took the chequered flag in pouring rain to win a hollow victory a hundred miles ahead of his friend Peter Collins in an Aston Martin he had shared with Paul Frère.

Mike Hawthorn with Betty in Rob's gullwing 300SL at Ibsley in 1955.

The debate about who or what actually caused the Le Mans disaster has continued ever since. Was the track dangerously narrow at that point? Was Hawthorn's impetuosity responsible, as he clearly thought at the time? Was it a misjudgement by Macklin? Or were Levegh's ageing reflexes simply unable to cope with the performance of the 300SLR? Could Fangio, had he been driving Levegh's car, have avoided the accident? Almost everyone who was involved, and quite a few who weren't, has an opinion. Rob Walker prefers to keep his own counsel, recalling each of the principal players with respect and affection.

'I first became aware of Mike Hawthorn when he began doing wonderful things with a Cooper-Bristol in 1952. I remember a Formula Libre race at Boreham where he was leading Villoresi in the works-entered Ferrari 375 in the wet, until the rain stopped and the greater power of the 4½-litre car simply overwhelmed him. I think he finished third in the British Grand Prix that year, and fourth in the Belgian Grand Prix at Spa. Then he got onto the front row of the grid at Zandvoort and finished fourth, I think, behind the three factory Ferraris. Of course by this time Enzo Ferrari had realised that if Mike didn't join them he might quite easily beat them, so he was signed up for the 1953 season and won his first Grand Prix for Ferrari at Rheims after that fantastic dice with Fangio's Maserati 250F which he eventually won by a car's length, having passed Fangio at the Thillois Hairpin on the last lap.

'Mike never drove for me, although five World Champions did: Jack Brabham, Jochen Rindt, Graham Hill, Alan Jones and John Surtees. Once at Brighton I lent Mike my B-Type Connaught for a demonstration run and then drove it myself in the speed trials. Near the end of my run I was doing about 140 mph when the car suddenly turned sharp left towards the stone wall, which was quite exciting at the time, but I managed to control it and get it across the finishing line. Afterwards

Rob seems apprehensive as Mike Hawthorn prepares to give the B-Type Connaught a run in the 1956 Brighton Speed Trials.

Rob, Stirling and Mike at Crystal Palace in 1956.

when I tried to drive the car back to the paddock I discovered that there was no drive at all; both driveshafts had failed and the rear wheels were only held on by the brake calipers! I suppose that Mike had caned it so hard during his demonstration run that the driveshafts had been ready to give up the ghost by the time it was my turn.

'I knew Mike pretty well and I was delighted when he became World Champion in 1958, although in truth he only did so because of Stirling's sportsmanship. At the Portuguese Grand Prix at Oporto Mike had finished second in his Ferrari behind Stirling's Vanwall, but had then been disqualified because he was said to have acted dangerously by push-starting his car against the direction of the race after he had taken to the escape road on the last lap. The Dino 246 still had drum brakes at that time and they used to get rather tired towards the end of a Grand Prix, and Mike must have been trying pretty hard because he thought Stirling was about to lap him. Actually, Stirling had decided to back off in order to spare Mike's feelings, but I suppose Mike wasn't to know that at the time. Anyway Mike appealed against his disqualification and a stewards' enquiry was convened to hear his appeal. I was having dinner with Stirling after the race when he suddenly looked at his watch and shot off in the middle of his pudding to testify on Mike's behalf. He told the stewards that he had seen Mike pushing his car on the pavement, which was not considered to be part of the track, and that therefore no offence had been committed; the stewards accepted Stirling's evidence and Mike kept his second place and his championship points.

'I've often wondered if Stirling really did see Mike on the pavement, or whether he just made the story up to protect Mike from the bureaucrats. Stirling was only interested in winning a race or a championship on merit; winning on a technicality just didn't interest him at all. In any event, his decision to speak up for Mike cost him the World Championship.

'At the last Grand Prix of the season, at Casablanca, Stirling had to win and set the fastest lap in order to become World Champion, with Mike finishing no higher than third. Of course Stirling duly won and set the fastest lap, but Phil Hill obeyed team orders and allowed Mike to pass him into second place, and so he won the title by just one point. But only because Stirling had supported him at Oporto. You can't possibly imagine something like that happening today, now can you?

'The scoring system for the World Championship was a bit odd in those days anyway; although Mike won the championship fair and square according to the rules, he had only won one Grand Prix during the season, whereas Stirling had won four, and even Tony Brooks – who finished third in the championship – had won three. But Mike's five second places won him the title. I think he would have retired at the end of that season whether or not he had won the championship; I don't think he enjoyed his motor racing very much after seeing Peter being killed in Germany.'

Fate brought Mike and Rob together near Guildford shortly after noon on Thursday 22nd January 1959. Earlier in the day Rob had left his home at Nunney Court near Frome to drive to his racing shop at Pippbrook Garage for a meeting with Dick Jeffery of Dunlop to discuss their tyre contract for the forthcoming season. Mike in turn had left his office in Farnham for London and a series of meetings of the sort that even a retired World Champion could not avoid. It was pouring with rain as Mike's highly tuned Jaguar saloon, which he called 'the Merc-eater', drew abreast of Rob's drophead Mercedes 300SL on the Hog's Back. The two friends waved and grinned at each other before accelerating hard through the gears onto the four-lane Guildford by-pass. Going into the right-hand bend past John Coombs' garage they were side by side, but after changing into top gear at over 100 mph Rob backed off, allowing the Jaguar to draw ahead by a car's length; 'That car was really very tricky in the wet and I thought to myself, "This is all very well for a World Champion, but I'm too old for this kind of thing." Then suddenly things began to get out of hand; I could see through the spray that the Jaguar

Daily Mirror

FRI
JAN 23
1959

FORWARD WITH THE PEOPLE

2½   No. 17,140

Mike Hawthorn's friend talks of death crash...

'WE WERE NOT RACING'

DAILY MIRROR REPORTERS

RACING driver Rob Walker, 40, told a dramatic story last night of the road crash in which his friend, world's champion driver Mike Hawthorn, 29, was killed yesterday.

Walker, from his own car, saw Hawthorn's Jaguar SKID while going down a slight incline on the Guildford by-pass . . . saw it HIT a traffic bollard . . . saw it SCRAPE the rear wheel of a lorry . . . and saw it CRASH into a ditch.

'Speeds?—I Don't Know'

Walker, near to tears, told the story at his Dorking, Surrey, garage.

HE SAID: "LET'S GET THIS CLEAR FIRST. WE WERE NOT RACING. WE WERE NOT 'DICING.'

"I don't know what speed I was doing and I don't know what speed Mike was doing but he was travelling faster than I was. The police asked me about speeds and I couldn't tell them."

Walker went on: "Mike was in his favourite Jaguar and I was in my new 140-mile-an-hour Mercedes. Mike had come up behind me on the Hog's Back.

"I didn't know it was his Jaguar at first. Then after turning out on to the by-pass Mike came alongside and waved.

"But this did not start the skid—that came some distance later.

"We were alone on our side of the road.

"As Mike swung in front of me his tail began to slide. I thought he would just flick the wheel and straighten up."

Walker continued: "I'll never know what caused that skid. It was such a simple one at first.

"I've seen him straighten a thousand more difficult ones on oil patches on race tracks.

No Answer . . .

"Eventually it was a complete side skid which went on and on. The car hit an island and then glanced off the rear of a lorry going the other way.

"Then everything flew in the air. I was about a hundred yards behind. It all happened as these things do on a race track—in a few seconds.

"I stopped opposite his crashed car and ran across, shouting 'Mike, Mike.' But everything was silent.

"The car appeared to have spun right round and gone into a tree backwards.

"The tree had been uprooted. It was all mixed up with the car.

"I found Mike on the floor at the back of the car. He was still alive but unconscious.

"He was dead before a doctor reached him. He must have died within a few minutes of the crash."

Walker added: "I think the wind might have been something to do with the crash. There were heavy gusts and one on the Hog's Back moved me fully two yards across the road."

ROB WALKER
Hawthorn overtook him on by-pass

CRUNCHIE

CHANT 6D
SIZE
ALSO 4°

● *They were to have wed . . . Mike Hawthorn and model Jean Howarth.*

THE GIRL WHO WAITED

THE girl who was to have married Mike Hawthorn walked weeping in the rain yesterday. . . .

She is model Jean Howarth, 22, daughter of a Huddersfield manufacturer.

And yesterday she said that she and Mike had planned to an-nounce their engagement shortly.

Jean was given the tragic news of Mike's death at her parents' home in Fenay-lane, Almondbury, near Huddersfield—where she was waiting for Mike to visit her this week-end.

She broke down, and then walked out into the rain. With her went

her Boxer puppy Ferrari . . . a present from Mike Hawthorn last November.

MIKE AND I: By DONALD CAMPBELL—See Centre Pages.
WHAT THE MIRROR SAYS—See Page Two.

had started to slide but I naturally expected Mike to correct it without any trouble at all – after all, this is what he'd been doing for a living for the past ten years or so. But then he hit the kerb and spun through 180 degrees so that we were facing each

other, clipped a traffic island which tore off his front bumper and flung it in front of my car, just missed a lorry which was coming in the opposite direction, and disappeared in a fountain of mud and water as he went off the road backwards, hitting a tree that virtually cut the car in half. I managed to stop pretty quickly despite the conditions and I can remember running up to the Jaguar in the rain and seeing Mike stretched out on the back seat, almost as if he was asleep. I said, "Come on, Mike, that was a bloody silly thing for a World Champion to do," and then I saw a slight trickle of blood coming from his mouth and I looked into his eyes and I realised that

he was either dead or dying. Within a few minutes a doctor who happened to be passing stopped to help, and then the police arrived, and it seemed sensible to leave the whole thing to the professionals.

Friday 23rd January 1959: grim headlines.

'The accident was never explained, though all sorts of theories were put forward. Jaguar could find nothing mechanically wrong with the car when they examined it afterwards, and they blamed the experimental Dunlop Duraband tyres which stuck like glue until the last moment and then broke away with absolutely no warning. Duncan Hamilton, who arrived on the scene some time after the crash, having heard about it on his car radio, thought that the very strong cross winds which he himself had encountered on the Hog's Back might have caught Mike out, but I never subscribed to that theory. Most people accepted, as I did, that even Mike Hawthorn was capable of driver error, especially in the appalling weather conditions on the day. Years later Chris Nixon discovered when he was researching his book *Mon Ami Mate* that five days before the accident Mike had had a hand throttle fitted to the car to enable him to rest his right leg on long journeys – just like the cruise control on modern cars. When I learned about this, I remembered my testimony at the Coroner's Inquest four days after the accident when I said that even as Mike's Jaguar was facing towards me, sliding backwards off the road, I could hear that the engine was still at full throttle. At the time I thought that was strange. I think now that what probably happened was that the hand throttle somehow stuck wide open, and that was what caused the accident. But of course we will never know for sure.'

Chapter 8
The Colotti Box

'I think that once Mike Hawthorn had become World Champion and Stirling could no longer be the first Englishman to win the title, he rather lost interest in the whole thing. Certainly when he drove for me, while we obviously wanted to win every race we entered, we were never really counting World Championship points. The press always made a great issue of Stirling's obsession with the World Championship, and with his continuing failure to win it, but I think it really was more media hype than anything else. Stirling never seemed to me to be nearly as obsessive about it as the papers made him out to be.

'Despite his enormous superiority in sheer driving skill Stirling was always seeking some little extra advantage over the others, some fractional edge, and he and Alf had decided that they needed to improve upon the Citroën-based gearbox fitted to the Cooper which they thought wasn't strong enough to handle the increased power given by the new, larger Coventry-Climax engines. John Cooper obviously felt the same, but he wasn't prepared to sell us his new, stronger gearbox. So Stirling and Alf decided to commission Valerio Colotti, a young ex-Maserati engineer based in Modena, to design a five-speed gearbox for us, and this gearbox was to give us endless trouble until we finally discovered that the gears had been badly cut. I'm not talking about just a small machining error; they had actually been cut to completely the wrong size so that they didn't even mesh together properly. It seems almost unbelievable now, but that sort of thing happened in Modena in those days. As a matter of fact, just about anything could happen in Modena in those days – but the root cause of the problem probably was that the gearbox was designed and built in too much of a hurry. It took us so long to sort it out that I actually suggested to Stirling that he should look for an alternative drive until we could be sure of providing him with a car that would not let him down; once we had got it sorted out, though, it was a super box, and very reliable.

'All the top drivers behave like this, even today. They always want to have something a little bit better, or a little bit different from the others, even if it hasn't been tried and tested. Even Ayrton Senna does it, and he has so much pure talent, just like Stirling before him, that he doesn't need to mess around with unproved modifications in order to win races.

'I remember once, at Monaco in 1960, Lance Reventlow asked Stirling to try the Scarab, and he immediately put in a lap six seconds quicker than Chuck Daigh's best time, even though he said the car was virtually undriveable on the slower corners. On another occasion, I think it was in 1961, we were testing our Cooper at

Alf, Tim Wall and John Chisman, watched by Rob, install the BRM engine into a Cooper chassis at Pippbrook in 1959.

Silverstone and we were sharing the circuit with the Austin Healey rally team. Pat Moss, Stirling's sister, was one of the works drivers. She was enormously enthusiastic about the performance of the Healeys and came into our pit to try and persuade Stirling to have a go in one. At first he told her to go away because he was busy but eventually she prevailed; he jumped into the car and on his first flying lap he was seven seconds faster than their quickest driver. He was that good.'

Back in 1959, again seeking a marginal advantage, Stirling Moss persuaded BRM to supply an engine for the Rob Walker team to fit to their Cooper chassis in the belief that it was more powerful and might prove to be more reliable than the Coventry-Climax motor. 'It wasn't too difficult to install the BRM but it was not interchangeable with the Climax which was a bit inconvenient as it meant we had to have a dedicated chassis for each engine. I honestly don't know if the BRM was a better engine, or worse; I preferred the Climax, but then I wasn't driving the thing. What I do know is that if it was Stirling's idea then it would go faster. I remember in that same year Stirling was determined to have coil springs fitted at the back of the Cooper. Alf said they wouldn't work, Stirling said they would and, of course, when we went down to Goodwood to test the coil spring car it was quicker than the one with the conventional transverse leaf spring. I think it was mainly a question of psychology, of Stirling believing that the car was better and therefore finding that in fact it was, but also I think it showed that he always had something in reserve which he could call upon, almost subconsciously, when the need arose.'

Stirling also believed that he could improve upon Coventry-Climax power for Formula Two, so Alf and John Chisman took a Cooper chassis to Germany where a Borgward fuel-injected engine was duly installed at the factory. As a condition of supplying the engine, Borgward insisted that it should be serviced only by one of their engineers – Fritz Juttner – seconded to the team; 'Fritz was a super chap, and terrifically dedicated. My mechanics used to tease him about being so in love with his engine that he even slept with it. Be this as it may, he looked after it so well that it ran faultlessly until the final race of the season in South Africa when a blocked injector allowed Paul Frère to beat Stirling into second place at East London.'

The engine deals with BRM and Borgward were negotiated by Stirling's manager, Ken Gregory, and it was an immense load off Rob's shoulders to have Ken's knowledge and experience available to him. Ken was very well organised and efficient, and he dealt with all the starting money negotiations and race entry formalities, leaving Rob free to deal with the preparation of the cars and the very complicated travel arrangements for the team. It was also an immense load off the shoulders of the mechanics to be able to leave the preparation of the Borgward engine to Fritz Juttner; they had their hands full with the preparation of two (sometimes three) Formula One and two Formula Two cars, as well as an Aston Martin DB4GT, for a very full season of racing.

At this time the R.R.C. Walker Racing Team consisted of Rob himself, his secretary Liz – who later married David Piper – Alf Francis, John Chisman, Tony Cleverley and an apprentice mechanic. Betty helped with the timekeeping during practice and kept a lap chart during each race, often assisted by Sid Henderson of Ferodo. Even by contemporary standards the team was not overstaffed.

Stirling and Rob had shaken hands – there was no formal, written agreement between them – on a simple financial arrangement; each of them had his own individual fuel contract with BP, but Rob's contracts for both fuel and tyres also earned performance bonuses which he shared with Stirling on a 60/40 basis in Stirling's favour. So it was with starting and prize money. This, Rob felt, was a fair reflection of the relative contribution each of them made to the team's success. 'The only time I ever had a money problem with Stirling was after the Portuguese Grand Prix at Monsanto in 1959. In those days we used to get paid our money in cash after the

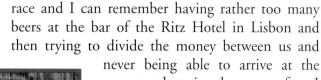

race and I can remember having rather too many beers at the bar of the Ritz Hotel in Lisbon and then trying to divide the money between us and never being able to arrive at the same totals twice, however often I counted it. It was an absolute nightmare; there were little piles of bank notes all over my bedroom!'

At Monaco earlier in the year Stirling had the choice of three Rob Walker Coopers; a chassis fitted with the BRM engine, another fitted with Rob's 2½-litre Coventry-Climax engine, and a third fitted with a 2½-litre Climax engine taken from his own Cooper Monaco sports car. The BRM-engined car was a disappointment; the 1959 version of the BRM power unit was said to be producing 270 bhp, almost 50 bhp more than the latest Coventry-Climax motor, but it was clear that far fewer horsepower were available from the earlier engine which was on loan to Rob at that time and, as well, the car suffered from gear selection problems. Stirling ran it for only three laps in practice, winning pole position in the car powered by his sports car engine and sharing the front row with Behra's Ferrari and Jack Brabham's works Cooper. Maurice Trintignant in Rob's second Cooper-Climax was on the inside of the third row of the grid.

Jean Behra led from the start with Moss tucked in behind him. Soon tiring of playing a waiting game, Stirling passed the Ferrari on the twenty-first lap and then, following Behra's retirement, left Jack Brabham's works Cooper trailing further and further behind until, almost a minute ahead on the eighty-first lap, the Moss jinx struck again and he retired with transmission failure. Jack Brabham duly won and recorded the fastest lap of the race; he was followed home by Brooks' Ferrari and Maurice Trintignant's Walker Cooper.

After the Monaco Grand Prix there were thinly

Main photo: *Stirling led the 1959 Monaco Grand Prix before the Colotti gearbox failed. Here he is seen at the Station Hairpin.*

Inset: *Maurice finished third at Monaco. Here he passes Harry Schell's BRM on the descent from Mirabeau.*

veiled suggestions in the popular press – as indeed there had been following earlier retirements – that Stirling had been pressing unnecessarily hard and had broken his car in a race he could have won easily had he paced himself more sensibly. Rob dismissed this suggestion with the words 'Stirling Moss could win a race in a wheelbarrow – especially with Alf Francis pushing it.' Gregor Grant, then Editor of *Autosport*, also disagreed that Stirling had contributed to the failure of his transmission. 'At no time', he wrote in his race report, 'did Moss appear to be caning his

Rob and Maurice confer at Zandvoort, watched by John Chisman, Tim Wall and Tony Cleverley.

motor car. His passage around the circuit was as smooth and delightful as anything I have ever witnessed. In point of fact, it was an exhibition of Grand Prix driving to which few drivers could aspire.' As well, statistics seemed to oppose the charge of car breaking which had been levelled at Moss; he was using his Colotti box rather less than his rivals. For instance, Tony Brooks changed gear in his Ferrari twenty-three times per lap; Stirling, aided by the massive bottom-end torque of the Coventry-Climax engine, changed gear only fourteen times per lap in his Cooper, and that would have made a difference of nine hundred gear changes over the full race distance.

As the season wore on Stirling and Rob began to get to know each other really very well. Unless Betty was attending a race with Rob, he and Stirling always travelled together. They were constant companions and, although different in age and temperament, discovered that they enjoyed each other's company hugely; they soon developed a very relaxed and easy relationship, and had terrific fun together. 'Whenever I drove with Stirling – anywhere in the world – we were invariably stopped by the police for one reason or another. I remember on one occasion, when we were driving from Milan to Modena in a rented Fiat, coming round a corner absolutely on the limit with the tyres squealing and being stopped by a couple of carabinieri who gave Stirling an extremely stern lecture before asking to see his licence. Of course they then realised who they had been lecturing and saluted about twenty times each before sending us on our way. On the return journey we were passing through a small village with narrow cobbled streets lined with houses, and I'll never forget Stirling saying, "I really had to grit my teeth in the Mille Miglia to keep my foot down and go through here at 160 mph." I can still hardly believe it!

'On another occasion we were driving from Zeltweg to Vienna in a 911 which

Porsche had lent us and I just knew we were going to get into trouble so I had prepared fifty Austrian Schillings, or whatever the fixed penalty was in those days, and had it all ready, just in case. Sure enough, Stirling was talking too much and missed one of those overhead traffic lights they have there, and crossed on the red. I could tell that Stirling was about to have a big argument with the policeman who stopped us, so I just handed him the money and he waved us on.

Betty and Maurice at Pau, 1959.

'Although he would become very combative with a policeman or any similar authority figure, Stirling never drove competitively on the road. He certainly drove very fast, but never competitively. If someone wanted to challenge him he just wouldn't react at all. I remember once when Stirling was driving my Facel back to London from Silverstone we passed a Jaguar XK120 on the M1 at about 120 mph. Of course the other driver recognised Stirling and got very over-excited and repassed us before blowing up in a cloud of smoke and steam. Stirling just ignored the whole thing. On another occasion the driver of the bus which was taking us to the airport after the Syracuse Grand Prix recognised Stirling and couldn't resist showing off; he drove absolutely flat out, barely slowing for the corners and scaring us all witless, until finally the bus burst a radiator hose and lost all its water. Luckily we had stopped near a river and the passengers, including Stirling and me, formed a human chain and used any available container to carry water to the bus so that we could get going again. People were always showing off or challenging Stirling on the road, and he would simply turn the other cheek.

'It was at some time in the summer of 1959 that I began to suspect that Stirling's marriage might be running into a spot of bother. He and Katie were staying with us at Nunney on the weekend of our church fete. Stirling had agreed to open the fete and over three thousand people turned up to see him do it, which wasn't bad for a sleepy little village in the depths of Somerset. One of the stalls offered clay pigeon shooting and my brother John challenged Stirling to a competition. John had his own shoot and shot four or five days a week throughout the season, and he was an absolutely outstanding shot. I'm not sure if Stirling had ever so much as held a gun before, let alone tried to shoot a clay pigeon, but his natural hand–eye co-ordination was so highly developed that he beat my brother easily!

Katie Moss and Betty at Rouen, 1959.

'Then Stirling wanted Katie to have a go. She had been the ladies' skeet shooting champion of Canada, and I would have loved to see her shoot, but for some reason or other she wouldn't. Stirling was absolutely furious with her – really livid – and he was even more furious when she beat him at croquet later in the day. He virtually refused to speak to her for the rest of the weekend, and it was all rather embarrassing. It was then that I began to wonder if something might be going seriously wrong between them.

Katie and Stirling Moss at Monaco, 1959.

'I have no doubt that although Stirling had more girl friends than you could shake a stick at when he was a bachelor he was absolutely faithful to his wife when he was married – although he was always eyeing the crumpet and I suppose it was a bit tactless of him to comment upon their finer points in Katie's presence. Even so, and even though Stirling was not the easiest person in the world to live with, I believe that the breakdown of the marriage was more Katie's fault than his. She was a very headstrong lady, used to having her own way, and she found the conventions of marriage somewhat burdensome. But I liked Katie; everybody did.

'Stirling was absolutely devastated when he and Katie separated. He was terribly confused by what was happening to him, and he didn't really know how to handle it. I would like to think that Betty and I helped him through this very difficult time by providing a home for him at Nunney; he used to come and stay with us and Betty used to tease him, and mother him, and teach him to paint. He seriously considered giving up motor racing at this time because he felt that his very demanding racing programme had been partially responsible for the breakdown of his marriage, but thank goodness we managed to dissuade him from doing so. We said that he should continue for two reasons; firstly, because motor racing would fill his life so that he wouldn't have time to sit around feeling sorry for himself, and secondly because what he did gave so much pleasure to so many people that he could not let them down.'

Meanwhile, there were races to be run, won, and lost. Maurice Trintignant's impeccably precise driving style triumphed again at Pau, where he won the Formula Two race in the rain by over a minute from Bruce McLaren's works Cooper. In the Dutch Grand Prix at Zandvoort, however, Maurice could only finish eighth while Jo Bonnier gave the BRM team its first-ever Grand Prix victory; Stirling again retired while he was in the lead, his Walker Cooper-Climax the victim of yet another failure of its Colotti box. But at least on this occasion he had the satisfaction of having recorded the fastest lap before pulling disconsolately into the pits.

A week later at Rheims, while the Walker team struggled to resolve their gearbox problems, Stirling drove a BRM which had been loaned to his father's British Rac-

Stirling retired with yet another Colotti gearbox failure when leading the 1959 Dutch Grand Prix at Zandvoort.

ing Partnership specifically for his use. The BRM team drivers, Bonnier and Schell, were none too pleased by this development, but Sir Alfred Owen was delighted to have Stirling appearing in one of his cars and overruled their objections. Alas, Stirling spun out of third place when his clutch failed seven laps from the end of a race which was run in almost intolerable heat and, once again, his only consolation was the fastest race lap. Trintignant finished twelfth in Rob's Cooper after stopping frequently at the pits to be doused with buckets of cold water and finally pushing the car home after spinning and stalling his engine. Several drivers suffered from heat exhaustion, but Tony Brooks stayed cool to win for Ferrari. Stirling won the supporting Formula Two race in Rob's Cooper-Borgward with Trintignant in fourth place in the Climax-engined car. At Rouen the following week the team-mates finished in precisely the same positions.

At the British Grand Prix at Aintree Stirling was once again driving the BRP BRM as doubt still remained about the reliability of Rob's Colotti gearboxes. This time, as well as sharing fastest race lap with Bruce McLaren, Stirling managed to coax the BRM into second place behind Jack Brabham, while Maurice Trintignant finished fifth in Rob's Cooper-Climax. This race was notable for the debut of the latest front-engined Vanwall, offered to Stirling at Rheims and now driven by Tony Brooks whose regular Ferrari entry was stranded in Italy by striking metalworkers, and a pair of Aston Martin DBR4/250s, also front-engined, for Salvadori and Shelby. John Cooper had given a lead in racing car design which would soon be followed by anyone who was seriously interested in winning, but neither Tony Vandervell nor David Brown seemed to have spotted the trend.

Maurice and Stirling.

At Clermont-Ferrand Rob joined battle again with Toto Roche. Stirling was in pole position in Rob's Formula Two Cooper-Borgward, and when Toto started the race while still standing on the track, Stirling had no alternative but to brake hard to avoid running him down. Chris Bristow in a Yeoman Credit Cooper-Borgward shot into the lead and it took Stirling three laps to catch and pass him, after which he was never headed. Rob's French gathered fluency as he berated Toto, telling him he was a disgrace to the sport and unfit to act as starter or, indeed, to officiate in any capacity. Curiously enough, the two men later became good friends; years later Rob was having some difficulty in negotiating starting money for the French Grand Prix and decided to confront Toto in his office at Rheims. Driving to Rheims from Spa after the Belgian Grand Prix, Rob and Betty were received with great courtesy. Champagne, of course, was produced, and a generous financial arrangement was agreed in a most civilised way.

Following his experiences at Rheims and Aintree Stirling decided that the BRM was, if anything, slower than the Cooper and hardly more reliable; he therefore elected to take a chance with the Colotti gearbox for the remainder of the Formula One season. He rejoined the Walker team in time for the German Grand Prix in August.

In 1959, largely for political reasons, the German Grand Prix deserted its traditional home at the Nürburgring for the Avus circuit in West Berlin. The Grand Prix was run in two heats on a circuit of very little character: two long, parallel straights formed by a section of the autobahn connected at one end by a hairpin bend and at the other by a steeply banked 180-degree corner, all that remained of the pre-war track. Berlin was an interesting city at this time, and Rob's first visit there was made more memorable by Bernard Cahier, who arranged a visit to what was left of Hitler's bunker in East Berlin, via Checkpoint Charlie. Rob was struck by the enormous contrast between the two halves of the city; in the west, the ravages of the recent conflict had been obliterated except where they had been deliberately preserved as a reminder of the awfulness and futility of war. The Hotel Kempinski was amongst the best in the world, maintaining a reputation for excellence which had endured since the turn of the century, and the stylish shops on the Ku'damm rivalled those on Fifth Avenue and Bond Street. Beyond the wall in the East, however, shattered buildings still lined the neglected streets, empty of cars, and those few wary pedestrians who were abroad wore drab, threadbare clothes. Those shops that were open had nothing to sell that any visitor from the West would want to buy, or that any resident of East Berlin could afford. It was a salutary experience.

French journalist Bernard Cahier.

'At the end of a fascinating day I remember all of us talking about the war over dinner. Maurice described his experiences with the Maquis in occupied France, I mentioned the Fleet Air Arm, and then someone asked Mimo Dei of Scuderia Centro-Sud what he had done in the war. "Oh," he said, "I hid in a cellar for three years; I don't like wars very much." He must have been the original Italian war hero!

'We didn't do too much practice at Avus; Maurice's car had a pretty tired engine – I think it had done two Grands Prix without being properly serviced – and Stirling's gearbox was equally tired. The circuit was so boring that there wasn't much we could learn about it anyway. However, Herr Schmidt asked us to go out and practise in order not to disappoint the crowd and although we didn't want to wear the cars out we agreed to do so.

'There was a sports car race the day before the Grand Prix in which Jean Behra was killed; he slid over the top of the banking and was thrown out of his Porsche and decapitated by one of the wires supporting the flag poles. His mistress saw the whole thing from the pits, which must have been pretty unpleasant for her. Carel de Beaufort also went over the top in this race, but his Porsche landed on all four wheels in the paddock thirty feet below and he rejoined the circuit further on. Later he was disqualified for failing to complete the full course!

'In the main race Stirling only lasted for two laps before the gearbox broke yet again. Now at this time there was a rule that if you didn't complete a certain minimum number of laps – I can't remember how many it was, but it was certainly more than two – then you didn't get your starting money. Herr Schmidt at first refused to pay us until I pointed out that we would have lasted the minimum distance easily if we hadn't worn out the gearbox entertaining the crowd during practice at his request. Fortunately he saw the justice of this position and paid up, otherwise I would have given him a very hard time indeed.

'Later in the race Hans Herrmann in the BRP BRM had a monumental shunt when his brakes failed at the hairpin. The car just disintegrated, but Hans was thrown clear and didn't have a scratch on him. Ken Gregory had rented a huge American Ford Galaxie for the weekend and he told me later that he loaded all that was left of the BRM into the boot!'

By the time of the Portuguese Grand Prix Alf Francis and Valerio Colotti believed that they had solved the gearbox problems which had plagued them for so long, and it was therefore in a spirit of great optimism that the Walker team arrived at Monsanto, north of Lisbon. Their optimism was not misplaced; Stirling's Cooper ran faultlessly to win the race easily, having lapped every other car on the circuit, and to record the fastest lap. Maurice Trintignant in Rob's second car finished fourth. During the race Jack Brabham made an uncharacteristic error of judgement when he tried to squeeze through a gap that wasn't really there in an attempt to pass local hero Mario Cabral. He was thrown out of his Cooper when it hit first the straw bales and then a telegraph pole, but fortunately escaped with no more than severe bruising. His failure to finish the race, however, eroded his lead over Stirling in the World Championship.

Next came the Italian Grand Prix. Once again Stirling started from pole position, and once again the Colotti box held together. Tyre wear was critical at Monza and, just as he had at Buenos Aires almost two years earlier, Alf conned the Ferrari team into believing that Stirling would have to join them in a stop for fresh rubber by holding up a wheel each time the Cooper passed the pits. Alf couldn't believe that they would fall for the same trick twice, but they did. Though he won, Moss was deprived of the opportunity of going for fastest lap by the inadequacy of the official timekeeping at Monza; it was not until the race had ended that he and Rob discovered that Phil Hill's Ferrari had bettered the record lap Stirling had established early in the race.

The point that Stirling would have won had he established fastest lap at Monza could have had a crucial bearing on the outcome of the 1959 World Championship. Despite the disastrous start to his season, Stirling's later successes created an opportunity, albeit a slender opportunity, for him to win the title at the final race of the year. As the contenders assembled at Sebring for the United States Grand Prix, it seemed that Stirling had to win the race and set the fastest lap in order to beat Brabham; Brabham could win by finishing second – so long as Stirling did not set fastest lap – and Tony Brooks, the outsider, could become champion if he won the race and made fastest lap with neither Moss nor Brabham finishing higher than third.

In the event one of the championship contenders was eliminated early on; Tony Brooks' Ferrari was rammed by his team-mate Taffy von Trips when he hesitated at the start, and Brooks was effectively out of the running after his inherent caution

Stirling winning the 1959 Portuguese Grand Prix at Monsanto, lapping every other finisher and setting the fastest lap in the process.

led him to stop at his pit to check the damage. Meanwhile, Stirling was in the lead – but not for long. After only six laps he retired, having suffered yet another transmission failure. This left Jack Brabham ahead in the race and the championship, but his luck was to prove no better than Stirling's; with only one and a half miles between him and the chequered flag, Jack's Cooper ran out of fuel and he pushed the car to the finish to be classified fourth. His team-mate Bruce McLaren became the youngest man ever to win a Grand Prix with Trintignant in Rob's second car

Stirling, Rob, John Cooper and Jack Brabham at Sebring for the 1959 United States Grand Prix.

snapping at his heels, having set the fastest race lap, vociferously encouraged from the pits by Alf Francis, Harry Schell and Stirling Moss.

Jack Brabham, just as Rob and Betty had predicted, was World Champion driver. Stirling Moss, whether or not he cared about it, was third and Maurice Trintignant was fifth and once again Champion of France. Rob Walker's cars had won ten major international races, including two World Championship events, and had helped Cooper to win the Formula One Constructors' Championship. Although the fallibility of the Colotti gearbox had spoiled what might otherwise have been a vintage 1959 season, there was still much of which the Walker team could be proud.

Chapter 9
The Lotus Blossoms

Towards the end of 1959 Jo Bonnier had appeared at Brands Hatch in a rather good-looking Formula Two Porsche – the forerunner of the car with which Porsche would enter the world of Grand Prix racing when the Formula changed in 1961 – which Stirling thought would be a better bet than the Cooper-Borgward for the following season. Ken Gregory was despatched to Zuffenhausen to work out a deal with Porsche management and a car painted in Rob Walker's dark blue livery was duly delivered to Syracuse for the first European Formula Two race of the 1960 season. On the occasion of its debut in Walker colours the car was accompanied by a number of Porsche factory mechanics supervised by the chief engineer of the competitions department, Dr Hilde, and by the competitions manager, Baron Huschke von Hanstein.

'It was a good financial deal because Porsche supplied the car and serviced the engine at no cost, but I'm not sure that it was really any quicker than the Cooper-Borgward. It was supposed to have quite a big horsepower advantage, but then this was offset by the fact that it was much heavier than the Cooper; in fact, it was built more like a road car than a racing car. It also took us quite a long time to get it fully raceworthy; for example the linkage to the synchromesh gearbox was rather sloppy, and the way the gear lever worked in the gate made changing gear a pretty hit-and-miss affair. I think this was probably what caused Stirling to drop a valve in the Syracuse race, when he was comfortably in the lead. Later on Alf fitted a gear lever, gate and linkage from a 250F Maserati and that improved things no end.

Baron Huschke von Hanstein of Porsche, Stirling and Rob at Syracuse in 1960.

'Alf was an absolute master of improvisation. At Syracuse the circuit had been resurfaced just before the race and it was so smooth that even after over forty practice laps the tyres on the Porsche were hardly worn, and Stirling reckoned they were still a bit slippery and unpredictable. Dr Hilde had driven to Syracuse in a prototype 2-litre 911 Carrera which Olivier Gendebien asked to borrow to drive to Catania for dinner with friends the night before the race. When Alf heard about this, he surreptitiously transferred the tyres from the race car onto the 911 and a hundred miles or so of Olivier's driving on the sort of road surface one usually finds in Sicily scrubbed the tyres to absolute perfection.

Stirling led the 1960 Syracuse Grand Prix before Rob's new F2 Porsche dropped a valve.

Alf Francis in the pits at Goodwood, Easter 1960.

'Earlier in practice all the BP cars had been suffering from carburetion problems and after trying all the obvious solutions without success Alf reckoned that the octane rating of the fuel supplied by BP must have been too high. He took two churns partly filled with the official BP fuel down to the local Agip station and topped them up with really rough two-star petrol to lower the octane rating, and after that we never had any more trouble.

'I recall another occasion at Monza when a rear wheel bearing seized on Stirling's

Cooper. We had a spare in the lorry, but without access to workshop facilities we couldn't get the seized bearing out of the upright. In the end Alf balanced the upright between two ordinary house bricks underneath the lorry, jacked the rear wheels six inches clear of the ground, put a piece of timber between the bearing and the chassis, and took the jack away. Six tons of transporter pressing down on the piece of timber removed the damaged bearing with almost surgical precision and we had the new one installed in no time.

'Alf regarded any obstacle we encountered when we were racing as a personal challenge to his ingenuity, and I never once saw his ingenuity defeated. I think his incredible gift for improvisation must have developed when he was with the First Polish Armoured Division in the war, when no doubt they had to use all sorts of tricks to keep the tanks going in very difficult circumstances.'

As the 1959 Grand Prix season had drawn to a close, Alf Francis had become convinced that he could design and build a better Formula One car than John Cooper. The resulting Walker Special was very much Alf's brainchild – although Rob has no doubt who paid for it. 'It had wire wheels and looked rather big and heavy to me. We tested it at Silverstone with Jack Fairman driving which made it rather difficult to assess its real potential. I don't think Stirling ever so much as sat in the car; Alf just couldn't persuade him to take any interest in it.' Further development seemed futile when Colin Chapman redefined all design and performance parameters with his first rear-engined car, the Lotus 18.

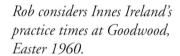

Rob considers Innes Ireland's practice times at Goodwood, Easter 1960.

The ill-fated Walker special.

This car, which had first appeared in Formula Junior guise, caused a sensation at the Argentine Grand Prix in early February 1960. While Stirling Moss in Rob's Cooper-Climax won pole position for the race, Innes Ireland in the Lotus, now equipped with a 2^1/$_2$-litre Coventry-Climax engine, was second fastest ahead of the BRMs of Graham Hill and Jo Bonnier and the three factory-entered Ferraris. In the race Stirling made a poor start and Innes shot into an immediate lead, only to fall back when he spun on the second lap. For forty-one laps thereafter, Stirling disputed the lead with Bonnier's BRM, first one and then the other thrusting his way to the front, until a broken rear wishbone forced the Cooper into the pits. Maurice Trintignant in Rob's second car had started from the third row of the grid and was lying fifth when Moss retired, despite the fact that he was suffering from appalling toothache. Rob called him in and sent him to the dentist to have his troublesome tooth removed while Stirling took over his car to finish third behind Bruce McLaren and Cliff Allison, setting the fastest race lap in the process. Innes Ireland had again led the race briefly in its closing stages before experiencing gear selection problems which dropped him to sixth position. Despite its lowly finishing position and its various mechanical disorders, the debate in the restaurants, cafés and bars of Buenos Aires after the race focused almost entirely upon the performance of the Lotus. Was it just a flash in the pan, or had Colin Chapman at last produced a world-beater? Perhaps the answer would be revealed at Cordoba.

The concluding event of the Argentine Temporada was called the Grand Prix of Buenos Aires City even though it actually took place almost 400 miles away from the capital at Cordoba. It was nominally a Formula Libre event although with one or two exceptions the field was as it had been for the Argentine Grand Prix a week earlier. One of the exceptions was provided by Stirling Moss who had returned to Europe to fulfil a prior commitment, leaving Maurice Trintignant to uphold the honour of the Walker team. Having observed him in practice, no less an authority than Juan Manuel Fangio had forecast that Trintignant, now fully recovered from his visit to the dentist, would win the race. And so he did, after both Brabham and McLaren had retired. Innes Ireland's practice was disrupted by the need to repair the Lotus chassis after he hit a kerb, and in the race the chassis collapsed as a result of the battering delivered by the very bumpy road surface. At the end of the day the jury was still out on the Lotus.

The race at Cordoba was to be Trintignant's last for the Walker team for some time; Rob had decided that it would be sensible to concentrate all the team's efforts on providing the best possible cars for Stirling to drive, and Maurice had therefore contracted with Aston Martin for Formula One, and had bought his 1^1/$_2$-litre Cooper-Climax from Rob to campaign privately in the 1960 Formula Two series. Rob had generously agreed that until Maurice could make other, more permanent arrangements this car would be prepared by the Pippbrook mechanics under the watchful eye of Alf Francis.

Maurice did well at Syracuse, in his first race as a private entrant, finishing second

Tony Cleverley, John Chisman and Stan Collier, Brussels 1960.

Maurice Trintignant in his ex-Walker F2 Cooper, Brussels 1960.

to Taffy von Trips' Ferrari after Stirling's retirement in the Porsche. Ireland's Formula Two Lotus also showed well in Sicily; he qualified second behind Moss and once again led from the start before Stirling overhauled him at the first corner. Ireland eventually finished fifth, and the case for the Lotus remained unproved.

Then came the Easter Goodwood meeting.

Practice for the Formula One race saw the 100 mph barrier for a single lap at Goodwood broken for the first time. No fewer than six drivers did so. Chris Bristow's Yeoman Credit Cooper-Climax was fastest, followed by Stirling's Rob Walker car, Schell, Ireland in the Lotus, Salvadori and McLaren. At the start Bristow led from pole position but the race soon developed into a straight fight between Ireland and Moss. Innes went ahead on lap four and from then on nothing that Stirling could do – and he tried absolutely every trick in his very considerable repertoire – could dislodge Innes from his lead. Despite the fact that Stirling set a new lap record in the closing stages of the race, Innes won the Glover Trophy by 2.8 seconds.

Innes Ireland and Gregor Grant of Autosport *with the Glover Trophy, Easter Goodwood 1960.*

*Stirling winning the 1960
Aintree 200 in Rob's F2 Porsche.*

In the Formula Two race it happened again. This time Innes took pole position in practice from Stirling's Rob Walker Porsche and although it was Moss who led from the start, Ireland was in the lead by the end of the first lap. And there he stayed, setting a new lap record and beating Stirling into second place by 6.4 seconds. Stirling was left to console himself with victory in the Grand Touring race in Rob's Aston Martin DB4GT.

At Silverstone, after Moss had won the Formula Two race at Aintree in Rob's Porsche, the Lotus once again proved to be the best car on the day.

A number of incidents marred practice for the International Trophy race for Formula One cars; in the most serious of them Harry Schell was killed instantly when he was thrown out of his car after leaving the road at Abbey Curve. 'Harry was killed about five minutes before the end of the first practice session as Betty and I were waiting for him to join us for a picnic lunch of smoked salmon sandwiches, which he enjoyed very much. Although he had never driven for my team, Harry was very dear to me. So many of my motor racing friends had been killed over the years that I had almost begun to accept it as a very sad but inevitable part of the game. But Harry's death hit me very hard. He was such a lovely man, so full of life and fun, and I really felt a deep sense of loss when he died.'

Earlier Stirling had hit a puddle of water as he accelerated down the pit lane at the start of his first practice lap, lost control of his Cooper and crashed into Roy Salvadori's stationary Aston Martin, severely damaging both cars. Under the circumstances Rob felt that he should offer to pay for the damage to the Aston, but David Brown wouldn't hear of it.

On race day Stirling started from pole position with a time set in the hastily prepared spare car, while Innes Ireland occupied a poor grid position after having a practice accident of his own. Innes made a spectacular start and was lying fourth by the end of the first lap. Thereafter he harried Moss continually before taking the lead on lap twenty-five. After Stirling retired with a broken front wishbone, Innes raced home ahead of Jack Brabham's new Cooper and Graham Hill's BRM, setting a new lap record in the process.

Harry Schell.

'I think that to this day Innes believes that he was a better driver than Stirling and that he won those races at Goodwood and Silverstone on pure merit. They're funny people, these racing drivers. At one level they are incredibly realistic, and yet at another level they can't accept reality. But I suppose if you don't believe you can be the best, then you might just as well pack up and go home.

'Stirling and I realised, of course, that the Lotus 18 was a simply fantastic car which conferred an almost insuperable advantage on its driver, and after Goodwood we wanted one very badly. I think that I may have spoken to Colin Chapman in the pits at Goodwood and established that he was as keen for Stirling to drive the car as

we were. Colin was longing to win a Grand Prix and he realised that Stirling had a better chance of winning one for him than anyone else, whatever Innes may have thought. I don't think Innes was too happy about it, but he wasn't in a position to complain too much.'

In the event, Chapman did not have to wait long for his first Grand Prix win.

Rob Walker's new Lotus was delivered on 18th May 1960, minus its fibreglass bodywork, just in time for Stirling to test it briefly at Goodwood before setting off for the Nürburgring and practice for the 1000 km sports car race – which he won in a Camoradi birdcage Maserati shared with Dan Gurney. There was no time to install the Colotti gearbox before the team set out for Monaco three days later, so Stirling would use the same five-speed Lotus box as the works drivers. But, at his request, his chassis had been constructed to rather more robust specifications than those of the Team Lotus cars.

Practice at Monaco was the usual hectic affair with twenty drivers seeking to qualify for only sixteen places on the starting grid. Innes Ireland, who had never before driven at Monaco, would not have qualified but for Stirling's help; when it became clear that Innes might not make the cut, Stirling led him round the circuit for several laps indicating the optimum line and the braking points, and holding up the appropriate number of fingers to show which gear he should be in where. Stirling started from pole position ahead of Brabham, Bristow, Brooks and Bonnier, with Ireland on the third row of the grid. The Ferrari challenge had been emasculated when their fastest driver, Cliff Allison, had been shipped across the harbour to the Princess Grace Hospital after clipping the kerb at the chicane during the second practice period.

Jo Bonnier jumped the start in his BRM and led Stirling for the first seventeen laps of the race before the Lotus nosed in front. Then it started to rain. Stirling had never driven the Lotus in the wet and very prudently decided to take it easy while he explored the car's wet-weather behaviour, and he allowed Jack Brabham to overtake him. He soon regained the lead when Brabham, less cautious than he, spun at

Rob, Alfred Moss and Betty, Monaco 1960.

Stirling on his way to victory in the 1960 Monaco Grand Prix.

Ste Devote. Then on lap sixty it seemed that the Moss jinx had intervened yet again when Stirling's engine began to misfire. He rushed into the pits, the engine cover was hastily removed, Alf Francis spotted and refixed a loose plug lead, and he rejoined the race. Now seven seconds behind Bonnier, Stirling began a serious charge. He and Bonnier were about to lap Graham Hill's BRM when Graham lost it at the exit from the hairpin at Les Gazomètres and demolished the Radio Monte Carlo commentary box, showering the track with debris. As they both skittered through the wreckage Moss passed Bonnier, who was destined to retire with suspension failure before the end of the race, to finish almost a minute ahead of Bruce McLaren's Cooper. Stirling and Rob had given Colin Chapman his first Grand Prix victory – but only just; after the race it was discovered that both forward engine mountings were broken and the front end of the engine in Stirling's car was supported only by a water pipe.

Jack Brabham leads Stirling at Tarzan in the 1960 Dutch Grand Prix.

Inset: *The author keeping a lap chart in the Walker pit, Zandvoort 1960.*

Still milking the theme of Stirling's alleged inability to pace himself properly, ex-racing and rally driver turned journalist Tommy Wisdom claimed most of the credit for his win at Monte Carlo. In his column in *Sporting Life* he wrote that he had begged Stirling not to go out in front at the start. 'I told him that was the chief reason for his run of non-success [sic]. He was content to follow the leader and wait his chance rather than tear into the lead from the start . . . all because of a chat he had with me last night.' Rob Walker, on the other hand, never once suggested to Stirling that he should hold back at the beginning of a race. 'I would never have presumed to tell Stirling how to drive his race; I never really felt that Stirling pressed on particularly hard in the first few laps anyway, even though he used to tell me that the Lotus handled exceptionally well on full tanks. He usually began his charge after about ten or fifteen laps, when he felt well and truly comfortable with the car and the circuit.' But Fleet Street had no such inhibitions, and it was inevitable that the gratuitous advice which appeared regularly in the press would eventually unsettle Stirling.

So it was that at Zandvoort, in a conscious attempt to appease his critics, he elected not to lead the Dutch Grand Prix from the start even though, given his pole position and the remarkable accelerative powers of the Lotus, he could have done so easily. Instead he allowed Jack Brabham's Cooper to take the lead, and lay close behind him in second place for seventeen laps.

On the eighteenth lap Brabham passed the pits alone. On one of the fast, 140 mph swerves leading through the woods to the main straight Jack had slid wide and dislodged a granite slab marking the edge of the track. His rear tyre had flung it towards the Lotus at head height and it had struck Stirling's right-front wheel with a crash, shattering the wheel rim and bursting the tyre. Stirling was extremely lucky not to have had a big accident. It was an incident which would have unnerved a lesser man, but when he finally brought his stricken car limping into the pits Stirling was more indignant than frightened. 'I've done what they wanted,' he said, 'and look what happened. What do they want me to do – sit there and let him throw stones at me?'

Stirling was stationary at his pit for almost three minutes. As Colin Chapman had been unable to supply spare wheels for Rob's Lotus there seemed to Alf to be little point in cluttering up the pit with a jack he wouldn't use. By the time the wheel had been changed, using both a spare wheel and a jack borrowed from Team Lotus, Stirling rejoined the race in twelfth place – next to last – and a lap behind the leaders. Never more determined than in adversity, Stirling treated the crowd to a magical display of race driving. By lap thirty he was tenth, by lap fifty he was seventh, he unlapped himself on lap sixty-five and at the chequered flag he failed by only one second to wrest third place from Graham Hill's BRM, setting a new lap record in the attempt. Jack Brabham won the race, but all the cheers were reserved for Stirling Moss.

'The night before the first practice day for the Belgian Grand Prix at Spa I had a hell of a party with Alf and the mechanics in the only nightclub in town. Somehow or other we got involved in a bit of a fracas almost as soon as we arrived there, and some Belgian chap knocked out my only false tooth. One of my mechanics soon disposed of him, but then the owner of the club decided to close for the night to avoid further trouble. This didn't suit us at all well as we had just paid quite a lot of money to get in, so the owner offered to provide us with a private cabaret, a strip-tease, in an upstairs room.

'At about two o'clock in the morning I decided that the best thing I could do was to walk back to my hotel, and I asked Alf if he would look after the 300SL for me. He woke up in a field later in the day, at about noon, having slept in the car, with no idea where he was or how he had got there. Eventually we all met up in the hotel in which the boys were staying, and we were all lying around in the same room groaning gently when Stirling turned up, bright-eyed and bushy-tailed and not

exactly overjoyed to find his team in such disarray. That heavy Belgian beer drunk in any quantity is not good news at all.

'In the end we more or less pulled ourselves together for the late afternoon practice in which Stirling, I think, was third fastest behind Jack Brabham's works Cooper and Tony Brooks in the Yeoman Credit car. Jack was fastest on the straight, reaching 190 mph on those skinny tyres, but Stirling was quickest through the twisty bits. I went to bed very early that night and made a resolution never again to drink too much before a race – and I never have.'

Stirling was on his second flying lap of the final practice session on Saturday 18th June 1960 when, approaching Burnenville Corner at about 140 mph, he suddenly felt the car sliding and found himself unable to correct it. Then he was overtaken by one of his rear wheels and he can recall thinking, 'This is it; I'm going to die.' The next thing he remembers is lying beside the road slowly regaining consciousness and realising that he was in great pain and almost unable to breathe. His car had slammed with enormous force into a bank on the left of the road, throwing him out into the undergrowth, then veered across the road again to come to rest upside down, off the track on the right.

Bruce McLaren was the first on the scene. He had been a few seconds behind Stirling and had witnessed the tail end of the accident.

He stopped his Cooper as quickly as possible and ran to Stirling's car thinking that he must be trapped underneath it. Then he saw the crumpled figure lying on the other side of the road and ran across, fearing the worst. Bruce saw that there was blood coming from Stirling's nose and mouth and found him shocked and not very coherent. He asked for artificial respiration, but Bruce was sensible enough not to move him. This was just as well, for Stirling's injuries included fractures of each tibia and fibia and three crushed vertebrae, as well as a broken nose, two black eyes and multiple cuts and bruises. As other drivers stopped at the site of the accident they agreed that they should keep Stirling still until, after about fifteen minutes, a doctor arrived, followed soon afterwards by an ambulance which eventually took him to Malmedy Hospital for examination.

Meanwhile, back at the pits, no one knew what had happened. There were no cars on the track; everyone had stopped even though no red flag had been shown. It was very quiet. The deathly silence in a situation which was normally a cauldron of noise was eerie, creating an almost theatrical sense of tragedy. In the end it became clear that three cars were missing and for a while it was thought that there might have been a multiple accident. At last, however, Chris Bristow came riding into the pits astride the engine cover of Tony Brooks' Yeoman Credit Cooper having suffered gearbox failure, and Michael Taylor was found to have had his own, quite separate accident when the steering column of his Lotus had collapsed. Throughout this period of uncertainty Rob sat quietly by a telephone and prayed that the news, when it came, would be good.

At last he and Alfred Moss, Stirling's father, were driven to Malmedy Hospital

Opposite: Stirling's three-wheeled Lotus spinning at 140 mph at Burnenville in practice for the 1960 Belgian Grand Prix. Inset: The wreckage of the Lotus after the accident at Spa.

2 BRITONS KILLED IN GRAND PRIX

Bristow Loses Control: Stacey Hit By Bird

MOSS BREAKS LEGS: WIN BY BRABHAM

From W. A. McKENZIE,
Daily Telegraph Motoring Correspondent

SPA, Belgium, Sunday.

TWO British drivers, Chris Bristow, 22, and Alan Stacey, 26, were killed in the Belgian Grand Prix motor race to-day. This followed serious accidents, in yesterday's practice, to Stirling Moss, 30, and Michael Taylor, 25.

The race, won by the Australian Jack Brabham, reigning world champion, at an average of 133.631 m.p.h., was one of the fastest on any road circuit in the history of motor racing. To-day's tragedies will arouse fresh controversy over the future of the sport.

Stacey's death seems almost certainly to have been due to a freak accident. M. Jean Bovy, a senior official of the circuit, confirmed that a bird hit Stacey's face, smashing his goggles.

The body of a bird was found on the track. There were traces of blood and feathers on the goggles.

It was at a spot called the Fountain of the Bird that Stacey, driving his Lotus at nearly 140 m.p.h., crashed. The car left the path, hit a bank and burst into flames. He died in the ambulance.

THROUGH BUSHES
Crash at Fast Bend

Bristow was well up, lying seventh in his Cooper, when, in the 19th lap, he took the long, fast bend known as Burneville, near Malmédy, at over 130 m.p.h., accelerated and overtook another car. Then he seemed to lose control.

STIRLING MOSS

where they found Stirling laid out in the operating theatre. They arrived just in time to hear the surgeon say, 'I'm afraid your face is in a bit of a mess, Stirling.'

'Well,' mumbled Stirling, 'I never was much of a beauty, but so long as my old man is OK, that's all that matters.' Rob knew then that despite his injuries Stirling's fighting spirit was undiminished.

Rob sat beside his hospital bed for much of that night and the whole of the next day. In the afternoon they listened to the race commentary on the radio and were horrified to learn that first Chris Bristow and then Alan Stacey had been killed. 'Bristow had been warned not to mix it with Willy Mairesse, who was really very wild and dangerous. He managed to resist temptation for about twenty laps but he was a pretty hard charger himself, as all those youngsters were, and eventually he got involved with Mairesse and lost it at Burnenville, just where Stirling had crashed. The car went end over end several times and Chris was killed instantly.

'People said that there were feathers adhering to poor Alan's goggles when they found him and everyone thought that he must have hit a bird at high speed, but I don't know if that's what really happened. He was terribly badly hurt and he died in the ambulance on the way back to the pits.'

The following day Stirling was smuggled out of a side door of the hospital at Malmedy to the military airport at Liège. From there, a chartered aircraft flew him, Ken Gregory, Rob Walker and Michael and Charlotte Taylor to Gatwick where Stirling's stretcher had to run the gauntlet of the *paparazzi* before an ambulance delivered him to

Opposite top: *The burnt-out remains of Alan Stacey's Lotus at Spa, 1960.*

A gendarme stands guard over the wreckage of Chris Bristow's Yeoman Credit Cooper.

St Thomas's Hospital beside the Thames in London. 'Stirling was anxious that the photographers should not take pictures of him looking so badly beaten up, so I used a clean white linen handkerchief to hide his face. It was not a question of vanity; Stirling was never in the least bit vain. I think he just felt that even he was entitled to some privacy under those circumstances.

'At St Thomas's Mr Urquhart, the orthopaedic surgeon, said after examining him that Stirling would be lucky to be driving again in six months. In fact he made the most amazingly rapid recovery and was driving a Lotus Monte Carlo in a sports car race at Karlskoga in Sweden in less than six weeks, and then he drove my Formula One Lotus in the Portuguese Grand Prix two weeks later. I think it really was almost a question of mind over matter; Stirling had the most extraordinary inner strength that simply wouldn't allow him to give in to physical frailty. He just set himself targets for recovery and refused to admit the possibility that he might not meet them.

'When the car was examined after the accident it was discovered that a driveshaft had broken, causing the collapse of the left-rear suspension. This component had failed several times before and Colin Chapman had already designed a stronger version which was available in time for the race – but that, of course, was too late for Stirling. At that time Lotus had the most appalling reputation for fragility, and if you spoke to Stirling or to any of the other Lotus drivers before a race they would admit to being worried in case something might break, but once they got into the car they just closed their minds to the possibility of mechanical failure – these drivers are just so competitive that they can exclude everything from their minds except going faster. This reputation dogged Lotus for many years; I remember talking to Jochen Rindt about it when he was driving for them and he said, "Listen, Rob, I want to win the World Championship so badly that I'm even prepared to drive for Colin to do so." And of course in the end it caught up with him and he became the champion posthumously in 1970.

'While Stirling was convalescing after his accident we missed both the British Grand Prix and the French Grand Prix at Rheims, so it was good to be back in action in Portugal. However, the car wasn't working particularly well and we started from the second row of the grid. It was the first time I had ever seen Stirling even slightly nervous before a race; I'm not sure that anyone else would have noticed it but, of course, I knew him so well by then that I was very sensitive to his mood.

'In the race the engine continued to pop and splutter and Stirling made several pit stops to try and put it right. In the end he bounced off the straw bales and spun into the escape road when a front brake grabbed. He push-started the car in exactly the same circumstances and in exactly the same place as Mike Hawthorn two years earlier, but unfortunately there was no one to speak up for him as he had for Mike, and he was disqualified.' Jack Brabham won at Oporto, and his victory was enough to guarantee his second World Championship.

In 1960 the organisers of the German Grand Prix at the Nürburgring decided to run it as a Formula Two race to give the Porsche team a chance of winning, and

Stirling leads John Surtees in the 1960 Portuguese Grand Prix at Oporto.

Innes Ireland, Stirling, Colin Chapman and John Surtees at Oporto.

141

Rob's car – repainted silver and entered by the factory – was driven to victory by Jo Bonnier. Displaying not dissimilar cynicism the Italians announced that their Grand Prix at Monza would be held on the combined road and banked oval circuits, in the certain knowledge that the British teams would boycott the race on safety grounds. Monza was a Ferrari benefit, just as the Italians had intended. The only serious Formula One race remaining on the calendar was therefore the United States Grand Prix at Riverside which, as we have seen, Stirling won to prove beyond doubt that he was back in business.

However, there were other races to be contested. Driving Rob's Porsche, once again wearing the colours of St Andrew's Cross, Stirling won the Formula Two race at Zeltweg after the race had been ended a lap early when about ten thousand excited fans swarmed over the track. 'It was clear that the crowd was totally out of control and almost without thinking Stirling and I ran to the transporter and locked ouselves in. The lorry was in gear and had the brake on, but even so it was shifted about a hundred yards down the runway by the sheer pressure of the mob. In the end we were rescued by mounted police, but it was a long time since I had been so genuinely frightened.' Stirling also won the Oulton Park Gold Cup and the Formula Libre race at Watkins Glen, which preceded the USGP at Riverside, both in the Formula One Lotus.

But none of this, Rob felt, was enough to justify his BP retainer. BP paid him £10,000 a year for the Grand Prix season and, given that his driver had been out of action for some weeks, Rob felt that he had not delivered his side of the bargain. Even though there had been no indication of dissatisfaction from BP he persuaded Dick Wilkins, a larger than life City figure and an old friend with more than a passing interest in motor racing, to finance the purchase of a short-wheelbase Ferrari 250GT Berlinetta with a particular view to winning the Tourist Trophy. This, he felt, would compensate BP for their loss of Formula One exposure and obviate the need which he would otherwise have felt to refund part of his retainer. At the same time it would allow Stirling to resume motor racing in something a little less demanding than a Formula One car.

The bookies paid Goodwood circuit a visit from their more natural habitat at the racecourse beside Trundle Hill and after practice for the TT offered even money on Stirling and Roy Salvadori, who was driving an Aston Martin DB4GT, two to one against Ireland in a similar car, three to one against Graham Hill in a works Porsche Carrera, and seven to one against Mairesse in a Ferrari. At those odds there were not many takers.

Stirling started from pole position and, despite limping heavily as he ran across the track at the Le Mans start, he was first away, saving fractions of a second by allowing the force of acceleration to shut the car door for him. For the first few laps Salvadori made a race of it but after their first pit stops Stirling began to develop a comfortable lead. It had become clear during practice that tyre wear would be considerable and that the time taken at pit stops for fresh rubber would have a decisive effect on the outcome of the race. 'In those days Aston Martin prided themselves on their pit stops, whereas Formula One mechanics were not required to be any good at that sort of thing. But Alf had spent ages training and drilling our mechanics and during the race we made Astons look foolish – we took seconds off them at every stop. Stirling made three routine stops for tyres, which took a total of just over two and a half minutes; Roy also made three routine tyre stops, but his took over four minutes! The only problem Stirling encountered came when he was badly baulked by Mairesse who had spun and chosen a bad moment to rejoin the circuit. When Roy burst a tyre, forcing him to make an extra pit stop, Stirling won easily, listening to the BBC race commentary on the car radio, and I felt that we had gone some way towards justifying our full BP retainer.'

Stirling wins in Nassau with Rob's short-wheelbase Ferrari 250GT Berlinetta.

The team ended the season in the sun; at Nassau they sailed, swam and won the Nassau Trophy with the Ferrari, and in South Africa they won both the Cape Grand Prix and the South African Grand Prix with the Porsche. But there were storm clouds on the horizon.

Left: *Stirling and Rob with the Nassau Trophy.*

Chapter 10
The Maestro

The advent of the 1961 season saw the introduction of new Formula One regulations which imposed a limit of $1\frac{1}{2}$ litres on engine size, combined with a minimum weight limit of 450 kg. The genesis of this change, ostensibly to reduce maximum speeds and therefore – or so it was argued – to improve safety, had occurred at a meeting in London of the then governing body of motor sport, the Commission Sportive Internationale, as long ago as October 1958. When the proposal was put to the vote only Britain and Italy were in favour of retaining the $2\frac{1}{2}$ litre Formula, and the motion was therefore carried by a majority of five votes to two.

The British constructors were incensed by this decision and confidently expected that the weight of their combined displeasure would enable the Royal Automobile Club to persuade the CSI to recant. It was not until mid-1960 – almost two years later – that it finally dawned upon them that their confidence had been misplaced and that the new Formula would go ahead with or without them. Only then did BRM and Coventry-Climax initiate the design of multi-cylinder engines which could not possibly be ready, therefore, until at least halfway through the new season. Until then all the British entrants, including Rob Walker and Stirling Moss, would have to rely upon the outdated four-cylinder Coventry-Climax engine which had served most of them barely well enough in Formula Two racing during the previous season.

Not so Ferrari, for whom Carlo Chiti had designed and developed a compact $1\frac{1}{2}$-litre vee-six which, when fitted to a mid-engined chassis and designated the Dino 156, had already raced in 1960 at Solitude, Modena and Monza, achieving more than respectable results on each occasion in the hands of Taffy von Trips. With a car which was thus well tried, tested and race proved, Ferrari confidently expected to do well in 1961. As well, Porsche viewed the forthcoming season with the justifiable optimism which had been generated by their success in the 1960 Formula Two series, culminating in Stirling's two victories in South Africa at the end of the year.

No doubt Porsche would have been even more optimistic had Stirling Moss responded favourably to an offer to lead the 1961 factory team, supported by Jo Bonnier and Dan Gurney. However, Stirling declined to do so, preferring instead to stick by Rob Walker and the mechanics with whom he had worked so closely for the past three seasons. There were those who regarded this as a somewhat quixotic decision, particularly as Stirling himself was on record as saying that he did not expect to be able to beat either the Porsches or the Ferraris in the machinery with which

Stirling at Hunzerug,
Zandvoort 1961.

Jo Bonnier with Innes Ireland before the start of the 1961 Syracuse Grand Prix. Behind him, Stirling and Rob stand beside the Lotus.

Rob could provide him and, indeed, tipped Jo Bonnier as the next World Champion.

Stirling explains: 'What a lot of people still don't understand is that throughout my entire career as a driver my first consideration was always that I should enjoy my motor racing; I only did it because I liked it. At the time [of the Porsche offer] I could think of no more enjoyable way of taking part in the sport than driving for Rob, so the question of driving for Porsche or anyone else simply didn't arise. Unless Rob had found, say, that he could no longer afford to continue, I would never have even contemplated driving for another team. It was absolutely out of the question. As long as Rob had wanted me to drive for him, I would have done so. My only regret is that we had to give up when we did – there was so much more that we could have achieved together.'

Others had been head-hunting Walker personnel also; BRM had offered Alf Francis an increased salary of £3000 per annum, a house, a car and carte blanche to develop the race cars as he wished if he would join them. But Alf, too, remained loyal to Rob Walker. He even asked Rob to attend a meeting with BRM at the Dorchester Hotel to turn the offer down on his behalf. If anyone was embarrassed by this request, it certainly wasn't Rob.

As the new season got under way in England, the disgruntled British constructors tried desperately to keep the old Formula alive by arranging a series of races for 2½-litre cars, but it soon became clear that this so-called Inter-Continental Formula would receive no support from outside the United Kingdom, and it gradually withered and eventually died of a terminal case of international apathy. In this series and in the preliminary Formula One skirmishes, Stirling and Rob enjoyed mixed fortunes.

Rob had acquired a new Cooper chassis for the Inter-Continental races and this soon proved to be a sound investment; at the Easter Goodwood meeting Stirling won the Lavant Cup by less than a second from Bruce McLaren, while at Silverstone he won the International Trophy race in the rain a lap ahead of Jack Brabham and the rest of the field. Later in the season he also beat John Surtees in the British Empire Trophy race at Silverstone despite having destroyed his clutch on the start line. Only at Brands Hatch, where Jack Brabham cruised to victory in the Guards Trophy race after the Walker Cooper had suffered transmission failure, was Stirling defeated under Inter-Continental rules.

Stirling and Rob fared less well, however, in the non-championship Formula One engagements which took place in the early season. John Surtees served notice at Goodwood on Easter Monday that the established stars would do well to watch their mirrors when he started his Yeoman Credit Cooper alongside Stirling's Lotus on the front row of the grid for the Glover Trophy race. The two of them fought tooth and nail for the lead until Stirling's engine began to misfire and he dropped back to fourth place. Surtees was followed home by Graham Hill and Roy Salvadori.

There were more carburettor problems for the Walker team at Brussels where the race on the new Heysel circuit was held in three heats. In the first two, Stirling could do no better than fourteenth and eighth places respectively, but halfway through the final heat his engine at last began to work properly and he finished second to Jack Brabham by only a tenth of a second. This was the first race of the season in which the British teams had encountered foreign opposition and their worst fears were confirmed when Bonnier's Porsche won the first heat easily before tangling with John Surtees while he was leading heat two.

Stirling won the Vienna Grand Prix on the Aspern airfield circuit without really

Below: *Stirling and Rob discuss the performance of the Zagato Aston, Easter Goodwood 1961.*

Bottom: *Stirling lapping the field to win the International Trophy race at Silverstone in 1961.*

The flight deck of the Bristol Freighter carrying the cars to Syracuse in 1961.

Rob at Syracuse in 1961.

having to extend himself against mediocre opposition, but at Aintree a week later the gremlins struck again. After a troublesome practice which saw him relegated to an unaccustomed position on the ninth row of the grid – with no less than twenty-two drivers ahead of him – Stirling could survive only two race laps before his engine's main bearings failed.

The Syracuse Grand Prix was scheduled to take place only three days after the race at Aintree so a Bristol Freighter was chartered to fly the cars from Gatwick to Catania while the drivers, mechanics, journalists and other camp followers travelled in a chartered DanAir Elizabethan. At this time private aviation in Europe was in its infancy, and few drivers held private pilot's licences. Amongst those who did were Jack Brabham and Innes Ireland, and each of them was invited onto the flight deck to try his hand at something larger than his Cessna. Jack's turn at the wheel passed without incident but when the time came for Innes to have a go Jack had a trick or two up his sleeve. First, he organised all the passengers to stand at the back of the aircraft so that Innes would have to trim the tail up to compensate for the uneven weight distribution; no sooner had he done so than Jack got everyone to rush forward so that the aircraft flew in a pronounced nose-down attitude until Innes had adjusted the trim again. Then everyone stood on the left so that the port wing dipped alarmingly – then on the right, and so

Rob, Tony Cleverley and Stirling wrestle with the Lotus gearbox after it had stuck in second gear on the warming-up lap for the 1961 Syracuse Grand Prix.

on. Eventually Innes got the message and in his best flight deck voice instructed his passengers to 'sit down, you lot, and belt up'.

The good humour and levity of the journey were soon forgotten in the face of the Porsche and Ferrari presence at Syracuse. Dan Gurney was fastest in practice in his Porsche, followed by Giancarlo Baghetti in the Ferrari Dino 156. Rob's Lotus was still dogged by carburetion problems and Stirling languished on the third row of the grid. Baghetti duly won followed by the Porsches of Gurney and Bonnier, while Stirling popped and spluttered his way to eighth place.

Battle was joined in earnest at Monaco where, as the Grand Prix circus assembled for the first World Championship event of the season, none of the British teams was particularly sanguine about the outcome. In the Rob Walker team, indeed, morale was lower than it had ever been. Their Formula One season thus far had hardly been successful; they had a chronic carburetion problem which they could not diagnose, let alone cure; they must have felt that their driver might be regretting his decision not to join Porsche and, to add insult to injury, the press was beginning to be overtly critical of them. In his column in *Motor Sport* published just before the Monaco Grand Prix, Denis Jenkinson had written, 'It is high time that Rob Walker stopped producing starting money specials for Stirling Moss to drive.'

Practice at Monaco promised to be even more hectic than usual; sixteen cars would be permitted to start, as always, but this year the organisers had guaranteed places on the grid to twelve drivers, which left ten more competing for the the final four places – including Richie Ginther of Ferrari and Hans Herrmann of Porsche.

Coventry-Climax had produced a more powerful, updated version of their four-cylinder engine for this race but it was still only good for 150 bhp, a disadvantage of at least 25 bhp versus the Ferrari vee-six. Rob's old Lotus 18 had a Mark II Climax fitted for Stirling, but Team Lotus appeared with two brand new Lotus 21s for Jim Clark and Innes Ireland. Each of these drivers was in trouble in practice; Clark crashed at Ste Devote on the first day and on the third and final day Ireland spun in the tunnel and was thrown out of the car, hurting himself sufficiently badly to spend the next few days in the Princess Grace Clinic before being shipped home. 'It was entirely my fault,' recalls Innes. 'We were using a new ZF gearbox for the first time, and I simply selected the wrong gear. Just as I was letting the clutch in I knew that I'd done it all wrong and that it was too bloody late. There was this tremendous locking sensation and I was out of control straight away. I can remember there was this fantastic noise of the car hitting things – this deafening, crashing noise in the tunnel – and then I was flying through the air. I don't remember actually hitting the road, but I do remember picking myself up afterwards and leaping pretty smartly over the barrier, which seemed to be the most sensible thing to do at the time.' Stirling Moss stopped to help and stayed with Innes until the ambulance arrived, before carrying on to win pole position – rather unexpectedly – from Richie Ginther and Jim Clark. In last position on the grid was Jack Brabham, qualifying for Indianapolis having restricted his availability for practice at Monaco.

'Alf was desperately worried about our carburetion problems which he just didn't seem able to solve. The night before the final practice day he collared the Weber representative and made him bring a brand new carburettor to our garage in Eze-sur-Mer, and together they stripped his and ours piece for piece, and examined and compared each of the the pieces in turn. Eventually they discovered that a small groove in the float chamber of the new carburettor hadn't been machined in ours, and that was the answer. I can't remember now whether we fitted new carbs to the car or had the old ones machined correctly, but it ran perfectly the next day and we never had any problems afterwards. I don't think Alf ever bothered to tell Stirling that he had spent the whole night working on the Webers, and I don't think that Stirling was particularly surprised next day to find that the car was running properly for the first time for months; he just naturally assumed that Alf would fix it in the end.'

On race day there was even more drama; as the mechanics were making their final inspection of the car, half an hour before the start, one of them noticed that a chassis tube was cracked right next to the aluminium fuel tank. 'Alf didn't hesitate for a moment. He moved the car away from the pit area, got the oxy-acetylene welding gear from the lorry and, having wrapped the petrol tank in wet cloths as far as it was possible to do so, he calmly began to weld the crack. It was a very brave thing to do, and typical of Alf. I watched him for a bit but after a while discretion overcame valour and I retired to a safe distance. I don't suppose Alf fancied being blown up any more than I did, but he never hesitated to do what had to be done, and I don't think his hand trembled once throughout the whole operation.

'Then, ten minutes before the start, Stirling decided that he wanted the side panels removed from the car to help keep him cool. Apparently Tony Cleverley and he had tried this during a very hot race in the Tasman series and it had worked very well. Anyway, I was rather worried that it would infringe some regulation or other so I rushed up to the Clerk of the Course, Monsieur Taffe, and asked his advice. He said it would be OK as long as the race number was clearly visible so we had to get some new numerals from the lorry and stick them on the engine cover. Eventually we pushed the car onto the grid well after the five-minute signal had been given.

Alf Francis (above) tended the Walker cars with great devotion and unfailing resourcefulness. Left: Alf welding the cracked chassis tube before the start of the 1961 Monaco Grand Prix.

'From then on it was up to Stirling. Richie Ginther in the Ferrari led from the start with Stirling in third place behind Jim Clark's Lotus. On the second lap

Stirling passed Jimmy going up the hill to Casino Square and set off after Ginther, who was already about four seconds ahead. Stirling was catching him slowly, taking a fifth of a second off him here and another fifth there until, after ten laps, he was right up Richie's exhaust pipes. He didn't seem to be in any great hurry to get past until Bonnier's Porsche began to close up on him and then he obviously thought it was time to get a move on.

'On the fourteenth lap he took the lead and for the next ten laps he pulled away at the rate of about a second a lap. I never really understood why the Ferrari drivers allowed him to do this in view of their subsequent performance, unless their cars just didn't handle as well as the Lotus with full tanks – or perhaps Stirling was just able to get more out of a car on full tanks than any of the others.

'By now Phil Hill had passed Ginther and set off after Stirling, gradually whittling away at his lead until by the halfway mark the gap between them was only seven seconds. At this point Phil made a desperate effort to close the gap still further, and I must say that I felt it was only a matter of time before we were caught and passed – although, of course, I knew that Stirling would resist for as long as the car kept going.

'Suddenly Phil began to tire and Tavoni in the Ferrari pit became very agitated and ordered Ginther to take up the challenge again. At first he started to close on Stirling, but when he got to within about three seconds it was as though Stirling thought, "Right; that's enough. Thus far and no further," and every time Richie put in a really quick lap Stirling would dig deeper into his resources and equal or better it – braking marginally later, going fractionally closer to the kerbs and walls so as not to scrub off speed in the corners, and getting back on the power a split second earlier. I knew we would win when Tavoni hung out a signal saying "GINTHER GIVE ALL", which must be terribly demoralising for someone who has been driving his balls off for ninety laps. I always

Stirling on his way to victory at Monaco in 1961.

Stirling in harmony with the Lotus – minus side panels – at Casino Square, Monaco 1961.

Zandvoort 1961. Stirling finished fourth behind two Ferraris and Jim Clark's Lotus 21. Here he leads Ginther (Ferrari) and Gurney (Porsche) at Hunzerug.

regard this signal as a sign of total despair, especially when it is given by Ferrari.

'In the end Stirling won by 3.7 seconds ahead of a very tired Ritchie Ginther. As he collected his trophy from Princess Grace and stood at attention for our national anthem, Stirling looked as cool, calm and collected as ever, but afterwards he told me that it was the first race he had ever driven in which he had not been able to relax for a single moment, and in which he had taken every single corner right on the limit. Throughout the race Stirling thought that the Ferraris were just playing cat and mouse with him and could have passed him at will; he never really believed he could win until he took the chequered flag. I thought it was Stirling's greatest drive; in fact, I thought it was the greatest drive, by any driver, that I had ever seen in my entire life.'

Stirling's victory made Denis Jenkinson and *Motor Sport* look very silly, and made their defence against Rob's subsequent libel suit impossible to sustain. Eventually damages of £1000 were agreed out of court, the money going to charity.

It was, however, an ominous portent for the future that Ferraris should have filled second, third and fourth places at Monaco; indeed for Rob Walker and Stirling Moss – perhaps the only British team capable of mounting an effective challenge against the Italians – it turned out to be downhill almost all the way from then on. At Zandvoort Taffy von Trips won for Ferrari; Stirling was fourth. At Spa Ferrari filled the first four places; Stirling was eighth driving an updated Lotus 18/21. At Rheims Giancarlo Baghetti won for Ferrari; Stirling retired. At Aintree Ferrari finished first, second and third; Stirling held second place while it was wet, but subsequently retired.

Then came the German Grand Prix at the Nürburgring.

The tortuous 14.165-mile Nordschliefe circuit of the Nürburgring – now, sadly, no longer used for Grand Prix racing – was without doubt the most exacting Grand Prix course in the world, climbing and plunging through some of the most spectacular mountain scenery in Europe. Over it all brooding, dark green pine trees stood glowering, their overhanging branches dripping wetly onto the track after rain, shading it from the sun and preventing it from drying quickly. Fair weather or foul, there was always an air of impending drama at the 'Ring, almost as if some long forgotten ghost of the Schloss Nürburg was gazing down from the lofty ruin from which the circuit took its name and demanding something more than an ordinary

Stirling and Rob at Zandvoort in 1961.

motor race. If this was indeed so, there have been many occasions on which he cannot have been disappointed; the most famous of them, perhaps, was in 1935 when the legendary Tazio Nuvolari trounced the hitherto invincible Mercedes and Auto Union teams, humbled them before 220,000 of their incredulous countrymen, in an outdated Alfa Romeo. It was a drivers' circuit; a circuit which, like Monaco, brought out the best in the best drivers of any generation; a circuit that separated the men from the boys.

It was, in other words, a circuit made for Stirling Moss. Even so, in August 1961 there can have been few observers who would have put their money on Stirling in Rob's Lotus to overcome the additional forty horsepower available to the Ferrari drivers from their new, even more powerful vee-six engines.

The second practice session, however, offered a glimpse of a more hopeful future; on Friday Jack Brabham appeared with a Cooper fitted with the long-awaited Coventry-Climax vee-eight engine which was reputed to be developing 175 bhp – still far short of Ferrari's 190 bhp, but at least a step in the right direction. The engine had been delivered to the Cooper factory in Surbiton precisely a week earlier, installed in the latest Cooper chassis by Monday, driven briefly at Silverstone by both Jack Brabham and Bruce McLaren on Tuesday, and then hurriedly shipped to the Nürburgring only to arrive too late for practice on Thursday.

On Friday morning the car would not start. It suffered the indignity of being towed round and round the paddock until Walter Hassan – the chief engineer of Coventry-Climax, who was on hand for the debut of his brainchild – discovered that a small pin in the distributor drive had sheared. Once out on the circuit the performance of the car was impressive despite appalling handling and constant bottoming on the Nürburgring's countless bumps. On Saturday Jack demonstrated the potential of the new engine by making second fastest practice time and becoming only the second man to break the nine-minute barrier at the 'Ring with a lap of 8m 58.2s performed in unofficial practice. Phil Hill was the first man to break nine minutes with a pole position time of 8m 55.2s; he and Jack Brabham shared the front row of the grid with Stirling Moss and Jo Bonnier.

All three practice days had been dry and sunny but Stirling's best time had been set on the super-sticky Dunlop high hysteresis D12 'Green Spot' wet-weather tyres. 'Alf Francis had painted the green spots which identified the wet-weather tyres black so that the other teams wouldn't see what we were up to. Actually, even Dunlop didn't know what we were up to until Vic Barlow visited our pit at the end of practice and was horrified to discover that Stirling had been running wet-weather tyres in the dry. When Stirling announced that he was determined to use them in the race, wet or dry, Vic was even more worried because of the risk of high wear and temperature build-up, and the possibility of a blow-out. Dick Jeffery, the Dunlop competitions manager, made the point pretty forcibly that they were wasting their time having a large technical presence at every race if we were going to disregard their advice, and I suppose if I had been him I might have felt much the same.

'Stirling had been very reluctant to tell me what he and Alf were up to because he knew I would worry about it, and he was right; I did. He and I discussed the situation in a very calm and civilised way over dinner that evening, and although I tried to persuade him that he took quite enough risks without adding to them unnecessarily, he felt that this was a calculated risk which was worth taking. He reckoned that the Ferraris had a 15 mph advantage over him in top speed, which meant that they were four seconds a lap quicker on the main straight alone, and he felt that he hadn't a hope of staying with them unless he could take advantage of the better adhesion of the sticky tyres on the twisty bits. In the end I was persuaded by Stirling's contention that as the sole supplier of racing tyres Dunlop were inevitably over-cautious, since they had everything to lose and nothing to gain from making a risky tyre choice, and by the fact that Innes had used them in the dry at Solitude without mishap, and we agreed to go ahead. I'm still not sure whether this was a courageous or a foolhardy decision.

'While Stirling and I dined together at the Hotel Lochmuhle and Alf and the mechanics enjoyed a rare early night, Coopers spent all night trying to sort out Jack's handling problems. Sometime on Sunday morning John Cooper retired absolutely exhausted to his hotel only to find every door locked. Some thoughtful person had left a ladder in the garden and John used it to climb up to his bedroom. Having crawled quietly in through his window, he was surprised to find a lady asleep in his bed. It was, of course, the wrong room, and John quickly took to the ladder again – or so he said!'

Before daybreak on race day seemingly endless streams of traffic converged upon

Stirling at the right-hander before the Karussel, German Grand Prix 1961.

the Eifel Mountains. Long before the start it was estimated that over 300,000 spectators crowded the most spectacular vantage points of the Nürburgring, hoping to cheer Taffy von Trips to victory. The day dawned to cloudless blue skies, although the possibility of some rain had been forecast. Sure enough, there was a shower during the preliminary race for GT cars, but as the start of the Grand Prix approached the circuit was drying rapidly. On Dunlop's advice Ferrari started on dry tyres but Stirling and Rob stuck to their decision to run their disguised Green Spots.

When Fangio dropped the flag Jack Brabham made a copybook start and led into the first corner, closely followed by Stirling Moss and Bonnier, Gurney and Hans Herrmann, all in factory-entered Porsches. For a variety of complicated reasons

Stirling takes the chequered flag in the rain to win perhaps his most famous victory.

Brabham had started with wet-weather tyres at the front and dry tyres at the rear of his Cooper. Halfway round the first lap this combination caught him out when he came across a damp patch under the trees; the front tyres bit and the rear tyres didn't and he found himself disappearing sideways through a beech hedge, the victim of massive oversteer. For thirty yards or so he raced parallel to Bonnier, albeit on the wrong side of the hedge, before eventually the Cooper came to rest, hardly damaged, against a tree stump. The only injury Jack Brabham suffered was to his pride.

Jack's accident had given Stirling Moss, following close behind, a nasty moment

and thus allowed Phil Hill's Ferrari to slip momentarily into the lead. Stirling repassed him just after the Karussel and led at the end of the first lap by two seconds. 'It was very difficult at the 'Ring to provide drivers with the information they needed using pit signals because as they came past the pits you could only give them the position as it had been at the end of the previous lap, nine minutes earlier, and of course in that time almost anything could have happened. Fortunately they came past the back of the pits about fifty seconds later, after going round the South Curve. The back of the pits were completely wired in but Alf managed to cut a hole in the wire just big enough to get his hand through holding two numbers, so we could give Stirling a corrected figure – it would be black if he was ahead and red if he was behind, just like the debit and credit on a bank statement and therefore easy to remember. So, for example, as Stirling came past the pits on lap two we gave him a signal showing that he had been ahead of Phil by two seconds at the end of lap one, nine minutes ago. Then Alf would stick his hand through the wire behind the pit holding black numbers eight and five, meaning that Stirling now led Phil by 8.5 seconds. This system really worked very well.'

By lap four the circuit was completely dry and Stirling led Hill by eleven seconds. Then Taffy von Trips mounted a challenge and by lap eleven the gap was down to 6.9 seconds. But at this point, just as he had at Monaco, Stirling decided that enough was enough; in their efforts to catch him both Ferrari drivers lapped the 'Ring in under nine minutes for the first time in a race, the lap record of 8m 57.8s being established by Phil Hill, but each time they made a little ground so Stirling responded by making a little more.

Then the rain came, first as a thin drizzle and later as a torrential downpour, and Stirling's wet-weather tyres came into their own even though they were dangerously worn. Only 1 mm of tread remained at the end of the race – insufficient for a family car to pass an MOT test today. He won by twenty-one seconds from von Trips with Phil Hill third.

'Stirling provided me with one of my proudest moments when he stood on the winner's rostrum in the pouring rain, with an enormous laurel wreath around his shoulders, while 300,000 Germans listened to our national anthem. It was made all the more moving because the grandstand in front of the pits seemed to be packed with soldiers from the British Army of the Rhine waving Union Jacks of all shapes and sizes, including the biggest one I've ever seen.

'When Stirling won at Monaco I thought that neither he nor anyone else could possibly drive a finer race; then at the Nürburgring I thought he had. Looking back on them today, I really don't know which of these two drives was the best. What I do know is that both of them were absolutely magnificent.

'Stirling was racing at Brands Hatch the day after the German Grand Prix, at the August Bank Holiday meeting, and he had been offered a lift home in a helicopter which was due to leave as soon as the race had ended. I insisted that he should stay for the prizegiving ceremony in the evening; in those days prizegiving was an important, formal affair and I felt that as the winner he had an obligation to be present. Today, of course, the drivers can hardly wait long enough to spray each other with champagne (what a stupid waste of good champagne that is!) before disappearing. Stirling was a bit miffed about missing his ride home, but saw the point and conducted himself at the ceremony, as you would expect, most graciously.'

Prior to the Italian Grand Prix at Monza a new Coventry-Climax vee-eight engine had been installed in Rob's Lotus. The frame behind the driver had been completely rebuilt, partly to accommodate the new engine and partly to provide additional strength; after the race at the Nürburgring several ominous cracks had been discovered in the Lotus chassis. As always the engine had been delivered late

Innes Ireland enjoys a banana at Monza.

and it was touch and go whether the car would be ready in time. In the event it was towed to Monza on a trailer behind Rob's Facel Vega HK500, to which a draw bar had been hastily fitted, arriving just in time for the first practice period. The new engine proved troublesome in practice and was withdrawn from the race because of persistent overheating and coolant loss.

Even had the Climax vee-eight proved viable on its first outing, Stirling could hardly have hoped to mount a serious challenge to the Ferraris on their home ground; once again the race at Monza was to be held over the combined road and banked circuits, a configuration which favoured absolute horsepower above all else. On the day, after all his problems in practice, it was almost incredible to find Stirling running in second place before retiring with a collapsed front wheel bearing in the latter stages of the race.

The Italian Grand Prix, however, was also notable for other reasons.

First there was the great sportsmanship of Innes Ireland; realising when Stirling decided to use his four-cylinder Climax engined car for the race that, old and tired as it was, it was unlikely to win him many of the World Championship points he so badly needed, Innes volunteered to give up his newer Team Lotus car for Stirling to drive. Moss duly appeared on the grid in a multi-coloured Lotus – the upper half Walker blue, the lower half Team Lotus green – sporting Lotus yellow wheels. Innes drove Rob's car clad in the bodywork of the spare UDT/Laystall Lotus and retired after only six laps with a cracked chassis frame, showing just how much Stirling had benefited from his friendship and generosity.

Then there was the tragic death of Taffy von Trips who came to Monza leading the World Championship by four points from Phil Hill, with Stirling a further eight

points in arrears. He took pole position on the grid with his Ferrari team-mates filling the next four places behind him. In the lead on lap two, he moved to the outside of the road as Jim Clark made to overtake him at the exit from the Curva Sud, and the Ferrari's left-rear wheel made contact with the Lotus's front-right wheel to precipitate a major accident. Taffy's Ferrari shot off the road to the left, rode up a bank into a chain link fence enclosing the spectators at that point, travelled along it for some distance, rebounded into the road and turned over several times before coming to rest in the middle of the track. Clark ended up in a ditch to the right of the road, emerging from his car shaken but unhurt. But Taffy von Trips was dead along with fourteen spectators; only the low, frail chain link fence had prevented a tragedy on the same scale as that which had occurred at Le Mans six years earlier. Phil Hill won the race in the sole surviving Ferrari and became the first American to win the World Championship.

Ferrari did not enter the final Grand Prix of 1961 at Watkins Glen ostensibly as a gesture of respect towards the late Taffy von Trips, although there were those cynics who made the point that as Hill was already the World Champion driver and Ferrari had already won the Constructors' Championship, they had nothing to lose by

Taffy von Trips (top left) *won at Zandvoort in 1961 but was killed later in the season at Monza, where his team-mate Phil Hill* (top right) *clinched the World Championship.*

Above: *Rob and Jack Durlacher monitor Stirling's fortunes from the pit wall.*

staying away.

Stirling again elected to drive Rob's four-cylinder Lotus in the race, swapping the lead with Jack Brabham in his vee-eight-engined Cooper for forty-three laps before Jack was forced into the pits to check an overheating problem which eventually led to his retirement. Stirling himself retired later, the victim of main bearing failure after BP Canada had supplied the wrong engine oil, and Innes Ireland inherited the lead with forty laps to go. Ireland's victory was the fifth Grand Prix win for Lotus, but the first for the factory team. The preceding four victories had been scored by Stirling Moss driving for Rob Walker.

Returning to England, Stirling drove the first four-wheel drive Formula One car to success in the Gold Cup race at Oulton Park.

As long ago as 1950 the visionary Harry Ferguson had foreseen the day when most if not all manufacturers would offer permanently engaged four-wheel drive to purchasers of family cars. At the time it was a revolutionary concept, and there were many problems to be overcome; not least of these were power loss, increased tyre wear and higher fuel consumption.

It is sad that Harry Ferguson himself did not live to see the day in 1960 when — after ten years of research conducted at a cost of several million pounds — the company which he had founded believed that these problems had been solved. Tony Rolt was then Managing Director of Harry Ferguson Research Limited and it is hardly surprising that he elected to demonstrate and prove the validity of the Ferguson four-wheel drive system in the crucible of Grand Prix racing, or that he chose Rob Walker as his partner in this endeavour.

The Ferguson P99 appeared initially in Inter-Continental guise in practice for the British Empire Trophy race at Silverstone in July 1961, only eleven months after the Ferguson draughtsmen had first put pencil to paper to initiate its design. It was a front-engined car powered on this occasion by a 2½-litre Coventry-Climax engine. In addition to its revolutionary four-wheel drive system, it was also equipped with Dunlop Maxaret anti-lock brakes poached from the aerospace industry. The car was not expected to win races or even to be competitive; rather, it was seen as a mobile test bed.

Its debut at Silverstone was not auspicious. When Stirling had tried the car in practice, he decided to let Jack Fairman drive it in the race. His judgement was vindicated when Jack retired after two laps with transmission failure.

Jack Fairman also drove the P99, now powered by a 1½-litre engine, in the British Grand Prix at Aintree. He made a good start in the wet, as might have been expected, but later, following an accident involving Henry Taylor, he ran over some debris on the track which damaged the car's bodywork. A magneto lead trapped between the damaged bodywork and the chassis frame eventually chafed through and Fairman stopped at the Walker pit to investigate a serious misfire. When the trouble had been diagnosed and rectified Stirling took over, having abandoned his Lotus with mechanical failure, but he received a push-start from his mechanics and was immediately disqualified. However, he was allowed to go on racing on the clear understanding that he could not qualify as a finisher; at least the mobile test bed continued to be mobile – until Ferrari lodged a protest and Stirling was black-flagged.

The race at Oulton Park proved to be third time lucky for the Ferguson. Stirling Moss drove the car to his fourth Gold Cup win ahead of Jack Brabham's works Cooper and Bruce McLaren in Tommy Atkins' privately entered car. Having made a poor start after finding difficulty in selecting first gear, Stirling demonstrated that the P99 was equally at home in wet or dry conditions, taking the lead on the sixth lap and setting the fastest lap as the race drew to a close.

As usual, Rob and Stirling finished the season by taking their Ferrari 250GT Berlinetta to Nassau for the Speed Week. Stirling had driven this car to win the 1961 RAC Tourist Trophy at Goodwood, his seventh TT victory and his second for Rob Walker, and now he also repeated his earlier success in the Nassau Trophy race. Rob reported the week's events for *Autosport*, a foretaste of many good things to flow from his pen in years to come.

Stirling winning the Oulton Park Gold Cup in Rob's four-wheel drive Ferguson P99.

Chapter 11
Annus Horribilis

His successes in 1961 gained Rob the coveted Ferodo Gold Trophy, the most prestigious award in British motor sport. With typical modesty Rob says, 'If anyone deserved it, it was Stirling, but drivers weren't eligible for that particular award then, so I suppose they had to give it to me instead.' Or 'I think the committee met to make their final decision over dinner and I suppose the port had been round so many times that the decanter was empty and they all wanted to go home, so they had to settle on someone.' Rob's modesty notwithstanding, everyone else thought that he richly deserved to join a list of previous winners which read like a who's who of motor racing: Jaguar, Tony Vandervell, Connaught, Colin Chapman, Leonard Lee for Coventry-Climax, Dunlop and Sir Alfred Owen of BRM.

The award generated considerable media exposure for Rob who was not slow to

use the opportunity to speak out against the proposed imposition of purchase tax on racing cars, a move which would generate revenue of only a few thousand pounds for the Exchequer at the cost of penalising an important source of valuable automotive engineering prestige in key export markets. Only days after Rob's appearance on BBC's *Sportsview*, the proposed tax was quietly dropped by an embarrassed Chancellor.

The award of the Ferodo Gold Trophy and his successful campaign against purchase tax excepted, however, 1962 was a very bad year for Rob Walker.

'Early in the year, when Stirling and I were discussing our programme for the forthcoming season, I suggested that we should enter for the Pau Grand Prix which was to be held on Easter Monday and which I always regarded as the perfect dress rehearsal for Monaco. Stirling saw the wisdom of this suggestion but felt that as he had so few opportunities to perform before his British public he would prefer to go to the Easter Goodwood meeting which took place on the same day, April 23rd. In the end I decided to take the Formula Two car to Pau for Maurice Trintignant to drive, and offered to lend Stirling the Formula One car for Goodwood, and for a race which took place at Snetterton the weekend before Easter. As I had too few mechanics to service both cars at these three different meetings it was agreed that

Stirling struggling with a sticking throttle at Snetterton, April 1962.

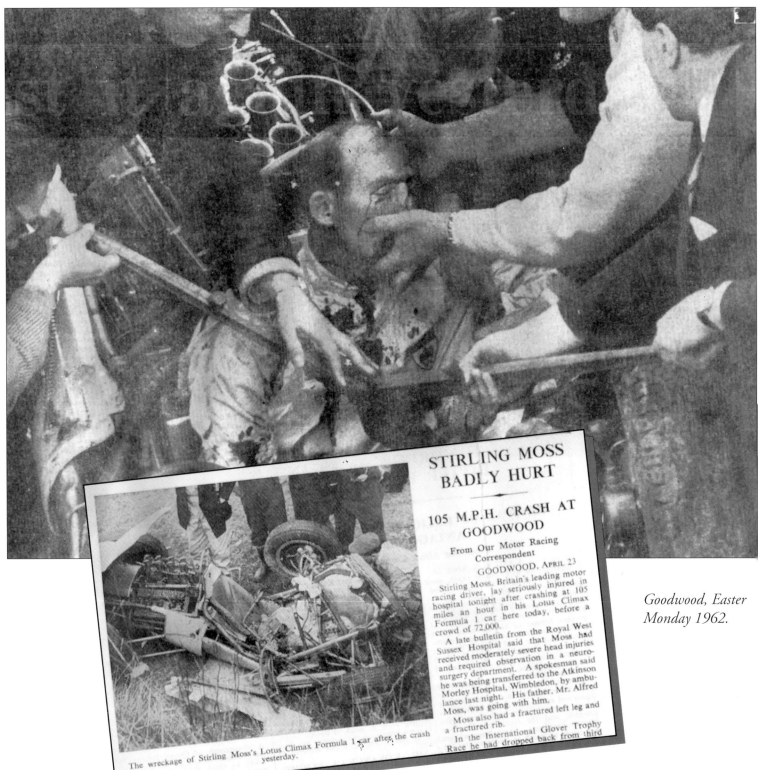

STIRLING MOSS
BADLY HURT

105 M.P.H. CRASH AT
GOODWOOD

From Our Motor Racing
Correspondent
GOODWOOD, APRIL 23

Stirling Moss, Britain's leading motor
racing driver, lay seriously injured in
hospital tonight after crashing at 105
miles an hour in his Lotus Climax
Formula 1 car here today, before a
crowd of 72,000.

A late bulletin from the Royal West
Sussex Hospital said that Moss had
received moderately severe head injuries
and required observation in a neuro-
surgery department. A spokesman said
he was being transferred to the Atkinson
Morley Hospital, Wimbledon, by ambulance last night. His father, Mr. Alfred
Moss, was going with him.

Moss also had a fractured left leg and
a fractured rib.

In the International Glover Trophy
Race he had dropped back from third

The wreckage of Stirling Moss's Lotus Climax Formula 1 car after the crash
yesterday.

*Goodwood, Easter
Monday 1962.*

the Formula One car would be prepared by BRP.

'Some time later Ken Gregory called me to ask if I wanted the entries at Snetterton and Goodwood to be made in my name. Initially I thought that I might as well chalk up another couple of victories but then, on reflection, I realised that it would be grossly unfair to my mechanics to be blamed for any possible mechanical failure when they had not been involved in preparing the car, so it was resprayed in BRP colours and entered by them. Later on I was to be very thankful that I had taken this decision, and that greed had not overcome common sense.

'Maurice duly won at Pau – for the third time running – and at the formal prize-giving ceremony that evening Jabby Crombac came up to me and said, "How is Stirling?" I said, "I haven't seen him for a few days, but he's absolutely fine as far as I know." Then Jabby said, "Haven't you heard? He's had the most terrible accident at Goodwood." And that's how I found out about it.

'I walked straight out of the prizegiving, found a telephone and called Ken Gregory in London. As always Ken was very calm and matter-of-fact and did his best not to alarm me unduly, although he did not attempt to conceal the fact that Stirling was very badly hurt. Ken said that at first it had been thought that Stirling would not survive, but the doctors were now slightly less pessimistic; he had been taken to the Atkinson Morley Hospital in Wimbledon and was receiving the best possible care. Next day Betty and I drove back to England in the Facel and on the car radio we heard a report on Stirling's condition broadcast every hour by the BBC World Service.'

Even so Rob was not prepared for what he found at the hospital, which shocked him profoundly; Stirling's nose and left cheekbone were broken, his eye-socket was displaced and his face badly cut. His left arm was broken, his left leg was broken in two places and his brain had suffered such severe trauma that the left side of his body was paralysed. He was in a deep coma. The latest medical prognosis suggested that recovery would be slow and perhaps no more than partial; Stirling might never regain full control of his left arm and leg, and his vision and speech might be permanently impaired.

The consultant who was in charge of the case was most anxious that when he emerged from his coma Stirling would find a familiar face at his bedside so Rob, Ken Gregory, David Haynes and Valerie Pirie, Stirling's secretary, arranged a rota system which involved each of them in daily four-hour shifts at the hospital. Alfred Moss spent the whole of every night with his son while continuing to work at his dental practice by day. Rob recalls that his sessions at the hospital were enlivened by solicitous telephone calls from Stirling's girl friends which seemed to come through thick and fast from all corners of the world, and by the delivery of so many flowers that Rob briefly considered setting up in competition with the hospital florist. After some weeks Stirling began to experience increasingly frequent periods of consciousness and was able to hold short but perfectly lucid conversations with his friends. To this day, however, he has little or no memory of this period of his recovery, and to this day he has total amnesia about his accident and about the events which preceded it. Thus it seems that the mystery surrounding the accident will never be solved. Thousands of people saw what happened on that fateful day at Goodwood, but the only person who knows why it happened cannot remember.

Stirling Moss, April 1962.

The Snetterton race which had preceded the Easter Goodwood meeting had been won by Jim Clark; Stirling had led the race and set the fastest lap before being delayed by a sticking throttle. At Goodwood his luck did not improve; he was lying fourth in the Glover Trophy race when, after only nine laps, he stopped at his pit with the car stuck in fourth gear. By the time he rejoined the race he was more than two laps behind the leader, Graham Hill.

Under these circumstances other drivers might have been tempted to settle for an easy ride, but not Stirling Moss; as his very presence at Goodwood testified, he was acutely conscious of his responsibility to his public, and he was equally conscious of his responsibility to his profession. Quite simply he took the view that the job of a racing driver was to race, to compete as hard as he knew how regardless of his position or his chance of victory. Thus it was that on lap thirty-four – the lap before he crashed – Stirling Moss set a new Formula One lap record for the Goodwood circuit.

On the following lap Stirling closed on Graham Hill's BRM at the entry to the 120 mph Fordwater Corner and then, as they approached the next, slightly slower bend, which was called St Mary's, Graham was startled to see out of the corner of his eye that the nose of Stirling's Lotus was almost abreast of his cockpit and very close beside him. The Lotus ran off the track onto the grass to the left and then continued in a dead straight line for some one hundred and fifty yards before hitting the protective banking head on. It took forty-five minutes for firemen aided by Stirling's mechanics to cut the car apart and extract him, dreadfully broken, from the wreckage.

It was hard for Rob to believe that driver error had been responsible for Stirling's accident. After all, he had coped with any number of potentially disastrous situations in the past with perfect equanimity: total steering failure at 160 mph on the banking at Monza in his Maserati 250F, for example, and total brake failure in the Mille Miglia, again in a Maserati, when approaching a 90 mph corner at 130 mph. But there's always a first time; Jim Clark never had a serious accident until the one that killed him.

Graham Hill was certain that Stirling could not have been trying to pass him at a point on the circuit where overtaking was virtually impossible. He believed that Stirling must have suffered an ignition failure (the distributor cap was found to be detached when the Lotus was examined after the accident) and had seen flames at the rear of the car suggesting that unburned fuel was being ignited in the hot exhaust pipes.

Another theory was that as Stirling had shifted down from fifth to fourth gear for St Mary's the throttle had stuck wide open and he had deliberately gone off the road rather than involve Graham Hill in his accident. But why were there no signs on the grass that he had applied the brakes – which were later found to be in perfect working order – to slow the car? Had the bumpy verge bounced his feet off the pedals? Then why hadn't he spun it? Even travelling at 120 mph it would have taken almost three seconds to cover those one hundred and fifty yards; that may not seem much to an ordinary mortal but to a racing driver of Stirling's ability it's an eternity. So, did something break which affected Stirling's ability to steer? When the car was examined after the event the broken front anti-roll bar was found to have jammed the steering but this, of course, may have resulted from the impact. Or did Stirling suffer some kind of momentary blackout? No one will ever know for sure.

In any event it was clear to Rob that Stirling would not drive again in the 1962 season, if ever. Indeed, it was not until more than a year later, on 1st May 1963, that Stirling sat in a racing car again. On that day he returned, in great secrecy, to Goodwood where Ken Gregory and Tony Robinson, the BRP chief mechanic, waited in the rain with a Lotus Monte Carlo in which he was to assess his readiness to return to the fray. The experiment was not a success; Stirling may have felt that as he negotiated St Mary's again he might have discovered some clue which would explain his accident, but this was not to be. What he did discover was that he could no longer drive a racing car with the instinctive flair which he had once possessed in such great abundance; he found himself having to think what he should be doing next – braking here, changing down there – and he was honest enough to know that retirement was his only realistic option.

Earlier in 1962 Rob and Stirling had discussed various ways of improving their competitiveness in the forthcoming season. The Ferguson P99, which might have been an option, had run out of funding so Stirling suggested that he should approach Enzo Ferrari for the loan of a car to be entered by Rob in his dark blue and white livery. Years before – in 1951, when Stirling was just beginning to make his name – Ferrari had offered him a Formula One drive at Bari, but when Stirling arrived in southern Italy he found that his car had been allocated to Piero Taruffi. To say that Stirling was put out by this discourtesy would be to understate the position substantially; he was furious. And in Rob's words he was 'an elephant' who never forgot a slight, real or imagined. In later years, however, the Commendatore had openly expressed his admiration for Stirling who, in turn, could not but respect the orchestrator of such a marvellously successful racing team.

After a visit to Maranello it was agreed, therefore, that Rob would have a new

Ferrari 156 for Stirling to drive in all the 1962 World Championship Grands Prix, but the accident inevitably altered the equation and the deal was rescinded. However, as a gesture of sympathy towards Alfred Moss Ferrari sent a Formula One car with a BRP green stripe painted on the nose to the International Trophy race at Silverstone for Innes Ireland to drive. Innes finished fourth, much impressed by the Ferrari engine, if not by the chassis.

In the aftermath of the aborted Ferrari deal Rob decided to buy two Lotus 24 chassis for the new season, having been assured by Colin Chapman that he would have exactly the same equipment as the factory team. Then, at Zandvoort, the monocoque Lotus 25 was unveiled. 'I remember John Cooper saying to Colin Chapman in the pits, "I thought you were going to sell Rob cars just like yours, Colin," and Colin said, "Well they are virtually the same, just a few minor differences here and there," and John stuck his head inside the monocoque and said, "Oh yes, I see what you mean; they're exactly the same – you just forgot to put the chassis in this one!" The Lotus 24 was an absolute dog; it handled very well until it reached the limit and then it broke away with no warning whatsoever. Whether or not Stirling could have coped with it if he had been given the chance we will never know, but it certainly proved to be too much of a handful for all sorts of other people.'

Rob invited Maurice Trintignant to handle the Lotus 24 for the remainder of the 1962 season but it soon became clear that this would not prove to be a satisfactory long-term arrangement. 'To be absolutely honest, Maurice was just past it. He was forty-five, just a couple of months younger than me. I know that Fangio won his fifth World Championship when he was forty-seven, but Maurice was no Fangio. He could string together half a dozen quick laps but he no longer had the stamina or the concentration to drive competitively for the full race distance.

'He was extremely unlucky at Monaco when the throttle stuck wide open on Richie Ginther's BRM at the start and he just punted Maurice off on the first corner, the Gazomètres Hairpin. There was nothing either of them could have done to avoid the accident. In a way Betty and I were quite relieved to be out of the race early as it enabled us to catch an earlier flight from Nice to London and so get to Eton for the Fourth of June celebrations next day with rather more breathing space than we had expected. We left the circuit as soon as it became clear that Maurice was unhurt, walking to the footbridge on the outside of the Armco with the cars brushing past us at 130 mph, and it was more than a year before I discovered that a photographer had been killed by one of Richie's rear wheels which had been torn off in the shunt. I think that Bruce McLaren won the race after Graham had led for eighty-five laps before his engine packed up.

'At Rouen we had a lot of niggling little problems which disrupted practice for us. Saturday was a free day before the race on Sunday and when, after lunch, we seemed to have solved most of our problems, Maurice announced that he was going to check that all was well with a few unofficial practice laps. I said, "Don't be silly,

Maurice Trintignant, 1962.

173

Maurice, this is the main road to Paris," but he just shrugged and said, "It will be arranged." Maurice set off from the garage in the Lotus 24 with me and the mechanics pursuing him through the traffic in the Facel and when we all arrived at the circuit he marched up to the chief of police, shook him by the hand and demanded that the road should be closed so that he could practise. Sure enough in a matter of moments gendarmes and officials all round the circuit were holding up the traffic and erecting barriers and so on, and Maurice was off. I couldn't believe it! I went down to the hairpin at Le Nouveau Monde, taking care to hide my passes in

Spa 1962: Trintignant and Bianchi confer while Tony Cleverley and John Chisman work on the Lotus.

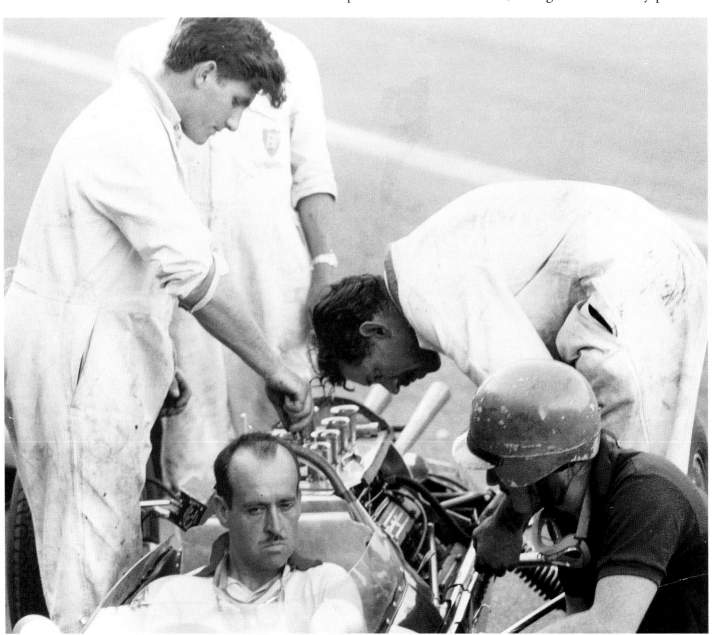

case I should be recognised and lynched for my part in causing an enormous traffic jam, only to find that no one in the five-mile tailback which had built up seemed in the least bit put out; as far as they were concerned if their champion wanted to practise it was fine by them, and they waved and cheered every time Maurice came round.

'I couldn't help hoping that the local police chief's arrangements were better than those of his counterpart at Rheims two years earlier when Bruce McLaren and Giancarlo Baghetti, slipstreaming each other at 180 mph down the Thillois Straight, had come face to face with a local farmer driving a Peugeot 403 station wagon full of chickens. I don't know who was the most frightened – Bruce, Giancarlo, the farmer or the chickens!'

At Rouen the race ended in disaster. On the final lap the gendarmes for some reason best known to themselves decided to cordon off the front of the pits. John Surtees arrived at the finish, his car unable to complete another lap, and was prevented from turning into his pit by the line of gendarmes. Thus the track was partially blocked when Maurice Trintignant arrived, braking and steering to the left to avoid Surtees. Next came Trevor Taylor in his Lotus 25, arriving flat out over the blind crest to find the track completely blocked. 'It was the most horrific accident I have ever seen, and it took place right in front of me. Trevor just rammed Maurice at 140 mph and bits of both cars flew in every direction. It was an absolute miracle that no one was killed, and I couldn't believe it when Maurice stepped out of the wreckage unhurt. As you might imagine, he had some pretty choice words to say to his friend the chief of police afterwards.

Trevor Taylor.

'Trevor Taylor was terribly accident-prone – in fact I don't think I've ever known a driver who lived a more charmed life than him. The worst of his accidents happened at Spa earlier in the year when he was dicing with Willy Mairesse. His Lotus jumped out of fourth gear at Blanchimont as a result of which both cars went off the road at high speed. The Ferrari threw Mairesse out and then turned over and set itself on fire, and Taylor's Lotus demolished a telegraph pole which ended up lying across the cockpit. When I went round the circuit after the race the Ferrari was still burning. Mairesse lost a few teeth and Taylor was badly shaken – but really they were both extremely lucky not to have been killed.

'When we were at Monza in September Ricardo Rodriguez asked me if he could drive my Lotus 24 in the Mexican Grand Prix the following month as Ferrari was not going to enter. It was a non-championship race and the first Formula One race ever to be held in Mexico. I talked it over with Alf and we agreed that we might as well go ahead although as the starting money was not terribly good I decided that I would stay at home and leave it to Alf to run the team.

'Ricardo had been motor cycle champion of Mexico when he was thirteen, he'd started racing cars when he was fifteen and he'd become a works Ferrari Formula

The steering wheel from the
Lotus 24 in which Ricardo
Rodriguez died in Mexico City.

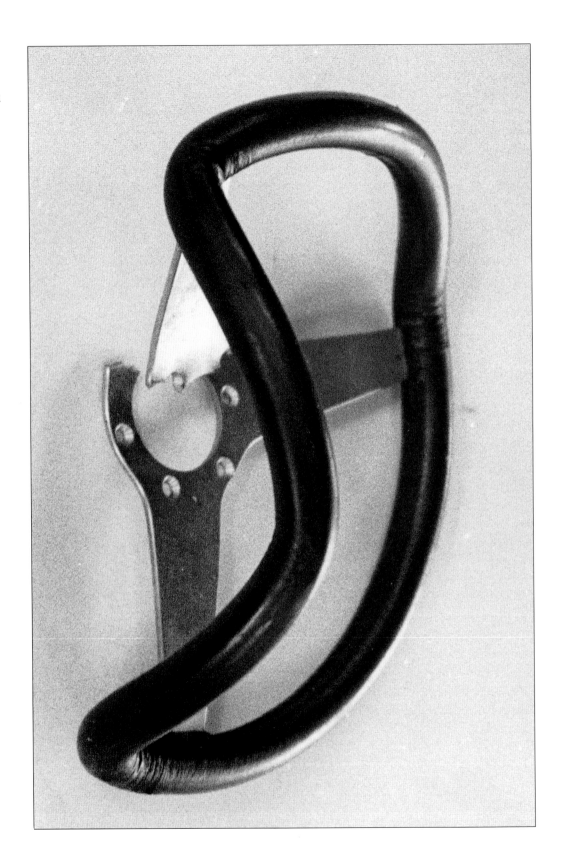

One driver by the time he was nineteen. He was regarded as being much more talented than his older brother – although Pedro became a great driver later on, and a very good friend of mine – and I think that the locals really expected him to win in Mexico City, which was a lot of pressure for such a young man to handle.

'On the first practice day Ricardo was thrilled with the Lotus 24 and told Alf that it handled much better than his Ferrari. He was fastest in practice until, while he was in the pits a few minutes before the end of the first session, John Surtees went slightly quicker. Ricardo got back into the car and as the mechanics were settling him in he crossed himself and kissed his father's hand, and then he went out to beat Surtees' time. On his first flying lap he lost it at about 120 mph on the bumpy part of the banking and he was thrown out onto the Armco barrier and killed.

'Ricardo was the first driver ever to be killed in one of my cars and even though I wasn't actually there when it happened it was still pretty traumatic for me. Alf assured me that nothing had broken on the car and that the accident had been caused by pure driver error, and this was confirmed by the Mexican scrutineers who examined the wreckage very carefully afterwards and could find absolutely no evidence of mechanical failure. I think that Ricardo was just overcome by the intense emotion of the situation and he was trying far too hard in a car which was notoriously difficult to drive anywhere near the limit.

'After the race Don Pedro, Ricardo's father, wrote an article for *Paris Match* saying that my car had been responsible for the death of his son, which made me extremely angry. At that time I had substantial life insurance cover for all my drivers, and for tax reasons the policies were set up to compensate me for the loss of the driver's services; I could then pass the money on to his next of kin, tax free, at my discretion. So I simply told Don Pedro that unless he retracted this accusation I would keep the insurance money.

'Of course he retracted it at once.

'Don Pedro had many friends in high places in Mexico – in fact the President of the country attended Ricardo's funeral – and they had seen to it that he was given responsibility for the collection of taxes from all the brothels, which I suppose must have been a pretty good job to have in more ways than one. Although he had become very rich in the course of his work, Don Pedro behaved in the most ungenerous way towards Ricardo's widow, Sarita, ostracising her completely after Ricardo's death and leaving her absolutely penniless. It must have made Papa Rodriguez very angry when I paid the insurance money to Sarita rather than to him. She was a great friend of ours, a spectacularly beautiful girl who adorned our pit whenever we raced in Mexico in later years.'

By now it was time to think about driver arrangements for the 1963 season. It

Ricardo Rodriguez.

Gary Hocking (right), *killed in practice for the Natal Grand Prix.*

was clear to Rob that he could not continue with Maurice Trintignant and while he was considering other options John Gooding of BP called him to ask a favour. Would Rob take on a young Rhodesian called Gary Hocking whom BP had under contract? He was a brilliant motor cyclist who had been both 350 cc and 500 cc World Champion in 1961 and was thought to have considerable potential as a driver. After thinking it over Rob agreed to try him out in the three-race South African season in December, and to take a longer-term decision in the light of his performances there.

Rob decided to enjoy Christmas at Nunney with his family rather than travel to South Africa, so Tony Cleverley took charge of the team. After the Rand Grand Prix at Kyalami on 15th December Tony telephoned Rob to report that they had found a real star in the making; Hocking had finished fourth after a race-long duel with John Surtees. Six days later, on the evening of 21st December,

Jo Bonnier . . . a very well-developed sense of self-preservation.

Tony telephoned again; Gary Hocking had been killed instantly when his Lotus had left the road at a corner known as the Devil's Leap during practice for the Natal Grand Prix at Durban earlier in the day. It was possible that he had missed a gear, but Tony thought it more likely that given his relative inexperience on four wheels he had been trying just a little bit too hard in a very unforgiving racing car.

Although he had never met Gary Hocking, Rob was devastated by this latest tragedy. After the funeral in Wales, where Hocking had been born and brought up before emigrating to Rhodesia, Rob found himself handing over the proceeds of yet another life insurance policy to the bereaved relatives of one of his drivers. In the bitterly cold compartment of the train which carried him slowly from Cardiff to London, frequently delayed by frozen points, Rob reflected that motor racing had brought him considerably more pain than pleasure in the past year. Maybe it was time to retire.

Betty and he discussed the pros and cons of retirement exhaustively in the following weeks. Rob didn't really want to retire. Except for the war years, motor racing had filled his life ever since he had learned to drive; he had never done anything else, and he couldn't visualise how he would spend his days if he gave up. Besides, he had the cars and the racing shop, and the livelihood of a number of people depended upon him. He didn't really want to retire – but he certainly didn't want to be haunted by another dead driver either. In the end he decided that he would continue, but with a safe driver.

'I chose Jo Bonnier mostly because I thought he had a very well-developed sense of self-preservation. He was a safe, reliable, experienced driver, and he was no mug; after all, he had won a World Championship Grand Prix only two years before. But more than anything else I chose him because I thought he was safe. Sadly, of course, poor Jo was killed in the end; he went downhill and found himself driving worse and worse cars and having to try harder and harder to keep up, and finally it caught up with him at Le Mans.

'My decision upset several people, not least of all Maurice Trintignant who was absolutely furious. If Gary Hocking had survived to drive for me in 1963, or if I'd chosen some other hot shoe, Maurice could have accepted it with good grace, but it really hurt him to be discarded in favour of Bonnier; he genuinely thought that he was the better driver of the two. He's forgiven me now, but it took a long time.

'The other person who was unhappy was Alf. He had got used to winning with Stirling, he hadn't enjoyed being an also-ran with Maurice, and he couldn't stand Jo Bonnier. In fact he had become totally disenchanted with motor racing, he was behaving in a very unco-operative and difficult way, and he and Tony were not getting along at all well together. Although it was very sad for me I

Tony Cleverley on the team scooter.

could see that the only way ahead was to make Tony chief mechanic and find Alf some new challenge. He was in partnership with Valerio Colotti in a company which was not doing at all well called Gear Speed Developments which manufactured Colotti-Francis gearboxes, so I suggested to him that it would make sense for him to go to Modena to look after his business interests there. It was an elegant solution for me but unfortunately it didn't work out for Alf. He and Colotti had a super product but not an ounce of business sense between them, and they went bust a year or so later.

'Of course Alf loved the whole Modena scene where people respected him and paid homage to him, and he stayed there for almost ten years. After the collapse of GSD he worked briefly as racing manager for ATS and then went to work for Count Volpi at Serenissima. In late 1971 I heard that Volpi had suddenly wound up his team and given Alf only two weeks' notice despite his eight years of loyal service. Alf was reputed to be in a bad way financially and so I created a job for

Alf Francis . . . from Dorking to Modena.

him at Pippbrook; I had given up the team by that time but I had kept the racing shop going to provide a job for John Chisman. He used to look after the Delage and the Delahaye, and we used to restore classic cars at cost, charging just enough to pay the overheads and John's wages but not trying to make a profit. I remember that we restored some cars for Sir Anthony Bamford – a Delage and a Miller, I think, and a Testa Rossa. Anyway, Alf joined John in the racing shop and they used to have a fine time together working on the cars and going down to the pub to reminisce about the old days over a beer or two.

'Eventually I found Alf a job restoring classic cars for a rich American collector who lived in Texas, and I rather lost touch with him after that. Whenever I did hear of him he seemed to be involved with yet another millionaire, and yet more exotic cars. I'll never forget that one year he turned up at Cap Estel with his current millionaire looking for a hotel room the day before the Monaco Grand Prix. Of course we told them that they hadn't a hope in hell of finding a room within a hundred miles of Monaco and the next thing we heard was that they were staying at the Hotel de Paris. Apparently Alf had tipped the concierge £500 and in no time at all they were installed in the best suite in the place.

'Eventually Alf set up his own classic car restoration business in Oklahoma, where he died of lung cancer in 1983 having been a heavy smoker all his life. He was a fabulous mechanic and a staunch friend. I feel privileged to have worked with him, and very proud of all that we achieved together.'

Chapter 12
Safety First

Hardly had Alf left Dorking in early 1963 than Rob was visited at Pippbrook by a very senior Customs official who, cautioning him that anything he might say would be taken down and used in evidence in any future proceedings, explained that the Colotti-Francis gearboxes which the team had been using for the past four years had all, without exception, entered the country without payment of import duty. Rob's obvious surprise and concern that such a serious offence could have been committed by his team, however unwittingly, clearly impressed his interrogator who eventually accepted that a genuine mistake had been made – probably by Alf, who was now beyond the immediate reach of British justice – and payment of the duty plus a nominal fine of £500 was agreed. It was made quite clear to Rob, however, that had matters been different he might easily have gone to jail.

Having disposed of this unwanted distraction Rob felt that he could concentrate on his plans for the forthcoming season. Although he would start the year with the Lotus 24, his quest for increased safety had led him to order a new Cooper to be powered by the revised 200 bhp Coventry-Climax vee-eight engine. Until the new chassis was ready John Cooper had offered to lend him the ex-Tony Maggs 1962 works car.

'We gave the Lotus 24 to Maurice for the Pau Grand Prix, really as a kind of peace offering, and Bonnier drove the ex-Maggs Cooper. Of course Maurice was absolutely determined to show that he was quicker than Bonnier, and he was; he started ahead of Jo on the grid, and he was lying third behind Jim Clark and Trevor Taylor in the Team Lotus cars when his gearbox broke on the ninth lap. But by then I think he felt that honour had been satisfied.

'Bonnier retired later with a broken universal joint, but he had one hell of a fright while he was still running. As he went past the casino in the Parc Beaumont he suddenly clapped his hand to his right ear as if he had been stung by a bee, but what had happened was that his ear plug had fallen out and he suddenly got the full benefit of the Climax vee-eight in his right ear and thought the engine had blown up!'

The 1963 Pau Grand Prix was the first occasion on which Rob became aware of Swiss driver Jo Siffert, an ex-racing motor cyclist from Fribourg, who was driving his own privately entered Lotus-BRM. Siffert retired with brake failure after spinning at the Station Hairpin, but he had been lying third at the time and Rob was quite impressed. Then at Imola, a week after Pau, Siffert finished second behind Jim Clark. Four days later at Syracuse he won, albeit defeating a field depleted by the conflicting Aintree 200 – but including Jo Bonnier in Rob's Lotus 24 who finished

*Jo Bonnier in Rob's Cooper-
Climax at Silverstone in 1963.*

*Jo Bonnier leads Jo Siffert into
the Station Hairpin at Monaco
in 1963.*

183

fifth, no less than seven laps behind. Young Siffert was clearly a man to watch.

Rob's fortunes hardly improved as the Formula One season progressed. Bonnier failed to complete the International Trophy race at Silverstone and a clutch problem relegated him to seventh place at Monaco, six laps behind winner Graham Hill. At

Spa, where a torrential downpour of the sort for which the circuit was infamous decimated the field, he was fifth. At Zandvoort he was twelfth. He failed to finish in the French and British Grands Prix, came sixth at the Nürburgring, seventh at Monza, eighth at Watkins Glen, and fifth in Mexico. Only in the non-championship Solitude Grand Prix had he shown any worthwhile form; there he harried Jack Brabham's winning Brabham-Climax until the very last lap when alternator failure forced him to coast to a halt just before the finish. He eventually coaxed the car over the line into ninth place. In a

Shielding his eyes from the rain, Bonnier navigates the Walker Cooper towards a distant fifth place at Spa in 1963.

World Championship season dominated by Jim Clark, Jo Bonnier amassed only six points to share ninth place with Lorenzo Bandini and Innes Ireland.

Jo Bonnier lived in Switzerland, a refugee from the punitive tax regime of his native Sweden. He was a marvellous linguist, fluent in six languages, but like many of his countrymen he found it difficult to communicate at a personal level, or to forge close personal relationships. He was regarded as a cold fish by some, as arrogant and aloof by others. As a driver he had fulfilled Rob's expectations on the score of safety but, as his results in his first season with the Walker team showed, he was also disappointingly slow.

He was no quicker in 1964. He made a good start to the season when in an

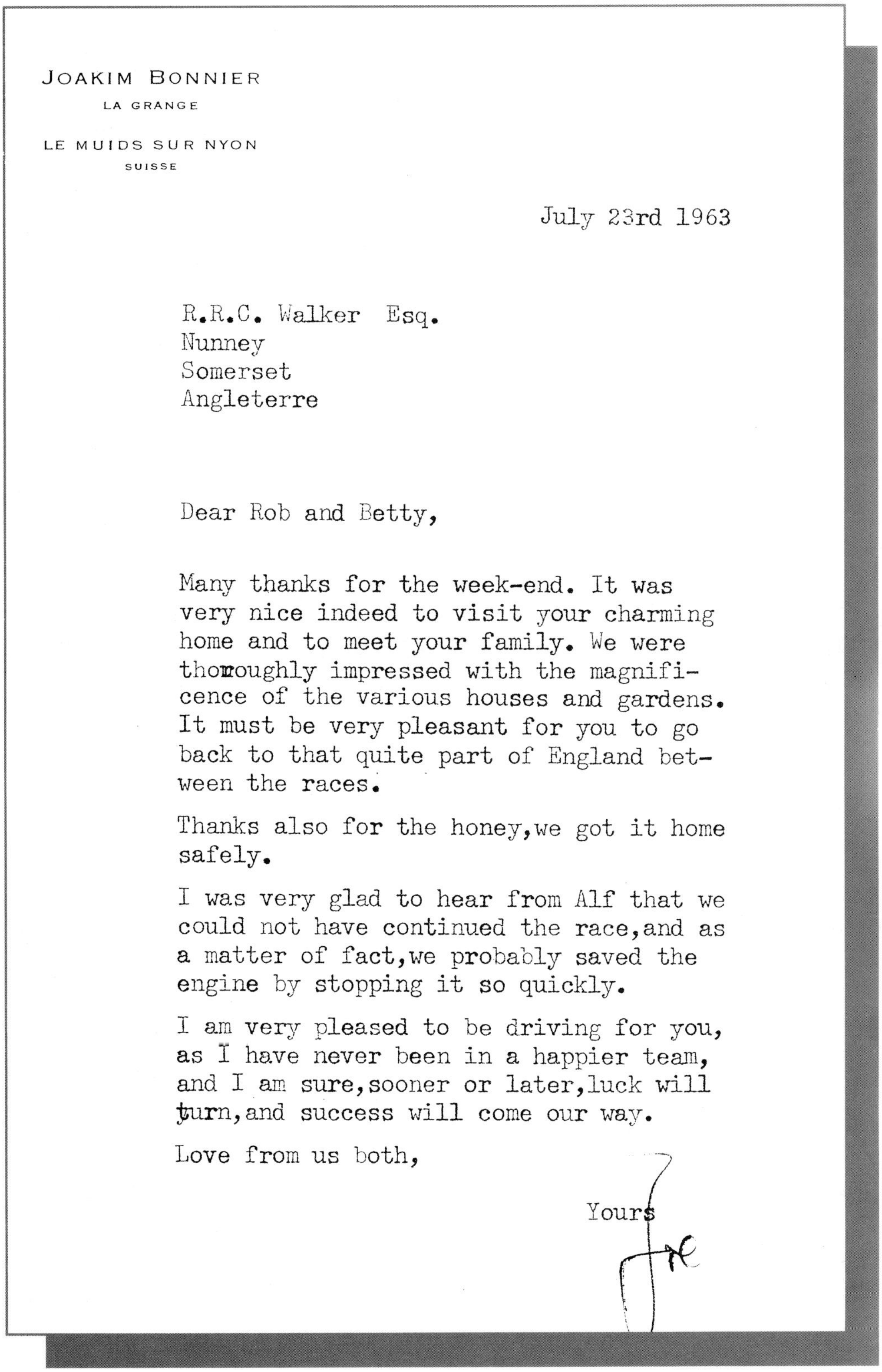

JOAKIM BONNIER

LA GRANGE

LE MUIDS SUR NYON

SUISSE

July 23rd 1963

R.R.C. Walker Esq.
Nunney
Somerset
Angleterre

Dear Rob and Betty,

Many thanks for the week-end. It was
very nice indeed to visit your charming
home and to meet your family. We were
thoroughly impressed with the magnifi-
cence of the various houses and gardens.
It must be very pleasant for you to go
back to that quite part of England between the races.

Thanks also for the honey,we got it home
safely.

I was very glad to hear from Alf that we
could not have continued the race,and as
a matter of fact,we probably saved the
engine by stopping it so quickly.

I am very pleased to be driving for you,
as I have never been in a happier team,
and I am sure,sooner or later,luck will
turn,and success will come our way.

Love from us both,

Yours

Hoping for better times. Jo Bonnier's letter to Rob following the 1963 British Grand Prix.

185

appallingly wet non-championship event at Snetterton he disputed the lead with Innes Ireland until the race was stopped after thirty laps because of the dreadful weather conditions. At the end Ireland's BRP-BRM was just ahead of Bonnier's Rob Walker Cooper-Climax.

'After that I think his best place was fifth at Monaco, and the most exciting thing that happened to him all season was when the Brabham caught fire at Silverstone during practice for the International Trophy race. We had been building a new BT11 with a BRM engine at the Brabham factory at Chessington and, as usual, it wasn't quite finished in time for the first practice day. On the second day Bonnier had done no more than two flying laps when he came past the pits at about 100 mph with flames pouring out of the back of the car. We found out later that an injector pipe had come loose and petrol had squirted onto the exhaust manifold. Jo pulled off the track at Copse and tried to climb out of the car before it had stopped, but he got his foot stuck under the steering wheel which slowed him down a bit. Eventually he put the fire out with an extinguisher which he grabbed from a marshal who didn't seem at all keen to use it himself. The car wasn't too badly damaged although we had to use the old Cooper for the race, which was tremendously exciting; Jack Brabham won by inches from Graham Hill, having overtaken him at Woodcote on the final lap. We finished last.'

By now Jo Bonnier was not only Rob Walker's driver but was also acting as his business manager. His principal function was to negotiate starting money, a role for which he was uniquely well qualified given his linguistic ability and his presidency of the Grand Prix Drivers' Association. 'He was quite shameless about using the clout which this position conferred upon him to obtain good starting money for the team, no doubt encouraged by the fact that under the terms of our agreement half of it would end up in his pocket.

'Jo and I generally got on perfectly well together but there was always a certain distance between us

Left: *The Walker garage in Mexico 1964; Bonnier, Cleverley and Nick Doel.*

Inset: *Jo Bonnier's Brabham BT11 on fire at Silverstone during practice for the International Trophy race in 1964.*

Jochen Rindt makes his Grand Prix debut driving Rob's Brabham in the 1964 Austrian Grand Prix at the Zeltweg airfield cicuit.

and he never became a friend in the way that Stirling had before him. I felt that there was no genuine warmth in our relationship; it was really much more of a business relationship between employer and employee than I had experienced with any other driver. I remember once at Brands Hatch he and I had some trivial dispute about something or other – I think it may have been something to do with timekeeping – and he became really quite stroppy about it. So I said, "Now look here, Jo, this is my team, I'm the boss, and what I say goes," and after that we never had any more trouble. But it would never have crossed my mind to say something like that to Stirling, for example, and he would never have put me in a position where I might have had to consider it. I suppose it was the nature of our relationship which prevented me from asking Jo why he always unzipped the fly of his racing overalls when he got into the car. I wish I had; even today I'd love to know.

'Jo had hit upon the very good idea of renting our second car to a local driver in each of the countries in which we raced, and making them pay through the nose for it. So, for instance, at the Nürburgring, while Jo drove our Brabham-BRM, the Cooper-Climax was entered for Edgar Barth who was then the European hill climb champion. I remember that he was dreadfully slow in practice and then blew the engine up on the second lap, so I don't suppose he really thought he'd got his money's worth.

'There was an even more embarrassing situation at Monza where we had been asked to give a drive to a local Italian hero who raced under the pseudonym of "Geki". On the first practice day we had rather a lot of problems with Jo's car and I'm afraid that apart from fitting him into his seat we paid very little attention to poor Geki. The result was that he didn't qualify in the first session and the next day it rained and so, of course, he had no hope of qualifying. In view of this the Italians flatly refused to pay us the agreed starting money for Geki until Jo said, "You chose the driver and if he's not good enough to qualify that's your problem, not ours," and they paid up without another word.

'At Zeltweg Jo had rented our second car to Jochen Rindt. He had been driving brilliantly in Formula Two, but this was his first Formula One race and he was absolutely thrilled about it. I remember that he had taken the trouble to find out when I was arriving and met me at the airport. He was such a charming young man, so full of youthful enthusiasm, and so grateful for the drive. He never forgot that I gave him his first Formula One drive and when the Österreichring was inaugurated some years later he said to me, "I want you to be the first person I ever drive round this circuit," and he took me round in a Mercedes 500SEL. It was very touching.

'Hap Sharp had rented the car for the races at Watkins Glen and Mexico City. He was a Texan oil millionaire who was a partner in Jim Hall's Chaparral team. He had done a lot of SCCA sports car racing and had also spent a fair bit of time testing the various Chaparral cars at Rattlesnake Raceway at Midland in Texas, but I don't think he had ever driven a Formula One car before. Fortunately he was a sensible chap and didn't overdo it. I remember that he was so happy to finish thirteenth in Mexico, even though he was five laps behind the winner, that he celebrated by drinking half a pint of neat Bourbon in the pit after the race.

'A week or two before the United States Grand Prix at Watkins Glen in October 1964 Bonnier had called me to say that Jo Siffert was having difficulty in obtaining an entry both there and in Mexico, and asked if I would help by entering Seppi's car in my name. Seppi and his mechanics would prepare his own Brabham-BRM as usual and it was simply a question of repainting it in my dark blue and white colours and having my name on the entry form, so I agreed. It turned out to be a wise decision because it was the beginning of a very good friendship and led directly to the proudest moment of my life.'

On the flight from New York to Elmira, the closest airport to Watkins Glen, Rob glanced sideways at the newspaper which the chap in the next seat was reading to be confronted by a photograph of himself standing beside the latest LTD in a full-page Ford advertisement. Rob couldn't resist teasing his neighbour by asking if he thought the photograph a good likeness; the inevitable double-take amused them both. 'The photograph had been taken at Stockton House where my mother lived after my brother John had taken over at Sutton Veny, and the advertising agency, J. Walter Thompson, had also shot a sixty-second commercial there which was later broadcast on network television in America. I'll never forget that as they were filming me one morning we were interrupted by Reid, my mother's butler, who had been with the family since before the war and had been at my wedding in 1940. By this time he was very old, stone deaf and not a little blind, and his hand shook so much that when he poured your wine at dinner you had to hold on to it to make sure that at least some of the wine ended up in your glass, but he still looked the part. Just as the camera was rolling for the umpteenth take dear old Reid emerged from the front door, blinking in the sunlight, and said in a loud voice, "Excuse me,

John Cooper, who signed Jochen Rindt to a three-year deal after Rob plumped for the more experienced Jo Siffert for the 1965 season.

gentlemen, has anyone seen her Ladyship? She is required on the telephone." I simply couldn't believe it when the director blew his top instead of thanking his lucky stars that he had been presented with this marvellous unrehearsed insight into life in an English country house!

'Anyway, we now had three cars entered for Watkins Glen and Mexico and while neither Bonnier nor Hap Sharp really did much good in either race, Seppi did. In America he drove a very steady race to finish third behind Graham Hill and John Surtees, having driven the last five laps with only fifth gear working, and I was sufficiently impressed to think about signing him up for the 1965 season.

'At the same time Jochen Rindt was desperately keen to drive for me, and I was torn between the two of them – I liked them both very much, and they were both marvellous drivers. John Cooper wanted Jochen as a works driver, but he would have preferred to come to me. In the end, after thinking about it long and hard, I told Jochen that I thought it would be best for both of us if he went to Cooper; he would be guaranteed an entry as a works driver, even though he was relatively unknown and had no Formula One credentials, whereas if he drove for me he would have to qualify for each and every race. I felt that having to qualify would put too much pressure on him in his first season of Formula One racing, and I didn't want to take that responsibility. He was very disappointed, but I think he saw the wisdom of this decision in the end. So I signed Seppi – who was guaranteed an entry in his own right at that time – to join Bonnier in my team. I suppose I should really have asked Bonnier to go at this point, but he was doing a perfectly good job as my business manager and at the time it just seemed easier to leave things as they were. I suppose you could say that I took the soft option.

'After Seppi had been driving for me for a while I used to visit him occasionally at his home in Fribourg where he had a small garage which dealt in all sorts of exotic cars. He had his finger very much on the pulse of the classic car market in Switzerland and always seemed to know where to find the best cars – and he was a wizard at striking a bargain. I think that he must have developed his bargaining skills as a boy when he supported his mother and two sisters while his father pursued other interests. He did so by picking wild flowers in the mountains and selling them in Fribourg market, and by following the Swiss army on manoeuvres and collecting spent brass cartridge cases to sell as scrap.

'During the course of one of my visits to Fribourg I fell in love with a beautiful Bugatti Type 35 which Seppi had in his showroom. I had always wanted to own a Type 35B, but this car was so absolutely perfect that I was prepared to overlook the fact that it was unsupercharged. It had those wonderful artillery wheels, a tiny aero screen and little mudguards to equip it for road use, all absolutely original. You could just imagine Isadora Duncan setting off in it from the Negresco in Nice, with her chiffon scarf blowing in the wind.

'Of course I couldn't afford it but Seppi and I worked out an arrangement whereby I would pay instalments whenever I could and he would keep the car in his showroom until I had paid the full price. It took a long time, but eventually the car

Rob's Bugatti Type 35.

was mine and Seppi delivered it to the racing shop at Pippbrook in his transporter. Unfortunately I didn't really enjoy driving the Bugatti very much because in its unsupercharged form the performance was absolutely abysmal. It looked wonderful, of course, but after a while just looking at a car becomes boring, however beautiful it is, and so I decided to sell it.

'That was when I ran into a bit of trouble. Seppi had avoided paying import duty when bringing the car into England by using a Swiss carnet which he thought the Swiss authorities would never expect to redeem. Unfortunately they did and I had been forced to hand it over to them or pay a fine equal to the value of the car. So the Bugatti then became an illegal immigrant with no documents of any kind and I couldn't sell it to anyone in England, even though a number of people were very

Rob at the wheel of his Ferrari Dino 196S.

interested in it. I went to the Customs and Excise office in London to ask how I could make it legal, but after a couple of hours of being passed from one department to another I got the distinct impression that no one really wanted to know about my problem, so I left. In the end I got hold of a friend of mine who was a senior Customs officer and asked his advice; "If nobody else knows about it," he said, "why don't you just keep quiet?"

'Then I had a bright idea. Christie's were about to hold their annual classic car sale in Geneva and I thought that if the car was sold in the country from which I had bought it that surely would solve the problem. It looked marvellous in the catalogue and I was very confident that it would fetch a good price, but it snowed on the day of the sale and the auctioneer, Patrick Lindsay of ERA fame, had to buy it in when it failed to reach the agreed reserve. Then the Swiss authorities gave me a week to get the car out of the country, which seemed a little unfair; there was a potential buyer in Paris but I discovered to my horror that I would have to pay duty to take it into France; considering that the car was originally built there, that seemed even more unfair. Just as I was at my wit's end I received a call from a Dutch buyer – who, like many of his countrymen, had a rather cavalier attitude towards rules, regulations and taxes – and within a few minutes my stateless Bugatti was his problem. I don't think I've ever been more relieved in my life.

'I also bought a Ferrari from Seppi. It was a Dino 196S which was a very rare car indeed; I believe that only three had been built, and one of them had been written off at the Nürburgring. The other was in France, in Pierre Bardinon's private collection at Mas du Clos. Seppi's car had come from Luigi Chinetti's North American Racing Team and still had the NART stickers on the sides. Earlier in its career, in 1960, it had been bought by Papa Rodriguez for Pedro and Ricardo to drive at Sebring and in the Targa Florio. It was a very pretty car, rather like a miniature Testa Rossa, but instead of the usual vee-twelve it was fitted with a six-cylinder Dino 246 engine.

'When I first saw the car it was in a very bad way; the bodywork was in appalling condition and it had been fitted with a big Buick vee-eight by someone who had commandeered the Dino 246 engine to put into a hill climb car. Nevertheless, Seppi recommended that I should buy it and have it restored. I said, "But what about the engine?" and Seppi said, "Oh, don't worry about that, Rob; that chap is certain to blow it up pretty soon, he won't be able to get any spares and then we can nip in and buy it and fix it up." And that's exactly what happened; the oil pressure relief valve stuck open during a hill climb, the engine blew in a big way, a con rod came through the side, and Seppi bought it for peanuts.

'John Chisman stripped the engine and welded the hole in the block. I think we had to have a new con rod made up, we got a new set of pistons and liners from Ferrari, and we rebuilt the engine and installed it in the chassis which by now looked absolutely stunning in Ferrari *rosso corsa* with blue leather upholstery. The car was a real joy to drive on the open road and was surprisingly docile in traffic. The acceleration was simply breathtaking and the close-ratio five-speed gearbox was a delight to use. Stopping was the only problem, as the brakes weren't up to much.

'When the restoration was finally completed Innes Ireland, who was then Sports Editor of *Autocar*, asked if he could test-drive the car for the magazine, and I agreed that he could drive it down from Pippbrook to Nunney for me. I'll never forget the first line of his story; "I've just fallen in love with a little Italian redhead," he wrote. Well, I don't suppose it was the first time, but I bet none of the others were as desirable as mine. I kept this car for a number of years but in the end the financial demands of the racing team meant that it had to go. I sold it in America but I think that it was later returned to Italy by Count Johnny Lurani, and I believe it is now in Australia having recently changed hands for £1,500,000. Whoever owns it is a very lucky man.

'In the fullness of time Seppi and I developed what I suppose you could almost call a father and son relationship. He was a superb driver who was just so brave he scared me witless, and I admired him enormously. When he was not in a French- or German-speaking country he was very dependent upon us, and he was the first driver for whom I was able to act as a true mentor. When Stirling was driving for me I was learning from him, but now the roles were reversed; Seppi was a young and relatively inexperienced driver, and I was able to pass on my acquired knowledge and experience to him. He always listened to what I had to say, and usually acted upon it.

'I recall that before the Syracuse Grand Prix in early April 1965 I told Seppi that when Stirling went out in front he was always content just to hold his lead until he saw an opportunity to make a break, and then he would go flat out to put a gap between himself and the others. Surtees, Clark and Seppi were having a tremendous battle for the lead, with Seppi in front more often than not, and I realised from my time sheet that they were about to lap Jo Bonnier in our other car. Just after the pits at Syracuse there is a kink that you can take absolutely flat out if you are very good and very brave, but if you're not quite so good or quite so brave then you just lift off a little bit.

Seppi leading Graham Hill in the 1965 French Grand Prix at Clermont-Ferrand.

'As Jo came past the pits I gave him a signal which simply said "SEPPI – CLARK – SURTEES" and of course Bonnier was no fool and knew exactly what I wanted him to do. He let Seppi past, lifted off fractionally at the kink and held up Jim Clark and John Surtees for just long enough for Seppi to make his break. After that they never would have caught him, but with only ten laps to go the back wheels came off the ground as he was going over the hump-backed bridge, just as he floored the throttle after changing up into fifth, and the car jumped out of gear and blew the engine. Jim Clark won the race after Surtees' Ferrari began misfiring. Afterwards Jimmy said to me that in the early part of the race the cut and thrust between Seppi and Surtees had been so intense – each of them doing things he didn't even want to think about

– that he had been more than happy to sit behind them and watch from a safe distance.

'Our next race was at Goodwood on Easter Monday when Seppi had a very nasty accident at the chicane. He clipped the brick wall on the right just hard enough to throw him into the wall on the left; the car was more or less written off and Seppi was taken to the ambulance hut where he lay on a stretcher being plied with cups of hot, sweet tea and seemingly suffering from nothing worse than a few cuts and bruises.

'Some time later, after I had returned to the pits, one of the nurses came up to me and said, "That driver of yours doesn't speak much English but he certainly seems to be complaining a lot," and asked if I could translate what he was trying to say to them. It turned out that he was complaining about pains in his back and so it was decided that he should have a precautionary X-ray at the West Sussex Hospital in Chichester, where it was found that his back was broken. If he had tried to stand up, or even to sit up, he would have become a paraplegic. He also had a broken ankle.

'Seppi was anxious to consult his own specialist in Switzerland as soon as he was fit to travel, so after about a week he was taken by ambulance to Heathrow where the little airport hospital was run by a matron who was built rather like a Japanese Sumo wrestler. Seppi looked very small and young and vulnerable lying on his stretcher, and this old battleaxe sailed up to him and said, "What have you been up to, young man? Fallen off your bicycle?" You can imagine her face when the head of Swissair in London turned up to escort Seppi to the aircraft where they had arranged for a special hoist to lift him into the first-class cabin which he was to occupy in solitary splendour.'

Jo Siffert.

Jo Siffert was still convalescing when the International Trophy race took place at Silverstone but, just five weeks after his accident, although far from fully recovered, he was ready to drive in the Monaco Grand Prix. Graham Hill won the race for the third year in succession; Seppi finished sixth, a truly remarkable achievement under the circumstances. In his report of the race for *Sporting Motorist* Douglas Armstrong wrote of him, 'One only had to watch him walk along in front of the pits and see him wince every time one foot touched the ground to realise what a courageous driver Rob Walker has got himself.'

Revelling in the challenge of the high-speed Enna-Pergusa circuit, Jo Siffert holds off Jim Clark during their torrid battle in the 1965 Mediterranean Grand Prix.

The rest of the summer belonged to Jim Clark; he had won in South Africa on New Year's Day and now proceeded to win in the rain at Spa-Francorchamps, in the sunshine at Clermont-Ferrand, at Silverstone, between the sand dunes at Zand-voort, and amongst the pine forests of the Nürburgring. On 1st August, after six Grand Prix victories, he was crowned World Champion for the second time. But in the Mediterranean Grand Prix at Enna two weeks later he encountered Jo Siffert now fully restored and at his best.

'Sicily seemed to be a special place for Seppi; for some reason he always got the bit between his teeth there and went really well.'

He started from the front row of the grid alongside Mike Spence and Jim Clark, and when Jim made a poor start Seppi and Mike raced wheel to wheel, inches apart, first one and then the other leading, with Jim Clark in third place. On lap twenty-seven Spence was hit in the face by a stone torn loose from the rapidly deteriorating track surface, and lost control. The Lotus 33 clipped the straw bales and ended up upside down amongst the reeds at the edge of the lake from which the Autodromo di Pergusa takes its name. Spence was trapped beneath the car and rapidly surround-ed by a crowd of chattering Sicilians. He switched off the ignition and shouted at them to lift the car off him but they simply stood and watched; he was stuck there until the arrival of the Team Lotus mechanics who had fought their way past obstructive carabinieri and run more than a mile to rescue him, unharmed but extremely angry.

Reassured by a signal from his pit saying 'MIKE OK', Jim Clark now took up the challenge abandoned by his team-mate, and he and Seppi fought a fantastic duel for the lead for the remaining thirty-three laps of the race. Clark nosed ahead for one lap, but Seppi repassed him as they lapped a tail-ender and thereafter held him at bay to win by three-tenths of a second. Siffert's average speed of 139.219 mph made the Mediterranean Grand Prix the fastest Formula One race ever run.

'I remember that near the end of the race Seppi came round the corner before the pits, which was a long sweeping right-hander which he was taking pretty well flat out, absolutely sideways, and I thought he had overdone it for sure. But he caught it and retained the lead. Afterwards Jimmy told me that he was absolutely certain that Seppi had lost it but he couldn't decide whether he was going to spin off to the left or the right and thought the best thing he could do was hang back and see what happened.

'It wasn't long before Betty and I became aware that Seppi's love life was extremely complicated. When we first knew him he seemed to be more or less happily married to Sabine, although there were always one or two other ladies waiting in the wings, but then he began a more serious affair with a girl called Simone, the daughter of a prominent Swiss brewer. In due course Simone became pregnant and Seppi was particularly anxious to conceal this fact from Sabine because Swiss divorce law at the time was heavily weighted against the "guilty party". He asked us if we would allow Simone to stay at Nunney until after the birth; we readily agreed to this but we soon realised that the gossip in a small Somerset village could easily get out of hand and so we shipped her over to Guy Ligier who lived at Vichy in the Auvergne. The baby was born at the time of the French Grand Prix at Clermont-Ferrand in 1969, and Seppi used to visit Simone at the hospital in Vichy between practice periods.

'In due course Seppi and Sabine were divorced without his affair with Simone becoming public, and Betty told him it was about time he married the girl. After some procrastination he decided that they would get married in England between the 1000 km sports car races at Spa and the Nürburgring, and asked if he could use our London address in Clover Mews when applying for the licence. He was staying with us the night before the wedding and I jokingly said to him, "I hope you haven't forgotten the ring, Seppi," and it turned out that he had! It was about five o'clock in the evening when we arrived at Richard Ogden's little shop in Burlington Arcade and we were still choosing a ring in the basement when they closed for the night, and we were locked in. For a while it looked as if we would be sleeping amongst all that expensive jewellery, but eventually someone came and set us free. Seppi was married on Thursday 21st May 1970 at Chelsea Registry Office. I think his best man was Rico Steinemann of Porsche for whom he had won at Spa a few days earlier after a terrific battle with Pedro Rodriguez.

'Our next race was also at Spa and somewhat to our surprise Seppi turned up not with his new wife but with a gorgeous Belgian girl called Nanette. He said that it was more convenient for Nanette to travel from Brussels than for Simone to travel from Fribourg, as if that explained everything. Nanette also made the more convenient journey to the 'Ring where there was high drama when Seppi's mother turned up unexpectedly. He used to call her "La Mère"; she was frightfully strict and Seppi was scared stiff of her, so he asked if he could explain Nanette's presence by saying that she was a friend of Betty's.

'All went well until the race was over and Seppi and Nanette returned to the Lochmuhle at Altenahr. On race day Betty and I used to check out of the hotel and load up the car before driving to the circuit so that we could leave immediately after the race and head for Spa, thus avoiding much of the traffic. Seppi found himself taking a fair amount of flak while trying to explain to La Mère why Madame Walker's friend was still at the hotel whereas Madame Walker herself had clearly departed! Seppi had almost as many girl friends as Stirling in his bachelor days, but while Stirling always gave up what he enjoyed most for three days before a race, Seppi enjoyed himself altogether too much on the morning of the 1967 Mexican Grand Prix; it was no wonder he only finished twelfth!'

Back in August 1965, however, Rob was still considering his options for the following season. The forthcoming Formula change to 3 litres atmospheric (or $1\frac{1}{2}$ litres supercharged) had decided Coventry-Climax to withdraw from the production of racing engines. This decision stemmed partially from financial considerations but both Coventry-Climax and its parent company Jaguar would have been prepared to continue had money been the only issue. As it was there were a number of commercial projects which required the attention of the technical, engineering and design staff who were devoting a large part of their time to the racing engines.

The withdrawal of Coventry-Climax created substantial problems not only for Rob Walker but also for the factory teams of Lotus, Brabham and Cooper. BRM offered to supply 3-litre engines to all of these teams in due course, but each of them felt that to be so dependent upon one of their principal rivals would create more difficulties than it would solve. In the end, Colin Chapman decided to use the BRM sixteen-cylinder engine as a stop-gap until the vee-eight which was being developed jointly by Ford and Cosworth Engineering became available to him, Jack Brabham settled on an engine based on a vee-eight Oldsmobile block and developed by Repco in Australia, and John Cooper opted for a vee-twelve Maserati engine. Ferrari, as always, would build his own engines, Harry Weslake was working on a vee-twelve design for Dan Gurney's new car, while the fledgling McLaren team, like Rob, were still undecided.

As a favour to his two drivers – one Swiss, one Swiss domiciled – and encouraged by BP who had few opportunities to capitalise upon their racing sponsorship in

Switzerland, Rob had agreed to enter his Formula One cars in the St Ursanne-Les Rangiers hill climb in the Swiss Jura. Rob devoted the journey to Switzerland to a final examination of his limited options, and by the time his Swissair flight had landed at Geneva he knew what he must do.

'Jo Bonnier met me at the airport in his Porsche and as we drove to his home at Les Muids sur Nyons, overlooking Lake Geneva, we were chatting about the forthcoming season – who would be driving what, and so on – and I said I thought the only car that would be available to me was the Cooper-Maserati. Then, summoning up all my courage, I said, "I really don't think that I can afford to run more than one car next year, Jo, and Siffert is going to drive it. I'm afraid that you and I will have to part company." I suppose there may have been a rather longer silence than usual, but his expression hardly changed. Those Swedes are just so controlled and unemotional; I remember when I went to Jo's funeral in Sweden some years later his widow, Marianne, was just the same – ice cool and absolutely impassive.'

As if to confirm Rob's judgement Seppi won the hill climb in appalling conditions, and Jo finished fourth. By the end of the 1965 season Bonnier had not scored a single World Championship point and Rob knew for sure that he had made the right decision.

Controlled and unemotional? Jo Bonnier and his wife Marianne.

Chapter 13
Dear Seppi

'According to Seppi the Cooper T81 chassis really handled very well, but the Maserati engine was too heavy, under-powered and unreliable – in fact about the only thing one could say in its favour was that it was available. One of the problems which plagued us the whole time we had the car was that it used to throw out huge quantities of engine oil – in fact we used to call it the "Torrey Canyon" after a supertanker which had run aground near the Scilly Isles and spilled most of its cargo into the sea. In the end we more or less cured this by fitting an enormous catch tank and feeding the oil back into the engine.

'The overheating problem was much more difficult to deal with; the car used to boil after about two laps of practice – or one at a long, ultra-fast circuit like Spa – and then it would take about half an hour to cool down before we could get the radiator cap off to top it up. After a while we found that we could release some of the pressure safely by slackening off one of the hoses, and eventually we fitted a special valve to the pipework which enabled us to pump water into the cooling system under pressure.

'I think our worst experience in 1966 was at Spa when we couldn't even complete a single lap in practice without boiling. I was really worried about qualifying for my starting money because I couldn't for the life of me see how we could possibly complete the required minimum number of laps. The race started in the dry but about halfway round Burnenville on the first lap they ran into a wall of water at about 140 mph, and they were all over the place. Mike Spence and Jo Bonnier went off the road and Seppi had just about dodged most of the others when he was clobbered by Denny Hulme – going backwards! Bonnier's car ended up balanced on the edge of a precipice, and Jo had to climb carefully out over the back of the car to prevent it from pitching into the void below. Further on, at the Masta Kink, Jackie Stewart, Graham Hill and Bob Bondurant all went off the road, and Jochen Rindt spun nine times at 150 mph before recovering to finish second to John Surtees' Ferrari. Even if Seppi had got through the first accident unscathed it wouldn't really have made much difference because the car would certainly have boiled sooner or later, but we never did find out if it would have lasted more than a lap before doing so.

'An accident like that was very serious for us because we only had one chassis and one engine. In fact when we dropped a valve in practice for the International Trophy at Silverstone we had to go to Monaco with our old 1½-litre Brabham-BRM because the Maserati engine couldn't be repaired in time. The Maserati people were all extremely nice and tremendously co-operative – quite unlike Ferrari – and after

img_1

At Silverstone in 1967 Seppi finished third behind Mike Parkes (Ferrari) and Jack Brabham (Brabham) in Rob's Cooper-Maserati.

this they helped us a lot by having a spare engine waiting for us at the factory whenever possible; as one engine was flown in for repairs so the other was flown out for us to install in the car. It took me quite a while to spot that both the engines had the same number and I suppose it was inevitable that sooner or later they would end up sitting side by side in the Customs compound at Milan airport with two identical carnets. I think we decided to let Maserati talk their way out of that situation without any help from us; we reckoned that the Italians were probably rather better at that sort of thing than we were.'

The 1966 season was a miserable one for the Walker team. It was no comfort to them to know that the works Cooper-Maseratis were faring hardly better, although John Surtees did win the Mexican Grand Prix after he had joined the factory team following a disagreement with Ferrari at Le Mans. Siffert's best result was fourth in the United States Grand Prix at Watkins Glen. He also finished second in the non-championship South African Grand Prix at the beginning of the year, using the Brabham-BRM at a time when hardly any of the new 3-litre engines were ready to race, and he won the St Ursanne hill climb for the second year running, breaking the record by no less than 13.1 seconds. But perhaps the most telling indicator of the team's fortunes was a derisory offer of starting money from Herr Schmidt of the AvD, as a result of which Seppi and Rob declined to travel to the Nürburgring for the German Grand Prix.

The following year started slightly better with Seppi taking third place in both the British pre-season Formula One races, at Brands Hatch and Silverstone, and at Syracuse. Brands Hatch provided the first victory for Dan Gurney's AAR Eagle-Weslake, and saw the first appearance of John Surtees in the new Honda RA301. At Silverstone, while Mike Parkes' Ferrari ran away with the race, Seppi and Jack Brabham enjoyed a stirring battle for second place; Seppi got past Jack at about the halfway stage, but as the race drew to a close Brabham mounted a determined challenge. He was ahead on lap forty-nine, then it was Seppi again on lap fifty, then Brabham again on lap fifty-one. And that was how they finished a lap later, separated by less than a second. Drained by his efforts and relaxing his concentration rather too much and too soon, Seppi spun at Beckett's Corner on his slowing-down lap. At Syracuse he was easily beaten by the Ferraris driven by Parkes and Scarfiotti, his engine boiled almost dry by the end of the race.

When the European Grand Prix season opened at Monaco in early May, however, the team suffered a sharp reversal of fortune. Starting from pole position, Jack Brabham's Repco engine trailed a cloud of grey smoke as he climbed the hill to the casino on the first lap; moments later a connecting rod punched a hole through the block and Brabham spun on his own oil between Mirabeau and the Station Hair-

pin. Although most of the field dodged past the gyrating Brabham Seppi could not avoid him and damaged his radiator so badly as the cars came together that he could do no more than limp slowly to the pits to retire.

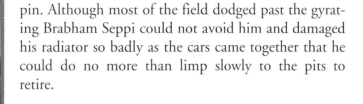

Lorenzo Bandini's Ferrari burns at the chicane while Chris Amon's similar car continues to finish third in the 1967 Monaco Grand Prix. Poor Bandini was to die from his injuries in hospital three days later.

As so often before, Rob's starting money seemed to be in jeopardy. But as he scrutinised the regulations a glimmer of hope emerged; a minimum of thirty laps was specified, but with no time limit. Tony Cleverley literally fought his way past the gendarmes obstructing the footbridge to collect a spare radiator from the transporter parked outside the circuit and, after a pit stop lasting almost half an hour, Seppi was duly able to complete thirty-two laps before his engine expired. Officials of the Automobile Club de Monaco were not exactly overjoyed to have been outfumbled by Rob Walker, but there was nothing they could do about it except pay up with as much good grace as they could muster.

As the race drew to a close, poor Lorenzo Bandini was killed when, in futile pursuit of eventual winner Denny Hulme, he crashed at the chicane, his Ferrari hitting the straw bales and lamp standards which lined the quayside at over 100 mph before landing upside

Seppi about to be lapped by Denny Hulme in the 1967 Monaco Grand Prix.

Driver briefing, German Grand Prix , Nürburgring 1967; l to r: *Hobbs, Surtees, Spence, Pedro Rodriguez and Siffert.*

down on the track and bursting into flames. It was a dismal start to the season not only for Rob Walker and Jo Siffert, but for the entire Grand Prix circus.

'The only races we did any good in for the rest of the season were the French Grand Prix, which was held on that Mickey Mouse Bugatti circuit at Le Mans, and the American Grand Prix at Watkins Glen, in both of which we finished fourth. Otherwise all our old troubles returned to haunt us and we discovered a few new ones into the bargain; in Germany we had a fuel starvation problem, at Monza we had a puncture, and at Mosport Park in Canada our starter ring broke up during practice. Having recovered some bits of our broken ring and scrounged some more from one of Rindt's engines which had suffered a similar fate, the mechanics worked all night to repair the ring, building up the welds and filing them into teeth, and then refitted it to the engine; it only had to work twice – once to try and once on the grid – but when we tried it next morning the welded teeth chewed up and it shattered again, so we were out of the race.

Denny Hulme was World Champion in 1967. Siffert was tenth. Rob Walker may have been the most successful private entrant – having started ten times, finished five times and scored championship points twice – but by his standards it had been a very disappointing season. And whatever crumbs of satisfaction he may have been able to derive from the handful of respectable performances delivered by his team must have been completely eclipsed by the devastating news that British Petroleum, his principal sponsor, was to withdraw from motor racing forthwith.

This news could not possibly have come at a worse time for, after two lean years with Rob, Seppi was beginning to wonder whether a works team might provide him with a more competitive drive. He wanted to go on driving sports cars for Porsche which ruled out the approach he had received from Ferrari; BRM had also approached him, but their last couple of seasons had not been particularly impressive and, in any case, Seppi really wanted to stay where he was – where he felt comfortable, at home, part of the family. But he must have a car in which he could win races. How could Rob find such a car? And now, how could he afford it?

It was in 1967 that Colin Chapman had introduced the Lotus 49 which incorpo-

Rob and Betty in the pits, Nürburgring 1967.

rated the new Ford-Cosworth DFV vee-eight engine as a stressed member of the chassis. Jim Clark had won with it at Zandvoort, first time out. 'As I talked over the problem of how to provide Seppi with a decent car to drive in the coming season with my business partner Geoff Thomas, we guessed that Colin would build new cars for 1968 and so, trading on the successes we had achieved together in the past, I asked him if he would sell me one of the 1967 team cars at a reasonable price. Colin not only agreed but also persuaded Walter Hayes of Ford to sell us a spare engine and give us some help to look after it, so suddenly we seemed to be in pretty good shape.

'Colin delivered the car to us quite early in the new season and Seppi flew over from Switzerland to test it at Brands Hatch. He had never before driven a car with quite such a high power to weight ratio and for the first thirty laps or so he just couldn't get the hang of it at all. Then he gradually began to work out how to do it and after about fifty laps his times were beginning to become quite competitive.

'Then came the disaster in practice for the Race of Champions, and the even greater disaster at the racing shop afterwards. For a second time I nearly gave up motor racing then – not for emotional reasons on that occasion, but simply because I couldn't for the life of me see how I could possibly afford to go on. BP had deserted me and my entire racing stable had been wiped out; there wasn't so much as a spanner left. Although the insurance company paid up in full, without question, we had been as badly under-insured as I suppose everyone always is, and there just wasn't enough money to get going again. However, everyone rallied round in the most incredible way; Betty's brother Val lent me £15,000; Colin Chapman offered to sell me Jim Clark's Tasman 49 which was on its way back from Australia by sea, and Jack Durlacher – who was my racing partner at the time – agreed to pay for it. When the ship which was carrying the car docked at Hamburg we managed to extract it from the hold and our transporter brought it home, and Woolworths in Dorking offered us an empty building to use as a workshop. The next race was not for six weeks and by the time it came round we were ready to go. Unfortunately the Tasman car was pretty clapped out and we never did any good with it, but at least we never missed a race as a result of either the accident or the fire.

'Colin promised us a new Lotus 49B in time for the British Grand Prix at Brands Hatch in July, but unfortunately we were not able to start building it until about three weeks before the race because certain key components were not available. We always built our own cars in those days, whichever factory they came from, for a number of very good reasons. In the first place, motor racing being what it was, the factory was always pushed for time and would inevitably give a lower priority to its customer cars than to the works cars; having our own mechanics there helped to alleviate this problem. Also our boys could benefit from the experience of the factory mechanics who had usually learned by bitter experience how to cope with the

Rob timekeeping at the 1968 British Grand Prix at Brands Hatch.

various idiosyncrasies of that particular car. And finally, in all honesty, we just felt that we bolted them together better than anyone else. There was also the question of money; it was a lot cheaper for me if my mechanics built the car because I didn't have to pay anyone else to do the job, and I was paying them anyway.

Seppi checks the front wheel bearings during practice for the 1968 British Grand Prix.

'The new car still wasn't finished when the first practice session started at Brands Hatch, even though my three mechanics had worked on it at the Lotus factory for the whole of the previous night. When they tried to start it at six o'clock in the morning they found that the electric fuel pump wasn't working so they simply loaded it into the transporter and drove the hundred miles or so from Hethel to Brands Hatch. They were still working on the car, putting the finishing touches to it, when practice started, and by the time they had finished and the car had been scrutineered everyone else had been practising for an hour and a half. Even though we didn't have the right gear ratios or the latest Firestone tyres fitted we thought we should run the car in what was left of practice just to make sure that everything was working properly, and much to our surprise it really went quite well.

'By the time of the second session that same afternoon we had sorted the gear ratios out and fitted the Firestone YB11 tyres which Seppi said made a huge difference, but after about ten laps the engine started to smoke badly. We were worried that the problem would prove serious enough to warrant an engine change which would have meant yet another sleepless night for the mechanics. However, Keith Duckworth found that the trouble was simply that a screw had fallen out of the head so we quickly fitted a new screw, topped up with oil and got back on the track for the remaining ten minutes or so of the session. I think we were eleventh fastest at the end of the day which was quite encouraging given that the car was straight out of the box.

'On the second day we were ready to go as soon as practice started and we quickly knocked about a second off our previous best time.

'Then at Seppi's request I asked Graham Hill if he would mind leading him round in the works 49B for a couple of laps, and Graham very generously agreed to do so. Siffert followed Graham for two laps and then missed a gear – which would have destroyed the engine in the days before we fitted rev limiters – and although he lost Graham in the process he had learned enough in those two laps to knock another second off his time. On his last lap but one, just as he had finished scrubbing his race tyres, he did 1m 29.7s, which was fourth fastest overall.

'We tried the car on full tanks in the untimed practice session later in the day and found that it was bottoming badly in places. I told Colin Chapman and Graham about this as I knew that they had not tried their cars on full tanks and I thought I might repay their kindness and get some free advice at the same time. Colin said we should reposition the rear shock absorbers and go slowly. We decided to disregard at least some of his advice.

'Graham had been fastest throughout practice, spurred on, or so he said, by the need to win a hundred bottles of champagne for the party he was giving on Saturday night. This prize for the fastest practice lap was billed as Veuve Clicquot and Graham was a bit miffed to be presented in the event with a hundred bottles of some less distinguished brand. Jackie Oliver was second fastest in the second works 49B, then came Chris Amon in the Ferrari, then Seppi.

'On the morning of race day I was approached by a scientist investigating the effects of stress on the human body and asked if I would allow Seppi to wear a portable ECG to record his heartbeat throughout the race. He had approached Colin Chapman with a similar request but had been turned down because Colin didn't want Graham to be bothered by any unnecessary distraction. Seppi had absolutely no objection to being wired up and the results were very interesting when we received them some time later; his heartbeat rose to about 170 while he was sitting on the grid immediately before the start, but otherwise it remained surprisingly low except for one flash reading of over 200 when he must have had a nasty moment somewhere.

Seppi before the start.

'Just before the race some very nasty-looking black clouds rolled up and a few minutes before the start there was a smattering of large raindrops which threw everyone but us into a total panic as they tried to decide whether to start on wet or dry tyres. We had done our usual trick of getting a forecast from the nearest RAF station that morning, so we were confident that it would not be a wet race. In any case our Firestone YB11 dry tyres worked very well in the wet – which was what they had been designed for in the first place.

'Both Oliver and Siffert made good starts and at the end of the first lap it was Lotus first, second and third – Oliver, Hill, Siffert – hotly followed by Chris Amon in the Ferrari. It didn't take Graham long to pass Jackie and leave Seppi to drive through a cloud of oil coming from Oliver's engine. Seppi was having real difficulty seeing through his goggles and he wiped them every time he came past the pits. At first we were rather confused by this strange hand signal but Tony Cleverley soon worked out what it was all about.

'On lap twenty-six Graham's right-rear suspension collapsed after a driveshaft failure and he was out of the race. Seppi was second, but still having real trouble with his vision. He decided to let Amon pass and take time to wipe his goggles properly. On lap forty-three Oliver's Lotus began spewing out even more oil; both Amon and Siffert were sliding around on it, but Seppi nevertheless managed to outbrake Chris to regain second place. Then Oliver's engine blew, and Seppi was in the lead with Chris breathing down his neck, less than half a second behind – a gap of about twenty-five yards as they passed the pits.

'The tension in our pit was almost unbearable as they went round like this for lap after lap, never more than a second apart. I tried hard to concentrate exclusively on my timekeeping and on giving Seppi accurate signals, and as I did so I was reassured to note that every time Chris put in a really quick lap and closed the gap by a fraction of a second, so Seppi would put in a slightly quicker one and open it up again. I first began to think we might win when Forghieri showed Chris the "GIVE ALL" signal. God knows what he thought Chris had been doing until then! Then Seppi started to pull away slightly as the Ferrari's tyres began to go off, but I choked on my sigh of relief when I saw Tony Cleverley lifting a fuel churn and a funnel onto the pit counter. In those days it was difficult to calculate fuel consumption exactly, especially when the car had been pressed to the limit for the entire race, and it took me a whole lap to pluck up courage to ask Tony whether he really thought we would have

to stop for fuel. It was a great relief to me to discover that he was simply acting as every first-rate mechanic would by preparing himself for any eventuality.

'In the end Seppi won the British Grand Prix by about two hundred yards – 4.4 seconds – from Chris Amon's Ferrari. His average speed for the whole race distance was faster than Jack Brabham's two-year-old lap record, and he set a new lap record into the bargain. It was Seppi's first World Championship victory and for me, after all the drama of our last visit to Brands Hatch, it was like a fairy tale. Without any doubt it was the proudest moment of my entire racing career.

'Much later, when the euphoria was beginning to wear off, I remembered that race day had been Chris Amon's birthday. I had walked up to the dummy grid with him before the start and had wished him luck and said I hoped that he would give himself a really super birthday present by winning the race. Little did I know then that less than two hours later I would be hoping and praying that he would finish second.

Under pressure. Seppi holds off Chris Amon's Ferrari at Druids Bend during their battle for the lead in the 1968 British Grand Prix at Brands Hatch.

'In a sense the rest of the year was a bit of an anti-climax. I remember the German Grand Prix because of the appalling weather at the Nürburgring – the fog was so bad that Seppi passed John Surtees on the straight without even seeing him. The race should never have been run under those conditions and I was incredibly relieved when Seppi retired after two laps. I remember the Canadian Grand Prix at St Jovite because the racer in Seppi got the better of his judgement; we were on pole and before the start I said to him, "For God's sake take it easy while the car is on full tanks because it's very bumpy here and these cars aren't all that strong." And then, of course, he got carried away in a dice with Chris Amon and something broke. He just went too fast too soon.

'And I remember the final race of the season in Mexico City. Seppi was going pretty well in practice, though maybe not quite well enough, when his throttle stuck wide open as he was entering the right-hander at the end of the straight and he was forced to go through the corner flat out. From then on he went through it flat out every time and started the race from pole position as a result. He made an

absolutely terrible start and he was in eighth place at the end of the first lap. By lap twenty-two he was in the lead but then a spring vibrated loose from the throttle slide and he had to make a pit stop. Tony Cleverley diagnosed the problem very quickly and fitted a replacement spring which he took from our spare engine, but by the time Seppi got going again he was in twelfth place some two laps behind the leaders. There was no hope of finishing in a respectable position, but that didn't stop Seppi from having a real go. He reminded me so much of Stirling in this way. In the end he finished sixth and set a new lap record. I think that if the throttle problem had occurred earlier in the race he might have won in spite of it; as it was

he didn't have quite enough time to make up the ground he had lost in the pits. In a way, I feel that Mexico was a Grand Prix which just slipped through my fingers.

'Before the race Colin Chapman had approached me and said, "If you are in front and Graham has a chance of winning the championship, will you let him through?" After the terrible loss of Jim Clark at Hockenheim in April it was very important to Colin and Team Lotus to win the championship. Even so, I was pretty non-committal about it and simply said, "Well, let's just wait and see what happens." And what happened after Seppi's pit stop was that Graham won the race and the World Championship.'

His performances in 1968 had made Seppi an even hotter, more desirable property and he was subjected to the blandishments of a number of teams before making it clear that he was going to stick with Rob Walker for the coming Formula One season. Actually, he had little option but to do so; Franco Lini offered him a blank cheque to sign for Ferrari but the deal involved both Formula One and sports car racing and Seppi still preferred to drive Porsche sports cars, although he was not above using the existence of this offer as a lever when negotiating a new contract with Porsche. Lotus demanded total concentration upon their Formula One effort and would not permit him to drive sports cars for Porsche, which was unacceptable to Seppi, and BRM was still not winning races. So Rob and Seppi found themselves collaborating for a fifth year in succession, and neither of them was unhappy about it.

The 1969 season, however, was not a resounding success for them. After finishing fourth at Kyalami in March, Seppi retired from the next Grand Prix at the Montjuich Park circuit in Barcelona just before the Team Lotus cars of Hill and Rindt crashed on the same corner after their rear aerofoils collapsed at 140 mph. Seppi had asked for a similar aerofoil to be fitted to his car but Rob, concerned by the fragile appearance of the new wing, had demurred. Halfway through practice at the next race at Monaco, the CSI banned wings in the interests of safety. Seppi finished third in his wingless Lotus 49B, but that and his second place at Zandvoort were to be his best results of the season.

At the Nürburgring he was classified fifth although he did not finish after crashing on the thirteenth lap; he was eighth at

Seppi at the wheel of the winning factory Porsche 908 in the 1969 BOAC 500 at Brands Hatch.

both Silverstone and Monza, and at Clermont he was ninth; he failed to finish as a result of mechanical failure at Mosport and Watkins Glen, and at Mexico he crashed out of the race. Neither crash was really his fault: in Mexico Piers Courage oversteered into his path while they were disputing sixth place, while in Germany he went off the road at the right-hander before the Karussel when the top rocker arm broke on the left-front suspension and suddenly he had no steering. To his surprise Seppi emerged unscathed after the car had ploughed through the bushes and trees beside the track. Later he described the accident in his rapidly improving English. 'I see the front wheel wobble and I think *"merde"*, and then I am in the trees.' Surely one of the most laconic accident reports ever delivered.

As the season drew to a close, Franco Lini once again approached Seppi to drive for Ferrari, and once again he could name his own price. Rico Steinemann realised that although Seppi might prefer to drive for Porsche the only sure way to com-

Seppi finished third at Monaco in 1969 in Rob's Lotus 49B. Here he is seen at Mirabeau Corner.

mand his continued loyalty was to find him a competitive Formula One drive and, if necessary, to pay for it. He approached Brabham on Seppi's behalf, but Jack had already signed Rolf Stommelen to complete his team. Effectively the choice was between BRM, March and, of course, Rob Walker who, although anxious to keep Seppi in the team, cared sufficiently about his driver not to stand in his way if he should receive a better offer.

'Seppi found it terribly difficult to decide what to do; on the one hand he felt at a disadvantage driving for me and thought he would have a better car if he drove for a factory team, while on the other hand we had been together for five years, the team

Joseph Siffert

Dear Rob,

At the beginning of this new year, I do send you quite sincerely my
best wishes of happiness, health and properity.

I would also like to thank you hartedly for all you did for me during
all the years I had the privilege to race for you.

The victory at Brands Hatch is certainly our greatest common remembrance;
but others too well proove the perfect organisation of your team and
the complete success of our collaboration. As for the bad remembrances,
they are so few that I already forgot them, and their positive result
was to reinforce more and more our friendship.

I would like you to tell Betty how much I always appreciated her kind
attention and her discrete care. Mrs Walker's presence in the team
make a great and beautiful family of it.

Last but not least, I wish all the ROB WALKER RACING TEAM a new season
full of success and satisfactions.

Looking forward to seeing you soon, I remain sincerely Yours

Avec toute mon amitie

(As decided at London, I am waiting for you in Fribourg on the 18th of
January)

1782 Belfaux / Suisse

suited him and he got along very well with everyone. Finally we were all running out of time; Seppi just had to make up his mind and he and I and Rico met for dinner at Prunier to talk the whole thing through yet again and try to reach a conclusion. We were still there at midnight, and he still hadn't decided; he wanted to sleep on it and he asked me to meet him for breakfast at his hotel at Heathrow, promising to give me his decision then without fail.

'By the next morning he had decided to go to March. I was bitterly disappointed because I really had thought that the odds were in favour of him staying with me. I think, in fact, that but for Rico he would have stayed. Porsche thought he was the finest driver ever to have driven for them, and they were desperate to keep him away from Ferrari. They wanted to see him settled in a successful factory team and so less vulnerable to another approach from Franco Lini, and I think that Rico really talked him into leaving me. Unfortunately going to March turned out to be the worst thing he ever did.'

A new qualifying procedure was instituted at the first Grand Prix of the European season at Jarama, and a series of misfortunes prevented Seppi from making the cut in

Seppi's March 701 at Monaco in 1970. It was to be a troubled year for the Swiss who failed to score a single championship point.

his March 701. Rob launched a petition to allow all the cars present to start which was duly signed by all the drivers and all but one of the teams – Ferrari being the exception, of course. The organisers didn't actually reject the petition, so on race day all the cars took their places for the start. As the five-minute board was shown two officials approached Seppi and told him to remove his car from the grid as it had not qualified, and when Seppi demurred he was dragged unceremoniously from his cockpit. A fierce argument followed but when the field got away to a delayed start Seppi and the other drivers who had failed to qualify were all spectators.

That incident was a mere foretaste of what was to be a completely disastrous year at March and at the end of 1970, disillusioned and without having scored a single championship point, Seppi signed for BRM in a move which was to result in his most successful Grand Prix season. He won the Austrian Grand Prix at the Österreichring where he also set the fastest lap, and finished second in America, fourth in France and sixth in Holland.

Jo Siffert's BRM disintegrates after hitting the bank at Hawthorn's Bend during the Brands Hatch Victory Race on 24th October 1971.

Below: *The last lap. Jo Siffert leading Tim Schenken's Brabham at Hawthorn's a lap before the accident.*

On 24th October 1971 Seppi started from pole position in the Victory Race at Brands Hatch, a Formula One event held ostensibly to celebrate Jackie Stewart's World Championship. He made a poor start, then had to take to the grass verge to avoid Ronnie Peterson, and he was lying tenth by the time the field reached Druid's Bend for the first time. Fifteen laps later he had fought his way up to fourth place when, just before the braking point for Hawthorn's Bend, his BRM suddenly turned

left at 180 mph. The car hit the protective earth bank head on, turned over, slid for some two hundred yards on its back, cartwheeled over the heads of a group of petrified marshals, landed upside down and burst into flames. Jo Siffert was killed instantly.

From the pits an ugly column of black, oily smoke could be seen rising above the far side of the track. All but a few of the cars had stopped at the scene of the accident, and all around the circuit the crowds fell silent, conscious that they were sharing a moment of great tragedy. John Surtees' car limped slowly into the pits; he had been close behind Seppi and had witnessed the accident from start to finish. One of his tyres had been shredded by debris from the BRM. He could offer Rob no hope that Seppi might have survived.

'John was absolutely marvellous. He realised how much Seppi had meant to Betty and me, and saw that we were both completely devastated by what had happened, and he took charge of us and made sure that we were collected by Betty's brother Val with whom we were staying. I lay awake all night regretting that I had not found an opportunity to talk to Seppi before the race, but Louis Stanley had been monopolising him and I hadn't wanted to intrude. As I thought about it in the darkness it was some small comfort to me to realise that Seppi had died as he would have wanted to – racing. Nearly fifty thousand people lined the streets of Fribourg when Seppi was buried there on 29th October; Jean-Pierre Oberson, his boyhood friend and devoted mechanic, walked behind the hearse carrying a red helmet with a white cross, and behind him came Seppi's gleaming factory Porsche 917 swathed in black crepe. It was a most moving occasion.

'It took me a very long time to find out the cause of Seppi's accident. In those days the regulations were that the scrutineers could keep a crashed car for only twenty-four hours and in that time they could find no obvious evidence of mechanical failure. Then BRM claimed the wreck and took it back to Bourne. The chief RAC scrutineer was a chap called Peter Jowitt who was the senior accident investigation officer at the Royal Aircraft Establishment at Farnborough, and he offered to go to Bourne to help the BRM team with their internal investigation, but they turned him down. BRM made no formal statement about the accident, although there was some criticism of the quality of the rescue operation at Brands Hatch, and their silence led most people to infer that Seppi had simply made a fatal mistake. From what John had told me I thought that sounded very unlikely and I was determined to get to the bottom of it, however long it took me.

'Nobody at BRM would tell me anything; I asked Tim Parnell about it several times but he wasn't giving anything away. Then years later, long after BRM had retired from racing, I was travelling by sea to Sweden for the race at Anderstorp and found myself having a beer in the bar of the ferry next to an ex-BRM mechanic. I plied him with drinks and we talked about old times, and when I thought he was sufficiently primed I asked him what had happened to Seppi's car. He told me that a rose joint holding a rear radius rod had broken, causing rear wheel steering, and at the speed he was going Seppi wouldn't have had a chance of controlling the car. When I told Tim Parnell later what I had heard and knew to be the truth, he confirmed what had happened.'

Twenty years after Jo Siffert was killed, on 24th October 1991, Rob Walker stood in the rain at the spot where he had died. 'Dear Seppi,' Rob thought. 'He should never have left me.'

Chapter 14
The Douglas Bader of Motor Racing

'At the beginning of 1969, just after Graham Hill had won the World Championship for the second time, I was chatting to Colin Chapman one day and he said, "You know, Rob, you ought to consider having Graham to drive for you." I was very surprised and rather puzzled by this; here was the proprietor of Team Lotus seemingly trying to interest me in his team leader, his World Champion driver. So I said, "But Seppi is driving for me, and I'm very happy with him," and that, I thought, was the end of that. But Colin brought up the subject several times more in the ensuing months, and I slowly began to realise that he thought Graham was over the hill and wanted to get rid of him so that he could concentrate on Jochen Rindt.'

As the season developed it became clear that Jochen Rindt and the Lotus 49 were a spectacularly quick combination while Graham Hill was more consistent than fast in the same car, although he did win the Monaco Grand Prix for the fifth time.

Then came Hill's accident at Watkins Glen in early October which completely overshadowed Jochen Rindt's first Grand Prix victory. Graham had been lying third in the early stages of the race but had fallen back to seventh place as the handling of his Lotus seemed to become progressively worse. After spinning on some oil he got out of the car to check for damage, but finding nothing amiss rejoined the race. The car was still handling badly and he became convinced that he must have a slow puncture; as he passed his pit on the ninetieth lap he signalled that he would be coming in next time round. On the ninety-first lap the punctured tyre suddenly deflated completely under braking and the car careened into the protective banking and turned over several times. Hill had been unable to refasten his harness after his earlier spin and as he was thrown out onto the verge his legs were trapped beneath the steering wheel. His right knee was broken, his left knee dislocated and, almost worse, there was massive ligament damage.

His doctors said that Graham would not race for a year, but they did not know the man. Colin Chapman saw an elegant solution to his problem and suggested to Graham that this might be a good moment for him to retire. Ford supported this view; they felt that even fully recovered from his injuries Graham would never be the driver he once was and that he would damage his reputation by racing again unsuccessfully – and his reputation was a commercial asset to the Ford Motor Company. But Graham was determined to be fit in time to drive in the South African Grand Prix at Kyalami in March 1970, five months in the future.

At the University College Hospital it was found that even the most potent of conventional pain killers were not effective in combating the agony of a succession of ligament operations and Graham was given morphia as a last resort, happily suffering no side-effects or withdrawal symptoms. Later he became an out-patient at Stanmore Orthopaedic Hospital where he exercised to the point of exhaustion on the rowing machine, on the exercise bike and in the swimming pool, in which the buoyancy of the water supported his damaged legs. Even then it was clear that his left leg would, as he put it, end up a bit bent and give his tailor a hell of a problem. Later, when he had discarded his crutches, Graham refused to ride in lifts and always climbed the stairs, however many there were, in order to exercise his wasted muscles.

'Although I was very disappointed when Seppi decided to go to March I wasn't totally disheartened because my various conversations with Colin Chapman had made it clear that Graham could be available to me as a replacement. I went to see him in hospital just before Christmas 1969 and I was so impressed by his determination to drive again that we reached an agreement on the spot. A few days later we were having our annual Christmas dinner for the team at a hotel near Dorking and to my astonishment Graham turned up on crutches, having escaped from the hospital in a chauffeur-driven car provided by Ford.

'Someone once described Graham Hill as the Douglas Bader of motor racing, and that was a pretty perceptive description. He was a folk hero, a sort of national institution, and throughout his convalescence the papers were filled with reports of his progress. It was a miracle that he drove at Kyalami; at the time he could barely walk without crutches, we had to lift him into the car and out of it, and it was absolute agony for him to use the brake pedal. And yet, driving a racing car for the first time since his accident, he was doing a competitive time within a couple of laps. It was almost unbelievable, and one of the bravest things I have ever seen. He was completely exhausted at the end of that first day but I can remember him saying, "You know, Rob, it's really nice to be back to normal again," as if he was talking about working behind the counter at NatWest!'

Graham's return to motor racing was a major media event and, recognising the importance of the occasion, the *Daily Express* had sent Basil Cardew to Johannesburg to provide on-the-spot coverage of Graham's first moments behind the wheel. 'After we had landed at Jan Smuts Basil gave us the telephone number of his hotel and asked us to let him know when we were going to practise. When we went out to the circuit later in the day we discovered that the car was ready to go and decided to do a few laps there and then. There was no reply from Basil's hotel room and, knowing how much he hated flying, we guessed that he must be recuperating from the rigours of the journey over a drink or two somewhere. We called every bar we could think of but simply couldn't track him down, so in the end we had to go ahead without him.' The next day the *Express* appeared without a contribution from Basil Cardew and was forced to call upon other sources to provide coverage of

Rob conferring with Graham Hill at Silverstone in 1970.

223

Graham brought the Walker Lotus 49C, covered with extinguisher foam from the Ickx/Oliver first-lap accident, into fourth place in the 1970 Spanish Grand Prix at Jarama.

Graham's return to the track. Then television took over; on 7th March 1970 *Grand-stand*, the popular BBC1 Saturday afternoon programme, was interrupted by a special announcement: 'Here is the news you have all been waiting for; Graham Hill has finished sixth in the South African Grand Prix.'

'Formula One racing was becoming more and more expensive and at the end of every season I found myself dipping deeper and deeper into my pocket to pay the bills. Although I still had my Firestone contract, BP were no longer supporting me and it was clear that I needed to find a new sponsor to help make ends meet. Gra-

ham's presence in the team was an enormous help and we were fortunate enough to make contact with Brooke Bond Oxo who agreed to sponsor us for a year in the first instance, with renewal options built into our agreement.'

Brooke Bond Oxo was a new company, recently formed as the result of a takeover, and the management was anxious to unite the disparate workforces by whatever means possible. The Brooke Bond Oxo Formula One car became a symbol of their unity, with Graham Hill a charismatic figurehead with whom everyone, whether factory worker, salesman or manager, could identify. A column was ghosted for Graham in the company magazine, and he made frequent visits to offices and production lines where he was universally adored. Various incentive schemes qualified company personnel to attend Grand Prix races, and champagne and smoked salmon were dispensed to Brooke Bond Oxo customers in hospitality tents at circuits throughout Europe, while Graham chatted them up. He was a marvellous ambassador for motor racing and for Brooke Bond Oxo, and he worked just as hard to meet the demands of the sponsor as he did to deliver the goods for the team. Brooke Bond Oxo first raced with Rob Walker at the 1970 Spanish Grand Prix at Jarama where Graham finished fourth in Rob's Lotus after dodging a first-lap accident between Jackie Oliver's BRM and Jacky Ickx's Ferrari which left the BRM burning at the trackside for the entire duration of the race.

'At Jarama our car had been updated to 49C specification and we had fitted a special master cylinder to make it easier and less painful for Graham to brake. The new Lotus 72, which Jochen Rindt was driving for the first time, had inboard disc brakes at the front and during the first practice period the left-hand brake shaft broke and Jochen went into the sand bank at the end of the main straight at 175 mph. We were occupying the pit next to Team Lotus and I was there when Jochen appeared, having walked back from the scene of his accident. He had obviously had a bad fright and he was still absolutely livid; his first words to Colin were "I'll never sit in that fucking car again as long as I live." I

Jack Brabham leads Jochen Rindt at Tabac on the final lap of the 1970 Monaco Grand Prix. He crashed on the last corner of the race, and Rindt won.

said to Graham, "What happens now?" and Graham told me, "Oh well, Colin will let him cool down for a bit and then he'll get him in a quiet corner and talk to him for ten minutes or so, and then he'll get back in the car and drive." And that's exactly what happened. Four months later he was killed when the same brake shaft broke at Monza.'

Monaco with its emphasis on braking was very difficult for Graham. He had a big accident on the second day of practice, tearing the front wheels off the car at Massenet on the approach to Casino Square. Although he was completely unhurt there was no chance that the car could be repaired in time for the race. Colin Chap-

Hill at Les Gazomètres, Monaco 1970.

man came to the rescue by lending Rob the spare Team Lotus car which, hastily resprayed blue and white, occupied the sixteenth and last position on the starting grid. Nevertheless, as a five-times winner of their Grand Prix, Graham was dear to the hearts of the people of Monte Carlo who reached out to touch him and pelted him with flowers as he limped down the hill from the Hotel de Paris to the start on race day. He finished fifth in a race won by Jochen Rindt – driving a Lotus 49C in preference to the new 72 – after Jack Brabham, securely in the lead, had made a major error of judgement and crashed on the last corner of the last lap.

'Colin Chapman had promised us the second Lotus 72 to be built and we had originally expected to have it in time for Monaco in May, but there were endless delays at the Lotus factory and in the end we only just got it in time for the Gold Cup at Oulton Park in September. So while Jochen won in his 72 at Zandvoort, Clermont-Ferrand, Brands Hatch and Hockenheim, we soldiered on with the old 49 which was becoming less and less competitive race by race. It was so clapped out after Hockenheim that we decided not to bother to prepare it for the Österreichring two weeks later, and I sent all my mechanics to Hethel to try and finish our 72 in time. In the event they didn't quite make it and Graham was left without a car for the race. He was not best pleased.

Graham Hill with Rob's new driver, British Grand Prix 1970.

'Earlier in the season there had been great drama at Brands Hatch where Jack Brabham had been within a mile or so of winning the British Grand Prix when he ran out of petrol and was passed by Jochen on the last lap. Then when Jochen's car was scrutineered after the race it was found that the struts supporting the rear aerofoil were bent whereas they had been straight before the start. The scrutineers jumped to the conclusion that the car had raced with the aerofoil above the permitted maximum height and that someone had bent the struts to lower it before it was taken to the scrutineer's bay after the finish, so Jochen was disqualified and Jack was declared the winner. Then Colin lodged a verbal protest against this decision and during the course of an argument which lasted for about three hours the struts were straightened, the wing was set to maximum deflection, it was measured very carefully, found to be perfectly legal, and Jochen was reinstated as the winner. It was all rather undignified and silly really.

'Brooke Bond Oxo were using chimpanzees in their TV advertising for PG Tips at that time and they brought one of them along to the paddock to have its photograph taken with Graham on the first practice day. I remember that as the photogra-

The start of the 1970 British Grand Prix at Brands Hatch. Rindt, Brabham and Ickx are on the front row.

The outdated Lotus 49 was still good enough to bring Hill sixth place in the British Grand Prix.

pher was waiting for Graham to turn up and the chimp was sitting on the car, John Surtees came up to me and said, "I see you've got a new driver, Rob – what's his name?" Brooke Bond Oxo had invited a huge number of staff and customers to Brands Hatch on race day and we did our best to put on a good show for them all, but unfortunately we blew up our only Ford DFV engine during practice and for a while it looked as if we might not even be able to start. Then Ron Tauranac of Brabham very kindly offered to lend us one of his spare engines and we managed to

Jochen Rindt on the winner's podium at Brands Hatch before being disqualified, then reinstated.

finish sixth.'

When Rob Walker's new Lotus 72C finally arrived, it turned out to be chassis number four. Jochen Rindt had been driving chassis number two since Zandvoort and was to do so again in the Italian Grand Prix at Monza. He was uncharacteristically slow on the first practice day, finishing behind the three works Ferraris, Jackie Stewart's March and Pedro Rodriguez's BRM. His mechanics changed his engine overnight and because of this he was not trying to set a spectacularly fast time in the opening minutes of the final practice period on the afternoon of Saturday 5th September 1970. This notwithstanding, he was travelling at about 190 mph when he hit the brakes some two hundred yards before turning in for the Parabolica, the 120 mph right-hander before the pits. Denny Hulme was about thirty yards behind and saw the Lotus wobble as Jochen braked, then turn sharp left to hit the guard rail virtually head on. Tragically the car struck the barrier at a point at which the Armco sections joined and, instead of sliding along and slowing progressively as it was supposed to, it was impaled on a projecting length of steel barrier and stopped dead in no more than a few inches. The force of the impact must have been enormous and Jochen Rindt was fatally injured.

The rescue operation was a disaster. Although the race organisers had undertaken to provide a helicopter to evacuate any injured driver, no helicopter was available and so, after a cursory examination and rather clumsy first aid treatment which probably did more harm than good, Jochen was loaded into an ambulance for the journey to hospital. Bypassing the Grand Prix Medical Unit, its sophisticated equipment and highly qualified doctors ready and waiting in the paddock in case of just such an emergency, the ambulance set off along roads choked with traffic; the police motor cycle escort headed for the Monza hospital a short distance from the track, but the ambulance driver preferred to head for Milan where better facilities were available. Before he could reach them, Jochen

Rindt succumbed to his injuries.

'I guessed immediately what had happened and, sure enough, when Colin examined the wreckage of Jochen's car he found that the left-hand front brake shaft was broken which, although this could have happened in the crash, was all the confirmation I needed to withdraw our car at once. Graham was initially very unhappy about this decision, but he saw the wisdom of it when Team Lotus also decided to withdraw John Miles and Emerson Fittipaldi. Later, when we got back to the racing shop, I had the brake shafts taken off our car and sent to Vickers Armstrong who did all our crack testing in those days, and their report described the shafts as "shattered". I rang them up to ask what this meant in layman's terms and they told me it meant that the shafts could have broken at any time in the next half-dozen laps at Monza. I reckon Graham had a very narrow escape.

'There were no Team Lotus cars at the Canadian Grand Prix at St Jovite. The

The first appearance of Rob's Lotus 72, at Oulton Park in 1970.

Italian authorities had impounded Jochen's car and Colin didn't want to take any chances until he had had an opportunity to examine it thoroughly. I think he would have preferred us not to race in Canada either, but we planned to fit some much stronger brake shafts which Lotus had made for us and we were pretty confident that these would solve the problem.

'Actually we might just as well have stayed at home because we qualified last after the car had caught fire just as Graham was about to go for a quick lap. What had happened was that an injector pipe had worked loose at the same time as the distributor cap had come off, and a spark just lit up all the petrol that was sloshing around. Fortunately the Graviner on-board extinguisher worked very efficiently so the damage wasn't too serious. I remember Jack Brabham coming into our pit and saying, "Tell me, Graham, how on earth did you manage to arrange for the injector pipe to come off at exactly the same moment as the distributor cap?" and Graham said, "Well, it's taken me years of practice, but I've finally got it right." Then after twenty-eight laps of the race he came into the pits complaining of poor handling. We discovered that a bolt had fallen out of the rear suspension and by the time we had replaced it we had lost so much time that although Graham was still running at the end of the race he was not classified as a finisher.

'It was after the Canadian Grand Prix, when we were driving to Montreal together, that Graham said to me, "If I'm going to drive for you next season you've got to get rid of your mechanics and start again." Graham was a very strong character who found to his surprise that he had met his match in Tony Cleverley. They first fell out in a big way at Zandvoort where it is terribly difficult to set the car up because the sand drifting across the circuit changes it from minute to minute. Graham just couldn't get the car to handle well and he was hopelessly slow. He kept stopping at the pit and telling Tony that the car was rubbish and badly set up, until finally Tony let fly at him, quite rightly; "There's absolutely nothing wrong with the car or the handling," he said. "It's the driver that's the problem. Why don't you just get in the car and drive it properly?" I suppose those few words altered the direction of both Graham Hill's motor racing career and mine, because Graham never forgave Tony and the situation between them went from bad to worse. I suppose the straw that broke the camel's back came when Tony refused to work all night to change the brake shafts in Canada; Graham was absolutely furious with him, even though the car was ready well before practice just as Tony had said it would be.

'I flew down to Los Angeles to visit *Road & Track* at Newport Beach on the day after this conversation and by chance John Surtees was on the same flight, on his way to a race at Riverside, and naturally we sat together on the plane so that we could have a chat. After a while he said, "You know, Rob, you're on your own, and so am I; we really ought to get together and save ourselves a lot of money."

'The coincidence of these two conversations struck home. John was right; motor racing had become terribly expensive and would no doubt become even more expensive in time to come. It was already costing me much more than I could easily

Graham consults Tony Cleverley at Silverstone in 1970.

afford and, indeed, on several recent occasions I had wondered how long I could carry on. I was determined to do so for as long as possible for the sake of my mechanics but now I thought, "I wonder if they are only staying on for my sake?" I talked the whole thing over with Tony and it soon became clear that each of us was really only doing it for the other one.'

In fact, Tony Cleverley was not at all surprised when Rob tentatively broached the possibility of winding up the team. 'I had seen the writing on the wall', he says, 'for quite a while. If we had had a really good, ambitious young driver, there was no reason why we could not have gone on, but Graham was not at anything like his best, and he wasn't going to get any better. I could see that unless we could get a top-class driver we would never get enough financial support to make it viable. I wouldn't have minded all the endless travelling, the sleepless nights and so on if we had been making progress, but we weren't; we were just marking time.'

So, after further discussions between Rob and John Surtees, a deal was worked out for the integration of the two teams. Rob helped Tony to start up a garage business, John Chisman stayed at Pippbrook to work on Rob's car collection, his third mechanic, Stan Collier – who wanted to stay in motor racing – found himself a job with another team, and the Rob Walker Racing Team was no more.

Graham's 'lobster claw' Brabham BT34 leads Pedro Rodriguez's BRM P163 and Chris Amon's Matra in the 1971 International Trophy race at Silverstone.

Initially Tony Cleverley, the only one of Rob's three mechanics to brave the outside world, found himself completely lost; having thought of nothing but motor racing for more than a decade he found that he had little in common with the regulars at his local pub. However, the stability of a happy marriage, healthy kids and a prosperous business soon convinced him that life after motor racing was not as barren as he had thought at first.

'Of course all this rather left Graham up in the air. He asked me if I could arrange a drive for him with Team Surtees and I dutifully put the question to John, although I couldn't envisage the two of them getting along together in the same team; they were as different as chalk and cheese. John very diplomatically said that he would think about it, and that's as far as it went. Eventually Graham drove for Brabham for a couple of seasons and then set up his own team with sponsorship from Embassy cigarettes. I think at first, while his own chassis was being developed, he raced Shadow DN1s and then Lola T370s, and then on the eve of the 1975 British Grand Prix at Silverstone he announced his retirement from active race driving so that he could concentrate on running the team.

'Graham and I always had a lot of fun together when he drove for me. I remember at Watkins Glen a fuel line broke in the cockpit of the 72 and absolutely soaked him with petrol, which was very uncomfortable. He stopped at the pits for some sympathy just after John Surtees had retired so we borrowed John's overalls and flameproof underwear for him to wear for the rest of the race. I wish I had a photograph of John standing in our pit in nothing but his Y-fronts, Graham stark naked and me pouring a bucket of water over his bare bum in an attempt to wash the petrol off him. It was absolutely hilarious.

'On another occasion he was driving me back to our hotel after practice at Mexico City when he shot a red light and was immediately stopped by the police. When they demanded six hundred pesos Graham got involved in a furious argument with them which only ended when he had beaten them down to a hundred pesos, which he asked me to pay as he had no money on him. They were absolutely horrified when I jumped out of the car waving a bundle of notes and quickly pushed me back inside. Then a hand sneaked in through the window and I put the money in it, realising as I did so that I had been pretty naïve to suppose that the hundred pesos was a fine!

'After the race in Mexico a year earlier we had all been invited to a celebration dinner at a bullring about an hour out of the city, and on the way there was a fantastic dice between the courtesy cars which had each driver's name painted in big white letters on the doors. They were three abreast on a two-lane road, up on the pavements, going the wrong way around roundabouts, all over the place, and as all the cars had the same engines, and pretty small engines at that, it was very difficult to overtake. I was travelling with Seppi on this occasion and there were four of us in the car which gave us a slight weight penalty, so we were about a car's length behind Jo Bonnier, Bruce McLaren and Graham as the bullring came into view. They were all so busy leaning on each other's door handles that they shot past the turning and we got there first.

'Graham often used to fly me to the races in his Piper Aztec, which he kept at Elstree, and I remember once when we were going to Hockenheim Colin Chapman and Jack Brabham in their aeroplanes were both looking for the airfield at the same time as us. Graham spotted it first and I asked him to tell me the secret of his navigational skill. "Oh," he said, "I just fly down the crease in the map." Sometimes Graham used to let me fly the plane when we were at a safe height, and it was quite fun to do a few turns and so on. Those were the only occasions on which I have flown an aeroplane since the war.

'I thought that Graham was an exceptionally good and careful pilot. On the return journey from Hockenheim we had to land at Southend to clear Customs, and a real pea-souper had cut visibility down to no more than three hundred yards, but Graham found the airport with no trouble at all and landed perfectly. No commercial aircraft had been able to take off from Southend all day and as it was at the height of the holiday season the terminal was absolutely packed with passengers who were pretty fed up when they saw that we could land and take off while they had to sit around until the fog had cleared. The fog was pretty bad at Elstree too, and of course there were no landing aids there, but once again Graham got us down without any fuss at all. Having had that dreadful crash in the fog at Horwich during the war, I had expected to feel pretty twitchy sitting beside Graham as we peered through the murk, but to my surprise I wasn't in the least bit perturbed by it. I had complete confidence in him.'

It was foggy again on the evening of Saturday 29th November 1975 as Hill made his approach to Elstree. His passengers on this occasion were Embassy team manager Ray Brimble, designer Andy Smallwood, mechanics Terry Richards and Tony Alcock, and Tony Brise – a newcomer to Formula One racing for whom Graham foresaw a brilliant future – who had been putting the new GH2 through its paces at the Paul Ricard circuit at Le Castellet. They all perished when the Piper Aztec ploughed into a hill some distance short of the airfield, disintegrated and caught fire.

'The fog at Elstree that afternoon was so bad that Graham should, of course, have diverted to Luton, but he was pushed to be on time for a dinner engagement in the evening, his car was parked at Elstree with his dinner jacket in the boot, and he had arranged for a Customs officer to be there so that he wouldn't have to waste time by landing at Southend to clear Customs. It would have been very inconvenient to divert to Luton and I don't suppose he considered it seriously for a moment. People say that in the end Graham took one risk too many, but I don't think he would have thought that he was taking a risk at all. He must have thought that he knew the airfield and the surrounding terrain like the back of his hand, and I have no doubt that he confidently expected to land safely. It was a tragic example of familiarity breeding contempt. It cost motor racing its finest ambassador, and it cost me yet another good friend.'

Chapter 15
Mike the Bike

Norman Bingham, the Marketing Director of Brooke Bond Oxo, was a motor cycling enthusiast and therefore undismayed by Rob's decision to part company with Graham Hill and join forces with John Surtees. Indeed, soon after the union between Rob and John had been agreed, Brooke Bond Oxo announced that they would sponsor the new team for an additional period of three years.

At the press conference at which this renewed sponsorship was announced Rob said of Brooke Bond Oxo, 'I cannot think of any firm with which I would prefer to be associated. Last year I promised them in good faith that I would have a new car at the Monaco Grand Prix in May; I didn't get it until September. I promised them that I would have the second Lotus 72 to be made; in fact I got the fourth. I assured them that I would have a Lotus 72 for the British Grand Prix at Brands Hatch, and they spent a great deal of money on corporate hospitality in this expectation; I turned up with an outdated Lotus 49. Not once did they complain at my failure to deliver what I had promised. They understood my problems and were prepared to live with them, and for this I am deeply indebted to them. In the coming season we will be racing the best and latest Team Surtees car and, as John will be driving it himself, I am sure that it will be as safe as he can possibly make it – which is very important to me and, I'm sure, to our sponsors also.'

In addition to the Brooke Bond Oxo sponsorship Rob brought to Team Surtees the only remaining Formula One Firestone tyre contract and also handed over his transporter, the Lotus 72 and the earlier Lotus 49, two Ford DFV engines and countless spares. In return Rob took a half share in the team and was to be paid a race by race fee throughout the three-year period of the agreement.

John Surtees.

The new team first raced at the 1971 South African Grand Prix at Kyalami which also saw the first appearance of the latest Surtees TS9 chassis. As always, the construction of the new car was running behind schedule and its initial shakedown test

took place at Goodwood only five days before the first practice session at Kyalami. A strike by French air traffic controllers delayed the arrival of the car in South Africa, and practice was further limited by various teething troubles. Under the circumstances John Surtees felt that to have qualified sixth fastest was no mean achievement.

John was baulked by Jackie Stewart at the start and found himself languishing in fourteenth place at the end of the first lap. By the mid-point of the race, however, he had clawed his way through the field to lie second to Denny Hulme's McLaren. He was about to mount a serious challenge for the lead when his gearbox began to overheat as the result of a fractured oil pipe and he gradually lost the use of gear after gear, finally retiring with only first available to him.

While this was a promising beginning for the TS9, Rob was less than happy. 'When I arrived in South Africa I realised that I had no active part to play in the management of the team and it was disappointing to find myself in the role of bystander after having run my own team with a certain measure of success. For want of something better to do I made myself responsible for timekeeping – although Patricia Surtees was a better timekeeper than I could ever hope to be – which at least prevented me from feeling a total passenger, and as the season wore on I learned to live with my new position in the pecking order. It was not a very happy year for me, but somehow I managed to get through it without having a row with anyone. There was one very nasty moment when I noticed that my name did not appear on the car's livery at Brands Hatch, but some letters made out of Scotch tape solved the immediate problem and good sense prevailed thereafter.'

The 1971 Race of Champions at Brands Hatch: Surtees' TS9 leads Wisell's Lotus 72 and Gethin's McLaren M14A.

Surtees enjoyed mixed fortunes in the British pre-season Formula One races, finishing third at Brands Hatch but retiring after a piston failed at Oulton Park. In the first Grand Prix of the European season, the Spanish Grand Prix at Barcelona, John qualified on the last row of the grid after a miserable time in practice, and he could do no better than eleventh place in the race. This set the tone for the rest of the Grand Prix season, poor grid positions being followed by race results which were equally disappointing – seventh at Monaco and the 'Ring, for example, eighth at Paul Ricard, eleventh at Mosport, and so on. By the end of the season Surtees had amassed only three World Championship points, as had his team-mate Rolf Stommelen. Even though John won the non-championship Oulton Park Gold Cup race from a mixed field of Formula One and Formula 5000 cars, this could not conceal the existence of an underlying problem. Rob had no hesitation in diagnosing it.

'It was quite clear to me that John couldn't possibly do all the things he was trying to do and hope to do any of them well enough to be successful. He was the chief designer, the head mechanic, the team manager and the driver, and the result was that he was not driving to anything like his full potential – in fact, everything was suffering. I thought that in everyone's best interests – especially John's – I had better try and get him out of the seat, so one day I said to him, "John, you're doing far too much. Why not chuck the driving? You can go on doing the testing so that you know how the car behaves and how to set it up properly, but let someone else do the race driving." Slightly to my surprise he didn't react too badly to this suggestion, perhaps because

Inset: *Rob at Silverstone in 1971.* Above: *John Surtees on his way to victory in the 1971 Oulton Park Gold Cup race with the Team Surtees TS9.*

under the strain of his fantastic work load he had begun to reach the same conclusion as I had.'

It was the appearance at Monza of Mike Hailwood in a third Team Surtees TS9 that gave Rob the confidence to suggest that John should give up race driving. Like John, who had been one of his boyhood heroes, Hailwood had been a multiple World Champion on motor cycles. He had first tried his hand at Formula One racing almost a decade earlier, driving Reg Parnell's Lotus 24 in a couple of races in 1963 and then spending the whole of the 1964 Grand Prix season with the Parnell team, acquiring a single World Championship point for his sixth place at Monaco. He hadn't altogether enjoyed the experience; he wasn't used to consistent failure, and he didn't care much for the Formula One people. So he went back to racing motor cycles.

Hailwood had been driving a Chevrolet-engined Team Surtees TS8 in the 1971 Formula 5000 series and had become quite interested in having another go at Grand Prix racing. John gave him the opportunity to do so at Monza where he started from a relatively humble grid position, but after about fifteen laps he found himself involved with half a dozen other drivers in an intense slipstreaming battle for the lead. The issue was in doubt until the last corner; François Cevert was ahead as they entered the Parabolica and left his braking very late. Ronnie Peterson did the same

Mike Hailwood in the Surtees TS9B in 1972.

and got sideways in the process, effectively shutting Hailwood out, and Peter Gethin nipped through to win for BRM. But not by much: he, Peterson and Cevert were side by side as they crossed the line with Hailwood only a matter of feet behind in fourth place. Afterwards he was to say, 'I've never come across this slipstreaming lark before – I didn't know what the hell we were all playing at!' Hailwood missed the Canadian Grand Prix because he was committed to a Formula 5000 race in England on the previous day, but he reappeared at the USGP at Watkins Glen where he was running sixth before retiring after a puncture caused him to leave the road, damaging his front suspension in the process.

'I thought that Mike's performance at Monza was quite remarkable given that he hadn't driven a Formula One car for nearly eight years, and the '71 cars were very different from the ones he had driven before. Yet in his first race he was right up there with the best of them; he was actually in the lead at various stages of the race and might easily have won it. I rated him very highly as a driver; he was cast from the same mould as Stirling and Seppi, and he always had a tremendous go. I have no doubt that he had the ability to win a Grand Prix, but he was probably too inconsistent to have had real World Championship potential.

'Mike hated Formula One when he first started; he couldn't stand what he perceived as the pretension and pomposity of it all, he didn't know anybody, and he felt that everybody looked down upon him as an ex-motor cyclist. I remember him telling me that Graham Hill was the only driver to offer him any help or encouragement. Although his father had been a millionaire who had seen to it that he was educated at a public school and had delivered him to his first motor cycle race, despite his protests, in a chauffeur-driven Rolls, the snooty and stand-offish Formula One people, as he thought of them, succeeded in making him feel inferior. I suppose that given my background he must have seen me as typical of the breed he disliked most.

'Mike took a Surtees Formula 5000 car to the Tasman series in early 1972. As Betty and I were visiting family and friends in Australia at the time, I decided to make the trip to New Zealand to watch the race at Christchurch in which Mike finished second. After the race I invited Mike and his friend Rod Sawyer to dinner at my hotel, and this was the first time we ever spoke more than a few sentences to each other.

'Later on at Jarama I was on my own as Betty had stayed at home at Nunney, and once again I invited Mike and Rod to dine with me at my hotel. I asked Mike if the transition from bikes to cars had been difficult for him, and with typical honesty he admitted that it had been much harder than he had expected. He said he didn't think that it was more difficult to ride a bike than to drive a car, or vice versa; they were just completely different, and the notion that the ability to do one well made it easier to do the other well was quite false. I found it very surprising to hear him say that he thought bikes were safer than cars, but he explained that in his experience most car crashes were caused by some component failure which reduced the driver's control of the situation, whereas bikes were much simpler and less prone to mechanical failure.

'As the evening wore on I seem to remember that we drank a great deal of sangria and I started telling them about the scrapes we used to get into in the old days, and gradually Mike began to realise that I was not as black as he had painted me. In the fullness of time I became terribly fond of Mike, and we had some absolutely marvellous parties together. After he was killed Pauline, his widow, asked me to give the address at his memorial service but I couldn't bring myself to do so because I felt sure that I would be overcome by the emotion of the occasion and make a fool of myself.

'I first heard about Mike's accident on the evening of Saturday 20th March 1981 when Rod Sawyer telephoned me to say that Mike had apparently taken his daughter to buy some fish and chips as a special treat when, on a stretch of the dual carriageway A435 near Portway, a lorry in the inside lane had begun a sudden U-turn through a gap in the central reservation just as Mike was about to overtake it. Even Mike's skill could not prevent his Rover from sliding beneath the lorry; Michelle was killed instantly and Mike was trapped in the wreckage of the car suffering from appalling head injuries. Professor Syd Watkins, the Formula One doctor, examined him at the Birmingham Accident Unit and gave him no chance of survival. He died the following day, without regaining consciousness. The lorry driver who had caused the accident was subsequently fined £100, with a judgement against him for costs amounting to a further £105.

'Mike always lived life to the full and, like Stirling and Seppi before him, he had

Mike Hailwood at Monaco in 1972.

an eye for the ladies. I will always remember an occasion at Anderstorp when at two o'clock in the morning of the first practice day a girl arrived in Mike's room having travelled some two hundred miles from Stockholm. I asked him what had happened. "Well, Rob," he said, "I couldn't disappoint her after she had travelled all that way – but for God's sake don't tell John." On another occasion at the Nürburgring four girls had turned up, three of whom he was doing his best to unload on his friends. I locked my bedroom door in case he found himself short of takers.

'I don't think John Surtees really approved of this sort of activity which he probably saw as a distraction his drivers would be better off without. To be honest I was never absolutely certain about the relationship between John and Mike. I don't think they can have been bosom pals because they were absolute opposites and had very little in common, but perhaps there was mutual respect between them.

'Mike wasn't frightened of anybody or anything. I recall that once after he had dined with Betty and me at the Villa d'Este at Cernobbio he was carved up by three Italian yobs as he drove his rented car back to Milan. Mike ignored them for a while, but eventually he'd had enough. When they stopped at some traffic lights he boxed them in against the kerb, then he dragged the driver out of the car and laid him out cold while the other two ran for their lives.'

In 1973, his final season with Team Surtees, Mike Hailwood's fearlessness was to win him the George Medal, the second highest civilian award for bravery. It happened at Kyalami on the third lap of the South African Grand Prix. As they

Mike Hailwood's TS14A before the chicane at Monaco in 1973.

approached Crowthorne, the fast right-hander at the end of the straight, Dave Charlton spun in front of Mike as he tried to overtake Carlos Reutemann on the outside. Mike hit him and spun, Clay Regazzoni hit Mike, and Jacky Ickx hit Clay. Hailwood's Surtees and Regazzoni's BRM were locked together, both cars on fire. The Graviner automatic fire extinguishers in the Surtees worked well, but for some reason those in the BRM did not. Regazzoni, unconscious, was trapped in the fire-ball which engulfed his car. With no hesitation whatsoever Hailwood plunged into the fire and succeeded in releasing Regazzoni's harness before being beaten back by the heat, his boots, gloves and driving suit soaked with burning petrol. After rolling over and over in the sand to put out his personal fire, Hailwood dived into the flames once again and this time, standing on the car, he grabbed Regazzoni under

the armpits and dragged him clear. Thanks to Mike Hailwood and two equally brave fire marshals Regazzoni suffered only minor burns, but he has no doubt that Mike saved his life.

'After everything had calmed down a bit Mike walked back to the pits and told me what had happened. I think I was the only one he told. Then he changed out of his driving suit, slipped quietly away on his motor bike and wasn't seen again until all the fuss was over. All the newspapers were going berserk trying to track him down but Mike didn't want to know. He hated being in the spotlight; he was a genuinely shy and modest man.'

Mike Hailwood left Team Surtees at the end of the 1973 season and his departure coincided with the end of Rob's three-year contract with both John Surtees and Brooke Bond Oxo. By now Mike and Rob were such close friends that when Mike joined McLaren Rob asked if he could join too and was delighted to be accepted. In 1974 Yardley's sponsorship of the McLaren team was in its final year and had been reduced to a single car which Mike drove, while Emerson Fittipaldi and Denny Hulme raced McLarens sponsored by Texaco and Marlboro. The two teams were both based at Colnbrook and both were equipped with the latest McLaren M23-Fords, but while they co-operated fully they were separately managed; Phil Kerr was the manager of the Yardley McLaren team, Leo 'Squeaky' Wybrott was the chief mechanic, and Rob became the timekeeper. This arrangement was to provide him with one of his happiest years in motor racing.

It was also quite a successful year for Mike; after a barren season with Team Surtees in 1973 during which he had frequently been out-performed by his Brazilian team-mate Carlos Pace, he amassed sufficient points to finish tenth in the World Championship even though his season was attenuated by a serious accident at the Nürburgring.

Mike Hailwood and Phil Kerr at Silverstone in 1974.

He had been contesting fifth place with the JPS Team Lotus cars of Ronnie Peterson and Jacky Ickx until two laps from the end of the race when at the Pflanzgarten, where the faster cars flew with all four wheels in the air for an appreciable distance, the McLaren landed all wrong at 155 mph. Fifty yards or so beyond the point at which it had landed on one front wheel, it slammed nose first into the Armco. The front suspension was driven through the monocoque crushing Mike's right ankle and breaking his right tibia, fibia and knee. Mike was fully conscious throughout the rescue operation which, even though he must have been in great pain, he directed. After being cut from the car he was taken to Adenau hospital before being transferred by air ambulance to St Thomas's.

'Several drivers I know might have blamed some sort of mechanical failure for that accident, knowing that it would be very difficult to prove otherwise, but not Mike. As usual he was completely honest and admitted that he had simply made a mistake. I went to visit him several times when he was in hospital in London; he was sharing a room with Howden Ganley and the two of them were having a whale of a time; the place was in absolute chaos, the champagne was flowing non-stop, and all the nurses were obviously in love with Mike. Although he was determined to be fit for the Canadian Grand Prix later in the season he never drove again.

'When Mike had finally accepted that retirement was inevitable Betty started to nag him about marrying Pauline who had been his steady girl friend for some time. Eventually he did so and they duly produced a baby son. I will never forget Betty asking him who the baby looked like, meaning of course which parent did he look like. "He looks like the milkman," Mike replied. Betty tried again and asked if they had decided on a name for the baby. "Fred," said Mike. Why? "Well, the milkman's name is Fred." From that moment on David Hailwood has always been known to us as Fred.

'In due course Mike and his family emigrated to New Zealand where he started a business with Phil Kerr and Denny Hulme, but it wasn't long before we began to hear that Mike was bored. Then we heard that he was racing motor cycles again, and winning. Then came the astonishing news that he was going to ride in the 1978 Isle of Man TT. To be absolutely honest I thought he was mad to try and make a comeback after not having ridden in a serious competition for seven years. It had been eleven years since he had ridden in a TT and now he was planning to return to the most dangerous motor cycle circuit in the world at the age of thirty-eight. I must say that I feared for him.

'Of course he won. He rode a 900 cc Ducati with all his old polish and brilliance. In 1979 he did it again, this time on Barry Sheene's old 500 cc Suzuki. He was also supposed to ride this bike at Donington Park later in the season, against the cream of the current crop of riders, but unfortunately he crashed in practice and broke his collarbone in five places. He was determined not to disappoint his fans, but when he arrived at the circuit on race day even he had to admit that racing was impossible. Instead he was driven round the circuit in an open Land Rover, supported on each side and almost fainting from the pain.

'What a man he was. What a star.'

With Mike Hailwood's retirement and the dissolution of the Yardley McLaren team, Rob's direct involvement with Grand Prix racing began to diminish. Instead he became almost a full-time journalist, writing race reports, annual driver ratings and more general articles about cars and racing for *Road & Track*. He also made both his timekeeping skills and his vast management experience available to a succession of emerging teams including Embassy Hill, Hesketh Racing, Penske Cars, Copersucar-Fittipaldi and Walter Wolf Racing, and his writing therefore carried the authority of the insider. For a brief period there was even a reincarnation of the Rob Walker Racing Team.

'One of the directors of Fraternal Estates, the company to which I had sold my garage at Corsley, was a chap called Harry Stiller. He was a self-made millionaire who was interested in motor racing and was running a Formula 5000 car at his own expense for a young Australian driver called Alan Jones. Harry thought that Jones had the makings of a Formula One driver and I can remember attending a meeting in early 1975 at which a number of us discussed the viability of a sponsorship package which would finance the purchase of a Grand Prix car for Alan to drive in the forthcoming season. The potential sponsor finally decided that Alan had not shown

sufficient promise to warrant his involvement and withdrew, and I'm sorry to say that I thought he had taken a very wise decision.

'Harry, however, was not in the least bit put off and, I suppose because he had more money than he knew what to do with, he decided to go ahead anyway. He bought the Hesketh 308 which had been driven by James Hunt in the preceding season, I agreed to enter the car in my name to give the entry some credibility, and Corsley Garage provided a very modest amount of sponsorship.

Future World Champion Alan Jones making his Grand Prix debut in the Harry Stiller/Rob Walker Hesketh 308 at Barcelona in 1975.

For some reason, once he had set everything in motion, Harry seemed to fade into the background and I found myself managing the team with the help of a couple of freelance mechanics.

'Our first race was the 1975 Spanish Grand Prix at Barcelona which was absolute chaos. At first the drivers refused to practise because the Armco crash barriers had not been installed to their satisfaction. I suggested to Alan that he should disregard the boycott and put in some practice laps to familiarise himself with the car; he said, "I'm all for it, Rob, but I'm just a new boy and I can't break ranks – they'd never forgive me," which was understandable enough, I suppose. In the end it was only the threat that all the transporters, cars and equipment would be impounded by the police that persuaded the drivers to practise in the third and last session. Only Emerson Fittipaldi stuck to his guns, fulfilling his contractual obligation by running three timed practice laps, in second gear all the way, and then refusing to start in the race.

'The race was even more chaotic than practice. Niki Lauda was shunted into the Armco on the first corner by Mario Andretti, Patrick Depailler also crashed on the first lap, and our race was over two laps later when Jody Scheckter's engine blew up and Mark Donohue clobbered Alan when he spun on Jody's oil. Then there was a real disaster; Rolf Stommelen was in the lead on the twenty-fifth lap when his rear wing collapsed and the car flew over the crash barriers and killed four people. Rolf broke both his legs, his wrist and some ribs. The race went on for four more laps while the Spanish officials argued about whether or not to stop it.'

All this notwithstanding, however, Rob had seen enough of Alan's driving to convince him that his earlier assessment had been wrong, and this view was reaffirmed at Monaco. The final practice session had been stopped to clear up the mess made by Mark Donohue when he spun into the guard rail at Ste Devote and there were only ten minutes left at the restart. Jones had not yet qualified. 'I went up to Alan as he was getting back into the car and I said to him, "You know what you have to do, don't you? And you know you've only got ten minutes to do it in?" He was as cool as a cucumber. "Don't worry, Rob," he said. "It'll be all right," and he went out and bumped Graham Hill off the grid by three-tenths of a second. It was his attitude that really impressed me and convinced me that he was going to be very successful.

'After Zolder where, through no fault of his own, Alan got involved in a first-lap tangle with John Watson and Jochen Mass, Harry Stiller suddenly realised that even he hadn't got enough money to run a Formula One car without support from a serious sponsor, and at the same time he also realised that he would have a lot less money unless he went into immediate tax exile, so that was the end of the team. Graham Hill took Alan on to replace Rolf Stommelen and I went with him because of our little sponsorship

Alan Jones, Silverstone 1975. By this time he and Rob were with Embassy Hill, and the Australian in fact scored the ill-fated team's best-ever result with a fifth place in Germany.

arrangement. Alan was practically broke at the time and his wife ran their house in west London as a kind of dormitory for any wandering Aussies who happened to be passing through. It wasn't much, but I suppose our small contribution must have helped to keep the wolf from the door. I dare say Alan was a bit better off when he was driving for Team Surtees and Saudia Williams, for whom he won the World Championship in 1980.'

In that same year, courtesy of *Road & Track*, Rob attended the Indianapolis 500 for the first time. He found it an enlightening experience. Arriving a couple of days before the race he was immediately impressed by the sheer size of the Indianapolis

Motor Speedway with its enormous concrete and glass grandstands, by the friendliness and willingness to help of everyone he met, and by the atmosphere of calm which pervaded Gasoline Alley, all quite unlike any European Grand Prix circuit.

It was not long before he was hailed by Mario Andretti who had qualified his Penske on the front row alongside Johnny Rutherford and Bobby Unser. Mario borrowed the official pace car for five laps of the oval track with Rob as his passenger. 'It was one of the greatest thrills of my life; although the speedometer was off the clock we calculated that we were doing about 130 mph and at that speed those banked corners look bloody sharp from inside the car. Mario pointed out the turning-in points for the corners and explained that he liked to ride high on the banking in his race car, within about three inches of the wall on the straights, or "chutes" as they call them. He said that on qualification day there had been a strong, gusty wind blowing across the track which must have made life quite interesting for him at well over 200 mph!

'I was also introduced to Johnny Rutherford and I remember asking him if he felt any added pressure starting from pole position, and if it was important, as at so many Grand Prix circuits, to be first into the first corner. He was totally relaxed about his starting position and said that he wasn't worried about being first into Turn One but that he would like to take the lead as soon as it was safe to do so in order to avoid the tremendous buffeting and loss of downforce that comes with slip-streaming someone at those speeds.

'Next day I paid a visit to the Hall of Fame Museum where the Director, Jack Martin, kindly gave me a personal guided tour of the sixty cars they have on display, of which twenty-five are past winners of the Indy 500, all in absolutely pristine condition. My favourite exhibit was the $1^1/_2$-litre supercharged "Tripoli" Mercedes which Rudi Caracciola tried to sell me for Tony Rolt to drive just after the war.

'American hospitality is famous, of course, and the hospitality at Indy must be the most generous and lavish in the world. David Thieme of Essex Petroleum gave a marvellous dinner party in a private room at the best French restaurant in town, and he was kind enough to invite me to be one of his guests. He had installed Roger Verge of the Moulin de Mougins in the kitchen with three sous chefs, having flown them all to Indianapolis by Concorde and private jet just to prepare that one meal! After dinner Roger Verge signed and presented one of his cook books to each guest, and as he signed my copy I told him that I had never eaten better in my life.

'John Mecom, for whom Graham Hill had won the race in 1966, invited me to watch the race and the carburetion tests – which we would call untimed practice – from his sumptuous private suite on the outside of Turn Two, its balcony overhanging the track. The tension before the start was terrific, and even though I was a mere spectator I could feel my spine tingling as Mrs Hulman, widow of Tony Hulman who had owned the Speedway for many years, uttered the famous words "Gentlemen, start your engines." Johnnie Parsons led them in the pace car for three laps and then they got the green light and they were off, with Rutherford taking an immediate lead from Unser and Andretti.

'It wasn't long before the yellow lights came on as Bill Whittington hit the wall on the exit from Turn One and ended up on the infield immediately below our balcony. I was very interested to see the rescue crews go into action as I had always heard that they were fantastically efficient at Indy. I remember Denny Hulme telling me that when he had his accident they were putting the fire out even before the car had stopped sliding. On this occasion, however, I was not particularly impressed; the ambulance was quite slow to arrive and then it took about fifteen minutes to cut him out of the car because the Honda generator which they were using to power the cutting tools wouldn't start. The whole thing fell far short of Formula One standards.

'In the end Johnny Rutherford's Chaparral won fairly easily after Mario and Bobby Unser had both retired and Rick Mears made an unscheduled pit stop because of a puncture. When the prizegiving and the lap of honour were over I collected the most fantastic press kit containing all the information I needed to write my story, said my farewells to the Mecom family and walked back to the Essex suite where Roger Verge was still signing cook books. It had been a long day for both of us.'

Chapter 16
Random Recollections

Two years later, in 1982, *Road & Track* invited Rob to cover the Talladega 500 in Alabama. NASCAR stock car racing has nothing in common with what happens at Wimbledon on Saturday nights; these stock cars lap the banked oval tracks which abound in South Carolina, Georgia, Alabama and Tennessee at over 200 mph. Stock car racing is more popular than baseball in the southern states because it is rooted in their history; the good ol' boys of the South made their living from distilling moonshine whisky and when the US government decided to tax their product, they were darned if they could see why they should co-operate. Their distribution system involved innocent-looking sedans and pick-ups concealing stainless-steel tanks containing a hundred gallons of hooch, and powered by engines which would not have disgraced a race car. Wild drives through the Appalachians pursued by the 'revenooers' were commonplace. Rob asked the legendary Junior Johnson if it was really true that he and his father had been locked up by the revenue agents for running illegal whisky. 'Sure,' he replied. 'But they caught us at the still – they never could catch us on the road.' Stock car racing is in their blood.

Rob's first appointment was at Bobby and Donnie Allison's racing shop at Hueytown where he was met by Donnie's sons, known collectively as the Peach Fuzz Gang. While he was there a battered Ford arrived driven by a diffident young man who was soon guiding Rob through the intricacies of the NASCAR rule book. It was not until much later that Rob realised that this was Neil Bonnet who had won the race two years earlier. 'He told me that the banking at Talladega was so steep that the car had to be doing over 110 mph to keep from sliding down. But there were advantages; for instance, any spilt oil was dispersed almost immediately and if it rained the track was dry the moment it stopped.' Once again Rob was fortunate enough to be driven for a few laps in the pace car, courtesy of Bill France, and found himself comparing the banking with that at Brooklands where he had driven forty-three years earlier. He reckoned that the Members' Banking had been at least ten degrees steeper.

Ron Bouchard won the Talladega 500 in a fantastic three-car photo-finish after five hundred miles of racing. Returning to his motel room afterwards Rob found an unlabelled jug of evil-smelling liquid inside a brown paper bag with a note from Junior Johnson saying, 'This is the real stuff.'

'As I flew back to England I remembered the story of the little old Irish lady returning from a pilgrimage to Lourdes with a bottle of whisky which she declared as holy water. When the Customs officer sniffed the cork and said, "This isn't water,

Rob's Australian forebears would approve of his choice of lager.

madam, it's whisky," she had clasped her hands together and said, "Faith, it's another miracle!" When I arrived at Heathrow I tried the same ploy, but unfortunately the Customs officer on whom I tried it had also heard the story, and I had to pay the duty on my bottle of whisky.'

Of the many Grand Prix venues with which he is so familiar, Rob has mixed feelings about Monaco. He has fond memories of the time when, as a young man before the war, he drove from Paris to Monte Carlo in his Delahaye coupé to stay at the Hotel de Paris for as long as he could support himself at the casino. Using a simple even chance system he managed to finance five luxurious nights there before deciding not to push his luck. Alas Rob's guardian angel deserted him at the Le Touquet casino on his way home and he was much relieved to discover that the Hotel Westminster would not only accept an English cheque in payment of his bill, but would also advance him enough cash for the ferry ticket to Dover.

'The journey down to Monte Carlo was always great fun; before the autoroute was built we always used to take three days over it, staying our first night at Chatillon-sur-Seine and our second at Gap. I think we stayed at the Cap Estel in Eze-sur-Mer for twenty-four consecutive Monaco Grands Prix and we became great friends of the charming couple who owned and ran it, who were called Robert and Carmen Squacciafichi; in fact their son came to stay with us in London when he was learning to speak English.

'The staff at the hotel stayed on there until they either retired or died, and they were always interested to see what kind of car we would turn up in next. I think the ones they approved of most were the Mercedes gullwings, the Facels and my two Ferraris, the Lusso and the Dino 246GT. We brought the cup back to Cap Estel three times and then we would have a great party, filling it with champagne and drinking from it on the terrace overlooking that wonderful view, as we relived every moment of the race. The driver always came to lunch with us on Monday and we used to stay on for a few days after all the other racing people had moved on, just swimming and soaking up the sun, and relaxing generally.

'But the traffic at Monte Carlo was simply dreadful. It used to take us hours to drive the few kilometres from Eze and, whatever kind of pass you had, parking was a nightmare. I remember one year when I was trying to reach my allotted parking space I inadvertently ran over a woman's foot. She didn't seem to be hurt much and as I was in a bit of a hurry I'm afraid I didn't spend too much time sympathising with her. When I got back to my car after the race I found that it had been clamped and when I went to the police station to get the clamp removed I discovered that the woman had filed a complaint against me. Eventually the police got bored with the whole thing, tore up all the forms which we had been laboriously filling in for the past three hours in both French and English, and unlocked the clamp. I was very glad to down my first champagne cocktail at Cap Estel that evening.

'It was qualifying that I really hated at Monaco. When Stirling was driving for me I never had any doubt that he would qualify, of course, but with almost any of my other drivers the strain was really very considerable. I'll always remember Maurice Trintignant trying to qualify the Scuderia Centro-Sud Cooper-Maserati in 1960, fighting Bruce Halford for the last place on the grid. The car was a real dog and Maurice simply couldn't set a decent time in it until he realised that the timing beam was within the braking area for the old Gazomètres Hairpin at the end of the lap. He worked out that if he kept his foot down and just didn't brake for the corner until he was past the timing box he would go through the beam quicker, even if he did end up in a heap in the straw bales as a result. It worked and he qualified sixteenth. It was a very clever if rather dangerous trick and it shows what risks people were prepared to take just to qualify.

'One regret that I will always have about the Nürburgring is that I never went round with Seppi. On one occasion we were staying together at the SportHotel, which was part of the main grandstand opposite the pits, and we had just found a table in the very busy and crowded dining room when I mentioned that sometime I would love to do a lap or two with him in his Porsche. Seppi stood up and said, "Come on, let's do it right now," but I was hungry and I knew that we would never find another table if we gave up the one we had, and so I let the opportunity pass. I'll always regret it. Always.

'On a different occasion we had been joined at the Lochmuhle at Altenahr by a wealthy Swiss brewer called Bernard Blancpain who lived in Fribourg. He was an Ancien Pilote and a great admirer of Seppi from whom he had recently bought a Porsche 911. On the morning of the race he asked Seppi to drive him to the circuit in his new car and we followed them along a short cut through the woods. About halfway there we came round a corner to find that Seppi had overdone it and the Porsche was upside down in the ditch. We got it back on its wheels again and carried on, and Seppi drove in the Grand Prix just as if nothing had happened.'

As we have seen, however, Rob's interface with officialdom at the Nürburgring was often abrasive. On one occasion he encountered a young scrutineer of evidently Prussian stock who asked why his car was painted blue and white. 'To be absolutely honest, it was painted blue and white because I thought it looked good, but I knew that wouldn't go down too well so I told him that they were the racing colours of

Rob reporting for Road & Track
at Indianapolis in 1975.

Scotland. He said, "I wonder what the FIA would have to say about that?" because at that time of course, in the days before sponsorship, all British cars were supposed to be painted British racing green. I replied, "Exactly the same as they would about a German car painted silver when your national racing colour is white," and that shut him up pretty quickly. Poor Jo Bonnier was not so lucky; he was forced to repaint his red Maserati 250F in the blue and yellow colours of Sweden before being allowed to race.

'A few years later we had another problem because when the official practice times were published they didn't show our best time. By then I reckoned that my timekeeping was really pretty accurate and if the official times and mine differed by more than about five-hundredths of a second then I reckoned that the official watches were wrong. I went to see the chief timekeeper whose arrogance absolutely incensed me; according to him it was impossible for German timekeeping to be wrong, ever. So I said, "You people haven't the first idea about timekeeping, you have no experience, you do it once a year whereas I'm doing it virtually every week," and I demanded that he should check Jo Bonnier's seventh practice lap, which he did with ill grace. And of course I was right. I then demanded an apology from him which he gave with even less good grace but, I'm happy to say, in the presence of all his subordinates.

'Having fought against the Germans at the time of the invasion of Poland in 1939, and then escaped to England in order to renew the contest on slightly more favourable terms, Alf's attitude towards them was even more entrenched than mine, and he always seemed to wind up getting into a fight with some official at the Nür-burgring – a marshal, a steward, or someone. I remember saying to him once, "Alf, I know you hate the Germans but for God's sake don't go and get into a fight with anyone this year – it's just more trouble than it's worth," and he looked at me and said, quite seriously, "Mr Walker, I don't really hate the Germans; even during the war I always had to shut them in a cupboard before I could bring myself to shoot them." Those were his exact words, and I believed every one of them!

'The Italian Grand Prix always coincided with our annual family holiday at Santa Margherita, so we always had the children with us there. In the early days we used to stay in Como but then we moved to the Villa d'Este at Cernobbio. The house and gardens were absolutely beautiful and the view across the lake was fabulous, but somehow I never really liked it. It was also a very long way from Monza, and the traffic was always terrible. Practice at Monza went on in those days until six-thirty in the evening, which meant that we weren't back at the hotel until nine-thirty and then had to change for dinner in the restaurant. It was all just too much of a hassle, really. In the end Innes tipped me off about a wonderful restaurant on the road to Bergamo which had three or four bedrooms, and we've stayed there ever since.

'I have one very fond memory of Monza which was when Alf and I pushed the Cooper, as is the custom, out of the paddock and along the full length of the pits into pole position. It was in 1959 and my brother John was in the grandstand,

257

Jim Clark and Colin Chapman in the pits at the Nürburgring, 1967.

Jimmy Clark's Lotus trailing its rear roll bar at Monaco in 1964.

surrounded by *Tifosi*, watching his first Grand Prix. They gave him a hard time whenever a Ferrari came round in the lead, but he had the last laugh because Stirling won.

'I think I saw Jim Clark at his very best at Monza in 1967. It was a very dramatic race which Jimmy was leading by the narrowest of margins from Denny Hulme and Jack Brabham in their Repco Brabhams until, on the twelfth lap, he had a puncture. He was in the pits for almost two minutes while the wheel was changed, and when

he rejoined the race he was a lap behind the leaders in fifteenth place.

His driving that afternoon was nothing short of miraculous; he not only unlapped himself but by lap sixty-two he was in the lead again. But the drama was not over; on the last lap Jimmy ran out of fuel and was overtaken by Jack Brabham and John Surtees. Then on the very last corner, the Parabolica, Jack slipped inside John under braking but ran wide at the exit and allowed John to nip ahead again to give the vee-twelve Honda its first Grand Prix win by two-tenths of a second. But the hero of the afternoon was definitely the third man home – Jim Clark.

'On another occasion, at Monaco, I remember the rear anti-roll bar on Jimmy's Lotus coming adrift; it took him about two slow laps to come to terms with the fact that the handling characteristics of the car had altered completely, and then he just drove around the problem and lapped as fast as he had before.

'I think that on the strength of either of those drives I would have to add Jimmy's name to those of Nuvolari, Fangio and Moss on my list of the five greatest drivers I have ever seen in action. He was obviously gifted with tremendous natural ability, but I don't think he was as skilled technically as some of the other drivers. He needed Colin Chapman to help him set the car up properly because he himself really didn't understand how to alter its behaviour; he would just tell Colin how the car was behaving and Colin would fix it. His record of twenty-five wins in seventy-two Grands Prix shows how well the partnership worked, but he couldn't have done it without Colin.

'Graham Hill, on the other hand, knew exactly how to set his car up and had to work very hard at doing so in order to compensate for his comparative lack of natural driving ability. I remember that before every race Graham would spend an hour and a half all by himself in the transporter going over his circuit notes and studying the map on which he had plotted every gearchange and every braking point. He normally concealed this tremendous dedication under a layer of bonhomie, but woe betide anyone who interrupted him while he was preparing himself for a race.

'Jack Brabham combined the best of both worlds; he was a very good engineer and could set a car up to suit himself quickly and easily, which was a great advantage, but he was also a very canny driver. He was not as fast as Stirling, as I think both of them knew, but he was a formidable opponent. I think that Jack is terribly underrated; he could easily have won more World Championships than any modern driver – not as many as Fangio perhaps, but things were different in Fangio's day – and it was only the worst of bad luck which prevented him from winning four times.

'Looking back on all the places I've been lucky enough to go to during the course of almost fifty years of motor racing, I'm hard pressed to decide which was the most enjoyable. I think it's probably a toss-up between Syracuse and Kyalami, although I liked Watkins Glen very much as well.

'The Syracuse Grand Prix was a non-championship race which meant that nobody took it terribly seriously, and we all used to stay at a marvellous hotel called the Villa Politi where they were very tolerant of our high spirits. On one occasion I can remember Innes Ireland driving his rented Fiat 600 up the steps and into the lobby, sliding as he braked on the rugs covering the marble floor, but nobody seemed to mind too much. The race was always held in March so that it gave us our first taste of sunshine after the usual miserable English winter, and I'll never forget the smell of orange blossom which seemed to envelop us everywhere we went.

'When we used to air-freight the cars to Catania, the drivers or mechanics would often drive them the fifty miles or so to Syracuse, and I have a marvellous memory of looking into the mirror of my rented car to see Maurice Trintignant in his Formula Two Cooper behind me, scattering chickens and donkeys as we passed through a dusty Sicilian village somewhere on the Gulf of Catania. There was virtually no crowd control at Syracuse; people used to wander about on the road while the race was going on, just like the Mille Miglia, and I can remember the drivers telling me once that there were people standing on the track on both sides of them as they went through the hairpin.

'Everybody used to stay at the Kyalami Ranch Motel for the South African Grand

Jack Brabham, Silverstone 1970. Fifteen years after his Grand Prix debut the three-times World Champion was still a front-runner.

Prix. In 1985, which was the last race to be held before the boycott, I stayed on there for a few days afterwards – swimming, sitting in the sun by the pool, and playing a little golf – and I got to know Gerhard Berger quite well, although I had a bit of competition from the airline stewardesses who also stayed there when they stopped over in Johannesburg. I reckon he is the principal beneficiary of Jackie Stewart's much maligned safety crusade; in the bad old days his crash in the Ferrari at Imola in 1989 would certainly have been fatal, and so would his practice accident at Spa in 1992. He aquaplaned going down the hill to Eau Rouge at 160 mph, hit the Armco on one side and then the other, the car disintegrated and burst into flames, and Gerhard just walked out of the fire completely unhurt. It was one of the worst accidents I've ever seen.

'If we had time when we were at Kyalami we would drive to the Kruger National Park to see the game, and we would always stay at a motel called Winklers

Gerhard Berger studying the latest qualifying times.

which was just outside the park at White River. The proprietor, Herr Winkler, owned a Ferrari which was looked after by Giulio Ramponi, and he and I used to have long chats about my Delage which he had worked on for Dick Seaman more than fifty years earlier.

'In the days when there were two Grands Prix in America, the most convenient place to stay for the Long Beach race was in the *Queen Mary*, the old Cunarder which was then moored in the harbour and operated as a hotel. The first time I stayed there I arrived rather late on the evening before the race in company with a number of fellow journalists including Michael Tee, Alan Henry and Nigel

Roebuck. We walked up the gangplank together and arrived in the reception area, which had been occupied by the ship's Purser in the good old days. When I said my name to the girl behind the desk she said, "Oh, good evening, Mr Walker; we've put you in the stateroom which you preferred when you used to cross the Atlantic with us, and Miss Ginger Rogers would like you to return her call." Alan's jaw dropped. "Is that *the* Ginger Rogers?" he said. Well, I suppose he wasn't to know that we had been friends for years. After a moment's thought Nigel said, "How much did you pay her to say that, Rob?"

Alain Prost.

'The Franzese family who owned the Glen Motor Inn where we all used to stay at Watkins Glen also owned the nine-hole golf course over the road, and every year they would organise a tournament for the drivers. In one of these tournaments I partnered Alain Prost the very first time he played the game, and nearly killed him in the process. I struck a very strong drive off the fourth tee, unfortunately hooking it into some trees which were close by; the ball came ricocheting back like a bullet and missed Alain's head by inches. However, it obviously didn't put him off because he now plays off seven and has his own golf course.

'Keke Rosberg said of Prost "Everyone thinks he is going to be World Champion unless he drives in the same team as Alain Prost." Keke should know – he was in the McLaren team when Alain won his second championship in 1986. I sometimes wish I could rate Prost higher than I do but, despite his very considerable achievements, I have never found him the least bit exciting to watch. Mansell described him as "just a chauffeur" and although he is obviously very much more than that he always looks as if he is driving very carefully and his car doesn't seem to be going fast, although I suppose it must be.

'I've never really enjoyed racing in Japan very much and the race I disliked more than any other was the 1976 Japanese Grand Prix at Mount Fuji. It came at the end of a long and arduous season and, for me, a long and arduous journey; I had been to Toronto for the Canadian Grand Prix at Mosport Park, then to Watkins Glen for the USGP, to Riverside for some reason or other, to Newport Beach to see *Road & Track*, and then finally I had made that horrendous flight across the Pacific and the international dateline to Tokyo. I was knackered when I arrived and I was enormously grateful to my brother-in-law Val who, as Chairman of RTZ, had arranged for his man in Tokyo to meet me at the airport and provide me with a chauffeur-driven car to take me to the circuit. I arrived ahead of the Penske team, with whom I was working at the time, to find that I had no reservation at the hotel. I was so jet-lagged that I could hardly think straight and I was immensely thankful when the team turned up, having escaped from the enthusiastic attentions of the Tokyo geishas, to rescue me. The

Penske team manager at the time was a Swiss ski instructor and hot dogger called Heinz Hofer who was incredibly good looking and charming. Everybody loved Heinz. I certainly did, because he got me sorted out in about two seconds flat.'

The race was run in a torrential downpour and James Hunt won the World Championship by finishing third after his only serious rival, Niki Lauda, had withdrawn, unwilling to risk his neck in the appalling weather conditions. 'I think that James was really very lucky to win the championship, as I'm sure he would be the first to agree. I think he just had a lucky break when Niki Lauda had that terrible accident at the Nürburgring and then thought that it was better to live to fight another day than to race in the rain in Japan.'

Nobody should infer from his decision in Japan that Niki Lauda was a coward. Far from it. He was a very brave man. It was enormously courageous to return to racing after the terrible injuries he had suffered at the Nürburgring, it was the act of a brave man to withdraw from the race at Mount Fuji with the championship within his grasp, and it was also the act of a brave man to walk away from the Brabham team in practice for the Canadian Grand Prix in 1979. He wasn't going well in a car unsuited to a circuit he didn't like, and when he asked himself, 'Why am I doing this?' and failed to come up with a sensible answer, he simply packed his bags and went home to Austria.

'I always think of Niki Lauda as being cast from the same

Niki Lauda.

James Hunt's McLaren M23C at Brands Hatch in 1976.

Ayrton Senna.

mould as Alain Prost: competent, careful, and not very exciting to watch. Watching Ayrton Senna, on the other hand, is very exciting indeed; the car looks as if it's absolutely on the limit and going very fast. And it is. I often think that one of the most important criteria for judging a driver's overall ability is his performance in wet weather, because going fast in the wet demands not only great courage but also terrific car control. Ayrton's touch is amazingly sensitive, and he has an uncanny ability to feel the most minute change in the attitude of the car. His drive for Lotus at Estoril in 1985 when he won in an absolute downpour and lapped everyone except Alboreto in the Ferrari was quite outstanding, and certainly qualifies him to fill the final vacancy on my list of the five greatest drivers.

'The Goodyear people say that Ayrton is the best judge of tyres in the business – he can tell exactly which is the best compound, how long they'll last, when they're going to go off, how to conserve them – and this perhaps explains why he took pole position so often in the days of qualifying tyres. I remember him telling me once that when he is doing a really fast lap he dismisses from his mind the corner he is going through at the time and is already visualising the next one; however he does it, it's certainly exciting to watch.

'I have heard Ayrton described as arrogant and aloof, but I have never found him so. In fact I like him very much. He has very strong self-belief, certainly, and he is a hard task master, expecting his mechanics, for example, to work just as hard and think just as hard as he does. But he treats them with respect; the first thing he does when he arrives at the circuit is to shake hands with each of his mechanics, and he always thanks them after the race – win or lose.

'Another driver I liked enormously was Gilles Villeneuve. He was absolutely brilliant, but temperamental, excitable and fearless to the point of recklessness. I thought he was bound to kill himself sooner or later.'

The genesis of the accident which killed Villeneuve occurred at the 1982 San Marino Grand Prix at Imola two weeks before his death. The Ferraris driven by Gilles and Didier Pironi were fancied to win the race and Ferrari team manager Marco Piccinini instructed the two drivers that if they found themselves ahead of the opposition by more than forty seconds they were to hold station and slow down. After forty-six laps Villeneuve was in the lead with Pironi close behind him, forty-six seconds ahead of Alboreto's Tyrrell-Ford. Piccinini gave both his drivers the signal, in English, '+46 SLOW'. Villeneuve obediently slowed and was astonished to find Pironi tearing past him at the next corner. On lap forty-nine Gilles regained the lead and dropped his lap time again as instructed, only for Pironi to shoot past him on the same corner as before. On lap fifty-nine Gilles was in front, but Pironi passed him on the last lap to win the race. Villeneuve was furious at Pironi's blatant disregard of team orders which Rob Walker describes as 'the most disgraceful behaviour I have ever witnessed in motor racing'. The two drivers never spoke to each other again.

Qualifying in those days was always a tricky business because each car was

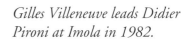

Gilles Villeneuve leads Didier Pironi at Imola in 1982.

allowed only two sets of qualifying tyres per session, and each set of tyres would provide optimum adhesion for no more than two laps. So the drivers either had to be lucky enough to find the track clear when going for a good time, or quite ruthless in forcing past any slower car.

A few minutes before the end of the final practice session for the Belgian Grand Prix at Zolder Gilles Villeneuve went out with new qualifiers to improve his time; Pironi was one tenth of a second quicker than him, a situation which, under the circumstances, was unacceptable. On his first flying lap he caught Jochen Mass, slowing down to return to the pits, at the first long, fast left–right combination in the woods. Jochen saw him

coming in his mirrors and moved over to the right to let him through on the conventional racing line. Alas, Gilles moved right also, their wheels touched and the

Enzo Ferrari.

Ferrari became airborne for fifty yards before landing nose first and cartwheeling several times. Despite instant and expert first aid, Villeneuve died in Louvain hospital without regaining consciousness.

Villeneuve's sportsmanship, his generosity and his wicked sense of humour had made him immensely popular with his peers, and his death cast a pall of gloom over Zolder equal in intensity to that which had engulfed Monza three years earlier when Ronnie Peterson was killed. 'I don't think Gilles Villeneuve would have been World Champion had he lived; he was just too wild. Nor would Seppi, for the same reason. The other drivers used to tell me that Seppi was so charged up at the beginning of a race that he was like an uncaged lion until he settled down after a few laps. He would never have beaten Jochen Rindt in equal cars; although he was incredibly quick, Jochen was also a very polished driver. But Ronnie would have been champion if he had lived. Like all those Nordic drivers he had phenomenal car control, maybe because he was brought up to drive on ice and snow, or maybe because he started driving karts when he was very young. Ayrton reckons that driving karts is the best possible preparation for Formula One because of the twitchiness which results from their extremely high power to weight ratio.'

Who was the best of all? 'Well, Enzo Ferrari, who was active in motor racing all his adult life and lived to be ninety, put it much better than I possibly can. He said something like "To compare all the great drivers from different periods is impossible. But if we must pick out specific names we can say that Nuvolari and Moss had similar styles. They were both men who, given any kind of machine, in any circumstances, on any track, would put everything they had into it and end up with the best results." I didn't often agree with Ferrari, but I do in this case.'

Jochen Rindt at Brands Hatch in 1968. Behind him stands an aspiring young Brabham mechanic called Ron Dennis.

Chapter 17
One of a Kind

Rob Walker made countless friends during the course of his motor racing career.

Even as a journalist he has made no enemies.

In his study at Nunney, Mike Hailwood's Griffin helmet stands amongst Rob's collection of trophies as a reminder that, unlike those of us who have lived more humdrum lives, he cannot enjoy sharing reminiscences with many of his closest friends: Jim Clark, Pedro Rodriguez, Gilles Villeneuve, Jochen Rindt, Ronnie Peterson, Graham Hill, Mike Hawthorn, Harry Schell, Peter Collins, Jo Siffert, Bruce McLaren. It's a cruel sport.

There is a story, perhaps apocryphal, of an ageing English dowager, rudely awakened by the screech of a Formula One engine warming up below her bedroom window for early-morning practice at Monaco, observing sniffily, 'In my young day the drivers were all gentlemen pretending to be mechanics; now they are all mechanics pretending to be gentlemen.'

Never in his life has Rob pretended to be anything but himself – generous, unpretentious, courteous, kind, the epitome of the English gentleman. Motor racing will never be quite the same without him, and will never again be enriched by anyone for whom there is such widespread respect and genuine affection.

Rob Walker is one of a kind.

Rob Walker, Nunney Court, 1993.

269